#PASSPORTREADY

THE ULTIMATE GUIDE TO SOLO FEMALE TRAVEL

ANNE MALAMBO

OvaViu
Publishing

OvaViu Publishing
Part of the OvaViu Media Group

FIRST EDITION
www.onthegowithac.com

ISBN e-book: 978-1-8381685-0-6

ISBN print: 978-1-8381685-1-3

Book cover design by ebooklaunch.com

Share your pictures/screen shots of the book and travel adventures under the hashtags

#IAmPassportReady and #GettingPassportReady

Tag the author @onthegowithac

To mum,

thank you for chasing your dreams, so that one day,
I could live mine.

♡

FOREWORD

Don't let this be the end, don't let this be the end, don't...

I found myself pleading with the universe—things were not looking rosy. I was lying flat on the ground, my body submerged in tall grass surrounded by the Mongolian wilderness, my left arm aching from the impact of the fall. I had just tumbled off a horse I purchased a few days earlier, and as far as I could tell, I was the only human being for miles around.

A wild desire for discomfort brought me here. A month earlier, I'd set myself the ambitious goal of completing a two-week solo horse trek in Mongolia. Equipped with intermediate riding skills and an advanced thirst for adventure, I bought two horses, collected some camping equipment, and set off into the wild. I knew it wouldn't be easy, but I hadn't foreseen that on day two, one of my horses would get spooked by a wild animal, throw me off, run away with the other horse carrying all my gear and leave me completely alone. I lifted myself off the ground and took in the scene. All around me were meadows, hills, forests, and not a single sign of human habitation. I watched my horses trot off into the distance, totally indifferent to my slowly growing despair.

This wasn't how I'd planned things. Just two years earlier, I was climbing the career ladder on London's start-up scene, earning a six-figure salary, and enjoying the city's energy to the maximum. I had just married someone who would have been my guarantee of affluence and stability for the rest of my days. I was always busy, successful by most standards, but extremely unhappy. The further I sank into that life, the more I felt I was living someone else's dream. I was starting to realise that I had accepted the status quo without ever questioning it, and was living the kind of conventional life I never wanted to have.

Here's the funny thing about the truth; once you see her, you cannot ignore her. She will stare you in the face like a wild animal and remind you to pay heed to her. After realising that the picture-perfect London life wasn't for me, I left everything behind and embarked on a journey around the world as a travel vlogger, even though at the time, I knew nothing about vlogging.

When I started out on this journey, my Instagram account boasted only 400 followers, which is perfectly respectable, but not exactly promising for someone who wants to make a career out of her travels. But I worked hard on creating my own niche, networked and strategised around the clock, tried to make videos that nobody else was making, and both my Instagram and YouTube following began to grow. The more I travelled and the more traveller friends I made, the more I aspired to break my own boundaries, seek discomfort, and grow. That was the travel style I wanted to pursue, and that's how I ended up in the heart of the Mongolian wilderness. Let's rewind to that scene for a moment.

In the path of tall grass, I was starting to feel hopeless. The bruise on my arm began to darken, and the trail of camping gear that my horses had left behind seemed to be openly mocking me. Maybe I had overestimated my abilities. Maybe I should have stuck to less risky adventures.

And then, I noticed something moving in the tall grass, several hundred metres away. Upon closer inspection, it turned out to be a woman who was walking towards me, my horses in tow. I ran up to her. She was forty or so years old, wrinkled from the sun, her fingers hardened by a life lived outdoors. She handed me the reins with a smile, and pointed at my cans and cutlery, scattered on the ground. Before I knew it, she was helping me collect all my gear, fixing my horse's bridle and sewing up the torn pack saddle.

It turned out she was a Mongolian nomad, who lived in a yurt to the side of the meadow. Her son had seen the accident, alerted her, and she ran over to check up on me. The entire time my new friend was there, I was operating in a kind of euphoric daze. I just couldn't believe my luck. Maybe my trek wasn't doomed after all. Maybe I could keep going. Half an hour later, she smiled, patted my horses, and gestured as if to ask me whether I was getting back on. I nodded to signal that I was. After leaving her with a small gift and bidding her farewell, I set off into the unknown again. The meeting left me with a fresh injection of hope and joy. I once again felt like I was there for a reason—like I had a mission to complete—a deeply personal journey into risk and discomfort, and an insatiable desire for growth.

I kept going for another week, camped alone in some of the most beautiful places I'd ever seen, figured out a new direction for my work, and found a completely new appreciation for nature.

Back when I was living someone else's dream, epic adventures like this seemed far beyond my reach. Chance encounters with kind people, treks in the wilderness, seeking discomfort? That was all stuff from travel books, but not ordinary life, and certainly not mine. But today, that is my life, and while it's not always a grand adventure, I see each day as an opportunity to learn something new, to grow. And that's something you can only do if you live consciously—mindful about every step you take, open to the world, seeking your purpose.

And with that said, I was so honoured to be able to write the foreword to Anne's book. Her expert travel advice and pearls of wisdom from other female travellers will bring you plenty of inspiration to create your own journey, however big or small. Your next adventure starts right here, between the pages of this book.

Safe travels,

Eva Zu Beck

Follow me: @evazubeck

PREFACE

A NOTE FROM THE AUTHOR

It is a truth universally acknowledged, that a woman in possession of a handsome man, must not be in want of adventure. At least, that's what my mother would say if we were in nineteenth century England. It was in fact, September of 2019, on a sunny afternoon in London. As we sat watching the news, a story about a woman who had gone missing in woodlands while backpacking began to run. Thankfully, she had been found alive and well. Midway through the report, her boyfriend appeared on the screen and gave his thanks to the rescue team. At the sight of his appearance, my mother exclaimed, "Oh, so she has that handsome man, what was she doing out there alone then? Why would she want to be doing anything alone?"

I sat silently and wondered; what if the poor chap hadn't been so dashing? Would his lack of good looks be license for the girl to roam freely? I dared not ask.

Unbeknown to my mother, I was three months away from embarking on one of the biggest solo adventures I would take since I began solo travelling in March of 2016. In four years, I had travelled solo to eight countries, all whilst having a full-time job. My trips had taken me to numerous cities across Europe and to Bali, Indonesia, where I got my PADI Open Water diving certification on the majestic island of Nusa Lembongan.

Although my mother has always been supportive of my travels, she had, like all mothers, her concerns. What she forgets perhaps, is that children are often a reflection of their parents, the apple rarely falls far from the tree.

From the age of eight, my mother had a dream; to get to the United Kingdom in search of a life with more opportunity. Some relatives would often laugh at her for having such an outlandish dream. Given the circumstances, it was a pretty absurd idea. How could a young girl, from a humble village in Zambia, whose parents had both died, think she could accomplish something so bold? She had a tiny waist-line and a pretty face, the smartest thing to do, would be to find a husband when she came of age.

My mother, armed with the wisdom her own mother passed on before she died, had other ideas. She was put through school by generous aunties who gave what they could to ensure she finished her education. She would later enrol as a ground officer in the Air Force. She had become a self-sufficient and well-accomplished woman, but wasn't any closer to reaching the United Kingdom.

It wasn't until the opportunity to train as a nurse presented itself, that she landed at Heathrow Airport in the early 90s, leaving me behind with her younger sister to build a foundation in the UK. Mission accomplished.

Before long, little baby me would join her, as would my father and elder brother. Her one dream changed the trajectory of our entire lives. The boldness and bravery of her choices cannot be understated, and it goes without saying, that it had an effect on me. I became more curious about the world as I grew, and wasn't going to bet on meeting a 'handsome' man so that I could go out and see it.

While I hope to one day find a partner who also loves travel, I do not believe a woman has to wait for anyone to seek adventure, neither should she forgo having some alone time when she is partnered. Despite the progress made to emancipate women from traditional roles, there is still something about a woman who can stand on her own that rattles people.

She's loose—she's wild—she's uncontrollable.

Most of us will become partners, wives, and mothers in time. These are not, however, our only roles in life. They are not labels that should confine and strictly define us, and they are not the end-all and be-all of womanhood.

I started writing a book detailing how to travel the world, but with the addition of the incredible women who submitted their solo travel stories, it became about so much more than that. The same way a passport permits you to cross from one border to another, you must give your inner-self permission to leave your comfort zone, and move towards a place of unfamiliarity and uncertainty, as this is where you will experience the most growth. You must give yourself permission to walk away from other people's expectations, and begin the journey of discovering who your most authentic self is. You must give yourself permission to chase your dreams and discover what will fulfil you, and understand that at different stages of your life, this may change— be open to that change. This, is what lays, at the heart of being #passportready.

On January 1, 2020, it was time to take off for my next big adventure. I arrived at Heathrow Airport Terminal 2, with a ticket to Northern Thailand. I would spend three weeks enjoying The Land Of a Thousand Smiles, before landing in Cambodia to marvel at the temples of Angkor.

Little did I know, that my January 2020 trip, could possibly be my last for a very long time. Little did anyone know, how quickly our lives would be turned around. Not only would international travel come to a screeching halt, simply walking to the local supermarket would be a highly coordinated operation.

As I made my way through Thailand and Cambodia, further east of the Asian Pacific, a new, unknown virus was causing unease in Wuhan, the capital of Central China's Hubei Province.

As I write this introduction, we are still in the midst of the Covid-19 coronavirus pandemic. Our towns, cities, and borders are slowly beginning to reopen, but travel has inevitably changed forever. The time to wander freely again will come, and so, perhaps this is the perfect time to reflect on ways we can be more sustainable, and engage in more ethical practices when we travel.

With the information provided in this book, I hope to give you the confidence to start planning your first trip, or, improve the way you travel if you already roam solo. Whether you're going on a short getaway, taking a gap year, or quitting the daily grind to become a full-time nomad, I want you to have the time of your life but, I also want you to be prepared for everything travel will throw at you. By the end of this book, I want you to be able to confidently say— #IAmPassportReady.

You've got this,

Anne Malambo

Follow me:@onthegowithac

Contents

FIRST THINGS FIRST

CHAPTER 1

WHY GO SOLO ANYWAY?

*"Women need real moments of solitude and self-reflection
to balance out how much of ourselves we give away.*
—Barbara De Angelis

So you want to travel solo. If you've told anyone about your ambitions, they've either given you a high-five and told you to go get it girl, or they've perhaps asked you if you're mad. Let's take a look at some of the advantages of solo travel.

Travel is an opportunity for self-reflection

Travel takes us away from everyday life and gives us a third-person perspective of where we are, and possibly a greater understanding of which direction our lives should take upon our return. Without the daily constraints of a nine to five life, we're given the time and space to focus on ourselves. We also get to see the world through the eyes of others, experience how they live, and reflect upon our own values, wants, and needs. This can be very powerful at any stage in life.

You don't have to wait for anybody

If you're waiting for a friend, boyfriend/girlfriend, husband/wife, or family members to travel with—you could honestly be waiting forever! Our lives run on different schedules, and it can be difficult to organise a trip with just one other person, let alone an entire group.

You can focus on your own interests

Everybody has different tastes and moves at a different pace. Travelling alone allows you to set your own agenda and change it at a moment's notice. Not enjoying a particular site? You can leave straight away. Want to speed through an attraction, or really take your time because you're enjoying it? Totally up to you. Solo travel is the ultimate self-indulgence—you get to make it about you, and do not feel that you are being selfish. I view travel as a form of self-care and self-preservation, neither of which are selfish.

You're a warrior without trying

As you walk through the world, you are shifting the cultural norms and expectations of what it means to navigate the world as a woman, and perhaps, without even realising, you give another woman permission to do the same. It wasn't until I stumbled across the online blogs of other solo female travellers, that the idea of solo travel even entered my mind. Seeing what these women had done/were doing inspired me to do the same. History is filled with intrepid women who broke barriers and dared to do more than just dream. Follow @passportreadyhistory on Instagram, where we curate a feed of inspiring profiles of travelling women.

**#PASSPORTREADY WORDS OF WISDOM
- ALEXANDRA, CHANGING SOLO STIGMA**

The empowerment you receive from being self-reliant makes solo travel worth it.

There is no waiting around—you go when you are ready. You make every decision from the get-go. You want to see an exhibit nobody you know is interested in? You go with zero guilt. You want to eat slowly without feeling bad for the other person? Graze away. Until you travel alone you do not realise how much of your behaviour you adjust for other people, and it is an incredible rush of joy when you put yourself first.

The unfortunate stigma attached to those who explore the world is that they are aimless and damaged in some way. On the contrary, those who go alone are often the most self-assured and resilient, or at least, come out the other side of their journeys much more so, and it is often people's feelings of security in their home life that allows them to feel like they can take time away. If you experience unwanted attention, my advice to other solo female travellers is to make your travel intentions clear. Nobody should expect anything of you, and it is their mistake for assuming. Travelling alone takes strength, and whilst I believe travelling is not for everyone, I believe it is unhealthy to become so comfortable that you inhibit new experiences and growth.

- Follow Alexandra: @alexandra_wallin_

You're not the only one doing it!

Solo female travel is booming and has never been so popular, and the figures don't lie. The term 'solo female travel' saw a 131% increase in Google Trends reporting in 2019. The same year, travel and entertainment website Culture Trip surveyed 10,500 respondents in the UK and US and found "a significant uplift in interest in solo travel". One in seven (14%) women said they had travelled on their own in the past five years, and more than a third of women (34%) were interested in travelling solo in the near future [1].

In 2018 on International Women's Day, tour company Intrepid Travel launched female-only group tours that have grown in popularity year after year. Not only do these offer women a female-centred travel experience, they create employment opportunities in countries where women would not be allowed to guide men. You will not be alone on your journey and are likely to meet many like-minded women like you.

You'll learn to live with less

To travel further, you must travel light, and you'll very quickly learn how easily you get by with only the critical essentials that can fit into your suitcase/backpack. You'll also better appreciate the value of experiences over things. Money can't buy you happiness, but it can buy you a plane ticket and a journey to the experience of a lifetime.

You'll gain a greater sense of confidence.

Making bookings, handling bank cards and money, moving around safely, navigating from one place to the next . . . all of it is on you. Don't let the thought of this scare you, use it as an opportunity to really stand on your own two feet and take full responsibility for yourself. You'll gain a new sense of independence and confidence having done so.

You'll see the world for what it is—not what you're told it is

It goes without saying that different media platforms have their own social and political biases, and nowadays, all thrive on generating clicks and views. Nothing gets you views like drama and conflict, even when it's not as dramatic on the ground. Travel takes you past the headlines and allows you to see for yourself what a place is really like, and more often than not, it is not entirely what the media portrays.

ALL YOUR WORRIES PUT TO BED

"Adventure should be part of everyone's life. It is the whole difference between being fully alive and just existing."
—Holly Morris

You're nervous—I get it. Even as a slightly more experienced traveller, I still get nervous before a trip. The best way to address your worries is to face them head-on, so let's dive into some of the misconceptions about solo female travel.

It's not safe

Simply using common sense and being a little more cautious is enough to keep you safe in most places around the world. Criminals look for opportunities, and that can be while you're in your home country, or abroad. You must follow the same rules of safety when you're abroad and research every location you visit.

Although the biggest worry for women travelling alone is male violence and assault, it is still a rare occurrence. The leading causes of tourists being harmed or killed abroad are in fact; traffic incidences, alcohol or drug-related incidences, drowning, and sickness. Women have been given the gift of incredible instinct, and sharpening your instincts is the number one tool for keeping you safe on the road. Exercising too much caution on the other hand, can deny you of some incredible travel experiences, so learn to read the room and find a balance.

The millions of women who travel the world and come back safe and sound, is evidence enough that you will be fine. As I have experienced, some of your biggest detractors will be people who have never travelled solo themselves. Do not allow others to project their own insecurities on you and dissuade you from following your dreams.

It's too expensive

Entirely untrue. There are many ways you can travel without breaking the bank and also many ways to travel the world for free. We cover all of this in the Money Matters chapter.

I'm afraid of being alone

Finding comfort in solitude is an incredibly liberating experience. When you're comfortable in your own company, you will not seek approval or validation from others, whether it be family, friends, or potential partners. The most dangerous thing we can do in life is to look to others to make ourselves feel complete. If you know that you can stand strong on your own, you are less likely to put up with mistreatment and abuse from others. You are also more likely to attract another individual who feels complete and at peace with themselves.

I'm an introvert

Travelling doesn't mean being an adrenaline junkie who jumps off of cliffs and goes diving with sharks—although there's nothing wrong with that either. The wonderful thing about solo travel is that you are truly free to make your journey your own. As I'll keep saying throughout this book: make the journey yours. Also, remember that you're not alone, there will be plenty of other introverts on the road, worrying about the same thing. Use this as an opportunity to come out of your shell, and freely go back in when needed.

I feel guilty for treating myself

Your friends and family should be supportive of your dreams and not make you feel guilty about wanting to travel. A person who is unfulfilled and lacks a passion for life isn't going to be much use to anybody. Each time I've come back from a trip, I am reinvigorated and feel that I can give more to those around me.

I can't quit my job

'Quit your job and travel the world' has become the biggest cliché in the travel space. It is not, however, necessary to enjoy frequent travel. In Chapter 3 of this book, we examine how you can travel whilst keeping a full-time job, how to quit the correct way if you're ready, and why gap years can be more enjoyable mid-career than as a younger traveller.

I'm too old

Age ain't nothing but a number, and you're never too old to travel solo. If anything, with age, hopefully, you'll have more funds, allowing you to enjoy more luxuries. If you find yourself surrounded by people much younger than you, embrace it. Use it as an opportunity to ask the kids what's going down with them nowadays, and see it as another opportunity to learn. There are, of course, plenty of ways to meet people your own age on the road and tour operators that cater to mature travellers.

Things will go wrong

Well, yes, in all honesty, they could. The little hiccups you face at home don't magically disappear when you're abroad, and for the most part, that's all they will be—little hiccups. The more prepared you are, the less likely it is that things will go wrong, and on the rare occasion that disaster does strike, you'll know what to do in those situations too.

HOW TO GET THE CONFIDENCE TO TRAVEL ALONE

*"Each time we face our fear, we gain strength, courage,
and confidence in the doing."*
—Theodore Roosevelt

The confidence to go it alone seems to come more naturally to some than others. Do not wait until you feel like Wonder Woman to go solo, because it is the actual doing that will ultimately help you to conquer your fears.

Home is closer than you think

You'll be surprised how quickly you will adapt to new surroundings. Humans are built for this. With an increase in globalisation, foreign lands are becoming less and less, well . . . foreign. You are likely to come across elements from home far more commonly than you think, especially in areas with high tourist traffic. Eventually, as I have found, you'll begin to crave more of the unfamiliar.

Travel close to home on your first trip

Schedule in time to do activities alone if this isn't something you do regularly. Dine at a busy restaurant, go see a movie, become a tourist in your own city.

One step further from this, plan a day trip an hour or two outside of your town/city if possible. My first official solo trip was a day trip to Stonehenge. Despite living in London all my life, I had never taken the relatively short journey to Wiltshire to marvel at this prehistorical masterpiece. You'll know very quickly by doing this if solo exploration is something you can enjoy.

Following my day trip to Stonehenge, I booked my first overseas solo adventure; a three day weekend to Budapest, Hungary. It was only an hour by plane, within Europe and affordable. Far enough to test the waters, but close enough for me to feel comfortable.

If in doubt, pick somewhere that's highly popular with tourists. It may be crowded and perhaps a bit more expensive, but you're likely to feel more at ease where you feel a sense of familiarity, than in a destination that requires more planning and experience to navigate. As the famous saying goes: 'Paris is always a good idea'.

Start interacting with other solo female travellers

There are hundreds, if not thousands of online communities where you can e-meet and have conversations with other solo female travellers. Facebook is a great place to find solo female travel groups. Whether in person or online in the digital space, finding your tribe will help to inspire and motivate you. Travel events are also a great way to meet other travel enthusiasts and experts who can share their knowledge.

Book a guided tour

Going on a tour ensures that you are always travelling in a group and with a guide. There is no shortage of tour operators on the market, the hardest part is picking one. When booking a tour, always take the time to read each prospective itinerary. Most tour companies do a good job of laying out exactly what you will see, where you will stay, and the overall physical stamina required for each tour. Also, read the fine print to see what additional costs you may be expected to pay for. Many tours, for example, do not include flights and make you pay a single person supplement. Tours are probably the best option for a nervous solo traveller, although, may not offer the most flexibility for some. Ask the operator what type of customer is likely to book their tours, so you get an idea of who you'll be spending your time with.

Also, take into consideration the number of people on the tour. Anything over twelve or so people is not going to be very personalised and focus on more touristy activities that can take mass bookings from large tour groups. An alternative to booking a full tour is booking day tours and activities during your trip. This allows you the flexibility of creating your own schedule and having days when you're with a tour group.

Feeling more confident? Great! Remember that on the other side of fear is the trip of a lifetime. Feel the fear and do it anyway.

A BIT OF REAL TALK

"Travel makes one modest.
You see what a tiny place you occupy in the world."
– Gustave Flaubert

It was four a.m. on the island of Koh Tao when my alarm went off. I needed to catch an early morning ferry back to the Thai Mainland. Two ferry rides, and a one-hour coach journey later, I reached Surat Thani Airport. From there, I took a flight to Bangkok, had a short layover, and then got on a second flight to Siem Reap, Cambodia. It would be nine p.m. when I finally reached my hostel.

No amount of adventure can make getting up at that time in the morning, and travelling for a full day on multiple modes of transport easy. It is exhausting!

These are the parts of travel that you don't see on the 'gram'. You can't wear a flowy dress and floppy hat when you're jumping from place to place, sleep-deprived, looking and feeling like you got kissed by a death eater.

Travel has its downsides, and you will have your down days on the road. This is not to discourage you, rather, acknowledging it will make those days easier to handle. On most days, you'll be having the time of your life, other days, nothing seems to go right. In many ways, this is no different from when you're at home. Escapism is a part of travel, but reality does not escape you just because you're on the other side of the planet.

Travel is not the end-all and be-all

There will be times in your life that you really just cannot travel, don't get yourself in a rut because you can't. The idea that anyone can jet off at any given time is often promoted in the online travel space, and this is simply not a reality for most people.

Acknowledge that travel is a privilege

Travel is a privilege that not everyone has access to. For some, the prospect of travelling is out of reach, or a dream that requires more time, effort, and work to achieve. The passport you hold also determines how you're treated when entering other countries. Some nationalities have the task of applying for visas in the majority of countries they want to visit. It is not, however, impossible, and there are many travellers who do so with careful planning and preparation.

Instagram vs. Reality

If you've ever scrolled down long enough through travel feeds, it can sometimes feel like you're the only person not in #Bali. Social media can be the most #FOMO (fear of missing out) inducing experience and make you feel like everybody else is having all the fun. This is especially true when it comes to travel. Remember that travel is one (and not necessarily essential) pillar of your overall journey to self-growth. Travel on its own will not fulfil you. In fact, chasing it like the cure to all of your problems will ultimately lead to dissatisfaction. Social media is merely a highlight reel of the best parts of someone's life and steer clear of travel influencers who say, *'look at me'* more often than they say *'learn from me'*.

Sometimes travel sucks

The world isn't perfect. The world isn't whatever you saw in a holiday brochure, and if you ask me, I'm glad it isn't. It's nice to sit in a resort and unwind for a few days, but if you really want to get the most out of travel, you have to be willing to get out of your comfort zone.

As Anthony Bourdain once said: *"Travel isn't always pretty. It isn't always comfortable. Sometimes it hurts, it even breaks your heart. But that's okay. The journey changes you; it should change you. It leaves marks on your memory, on your consciousness, on your heart, and on your body. You take something with you. Hopefully, you leave something good behind."*

Quit trying to find yourself

Finding yourself is a life-long journey that never really ends. It combines deep self-reflection, constant observation, mindfulness, self-discipline, and a thirst for acquiring new skills and knowledge among other things. None of these things require that you travel, instead, just a dedication to self-growth. So I would like us to end this narrative that travel helps you to find yourself. Can travel help us gain a new perspective on certain aspects of our lives —yes—but it will not help you find yourself. Your soul does not reside on a beach in Bali. Self-awareness will not suddenly come to you while trekking ancient ruins in South America, and your inner struggles don't suddenly disappear because you're further away from whatever is causing them.

The experiences you'll have on your travels will be enlightening in their own unique ways, and if you do feel that travel has helped you do find yourself, you likely did a lot of inner work, but remember, this is work you can begin to do right now if you choose, well before you get on a plane. As Robert M. Pirsig once said, *"the only zen you can find on the tops of mountains is the zen you bring up there."*

Your values and outlook on the world will continue to evolve over time—there is no end-point to this process.

**#PASSPORTREADY WORDS OF WISDOM
- PHOEBE, INNER GROWTH**

It's perhaps a tired cliché that when we travel, we find ourselves, yet when I think back to the person I was prior to travelling solo, I can confidently say that a different person emerges from the arrivals lounge each and every time. Be it haggling in a chaotic market, negotiating a tuk tuk fare or

even issuing a firm "no" when receiving unwanted attention, I quickly came to develop a greater instinct for safety and ability to judge a situation, skills which have come to serve me in all sorts of ways. Although it's compulsory to research your destination before setting off anywhere, all the travel guides in the world couldn't possibly teach you what you will learn for yourself on the road. To me, that is one of the most valuable things about travelling as a solo female; the perspective it can create and the confidence it can restore.

Follow Phoebe: @phoebe.worthington

Take destinations for what they are—not what you expect them to be

Remember that the travel industry is ultimately a business, a multibillion-dollar a year business. No one is going to advertise beaches full of plastic trash, poverty, and street hagglers waving cheap souvenirs at every major tourist site. Yes, on occasion, destinations will disappoint, or when you're confronted with social inequality—leave you heartbroken. Take everything for what it is, and try and learn from each experience.

Avoid chasing countries

Country counting has become a popular sport. There are communities within the travel space dedicated to seeing every country in the world and in as little time as possible. You might manage to step foot in every country, but every city, town, or surrounding island—never. You'll never truly see it all, I doubt anyone has, and that's okay.

Better to embrace the world slowly and take it all in, than rush through it and miss the best parts.

#PASSPORTREADY PROFILE
- KAYE, ALWAYS ON THE GO

"*To awaken quite alone in a strange town is one of the pleasantest sensations in the world. You are surrounded by adventure.*"

The intrepid British explorer Freya Stark may have uttered these sentiments a century ago, but her words still ring true today. I should know. I strapped on my backpack and took my first trip alone—the ubiquitous gap year Down Under—at the age of 18 and haven't stopped travelling solo ever since. There have been spells living and working abroad on my own in the Middle East, China, and the Cayman Islands, stints pursuing the digital nomad lifestyle in Colombia, Hawaii, America, Argentina, et al.

Sometimes I have travelled solo simply because I've been single, friends, and family haven't fancied my choice of destination, our finances didn't match up or our annual leave wasn't compatible. Mostly, however, I've travelled alone because I love to. When I step solo off a flight, I get to try a new and different life on for size. Nobody knows if I have been dumped, sacked, or succumbed to London's winter gloom: I can become who I want to be. In Buenos Aires, that was a tanguero (tango dancer) and, accordingly, I would rise in the afternoon to work, before grabbing a bite to eat and heading to a tango class around ten p.m.

After the class, I'd go onto a tango club to milonga the night away, arriving back home and climbing into bed circa the very Argentine hour of six a.m. In India and Sri Lanka, I'd lower myself onto a yoga mat for my very own *Eat, Pray, Love* moment, and in Hawaii, I would rent a surfboard. I may not be Hawaiian, but when I was riding the waves off the world-famous Waikiki shoreline, with the sun beating down on my back, I was able to pretend that I was.

When abroad alone, I adore waking up when I want and eating and drinking what I want—although often, I find that I am only on my own when I choose to be. That's the thing about flying solo: you're much more approachable when you're on your own than in a couple or a group. In Japan, I ticked off Kyoto's temples with Ruth—a Scottish woman who is still a friend to this day. I hiked up Diamond Head in Hawaii with a strapping American military man who I met when collecting my backpack off the carousel at Oahu airport. In the indigenous north of Argentina, I ate empanadas and explored the gorgeous Calchaquí Valleys with Laura, a German lady on her own adventure. I swam from island to island in the South Pacific Ocean with Thomas, a Swiss solo traveller, and enjoyed many crazy nights in Beijing with Americans, Amanda and Geraldine, who have become two of my closest friends.

My message? Don't be scared to travel alone—for flying solo teaches us as much about ourselves as it does about the different lands and diverse cultures we encounter. Certainly, my solo trips, with the same trusty backpack I bought aged eighteen, have changed my life for the better and stayed with me long after I returned home. So go. Now. Or in the words of Mark Twain: "Twenty years from now you will be more disappointed by the things you didn't do than by the ones you did do. So throw off the bowlines. Sail away from the safe harbour. Catch the trade winds in your sails. Explore. Dream. Discover."

Follow Kaye: @kayeoholland

www.kayeholland.com

#PASSPORTREADY PROFILE
- ARI, TAKING OWNERSHIP OF MY JOURNEY

My first solo travel experience was a lonely one. I was travelling to Cambodia for the weekend to see Angkor Wat for the first time. I had arrived with no set plans and spent most of the weekend alone, wandering the giant temples taking in everything I was seeing. I left feeling satisfied, but the lack of interaction left me feeling like solo travel wasn't for me.

Fast-forward to four years later, and I found myself travelling through Turkey for two weeks on the solo adventure of a lifetime. It left me longing for a style of travel where I could control the agenda as I pleased and see the places that meant the most to me.

As an extrovert, I was worried about how much I would or wouldn't be able to really interact with other people. Knowing this, I tried to place myself in situations where I was able to socialize with other people and also have some time to myself. My accommodation was a mix of hostels and nicer hotels, and I made sure to hire tour guides at the historic places I was visiting. Hiring guides cost a little bit more money, but the company and the knowledge I acquired was well worth the price. I also made sure to continuously push past my comfort zone. I started conversations with people I was waiting in line with, or who I saw in the hostels. Some of the interactions were awfully embarrassing, while others gave me some Instagram friends I'm still in contact with today. The more I had conversations with strangers, the more I felt emboldened to keep doing it. I realised that at the end of the day, these embarrassing interactions weren't going to ruin my day, just maybe leave me embarrassed for a few minutes.

By the time I came home, I felt more confident tackling situations that before made me feel uncomfortable. It didn't mean that I no longer felt that discomfort, but that I wasn't afraid of it anymore.

I think the key to solo travel is knowing that mistakes are going to be made, and things aren't always going to turn out the way you want them to, but it's that type of growth that makes these trips the most special.

Follow Ari: @alongwithari

www.alongwithari.com

CHAPTER 1 RESOURCES

FEMALE ONLY TOUR COMPANIES

www.explorerchick.com

www.girlsontravel.co.uk

www.purposefulnomad.com

www.rei.com/adventures/t/womens

www.origin-travels.com

www.adventurewomen.com

www.womens-travel-club.com

www.damesly.com

www.whoatravel.com

www.goddessretreats.com

www.fitandflygirl.com

www.womantours.com

www.wildlandtrekking.com

www.byond.travel/women-only-trips

www.intrepidtravel.com/uk/womens-expeditions

womenoverlandingtheworld.com

walkingwomen.com (also hosts group tours for lesbian women)

www.divadestinations.co.uk (caters specifically for lesbian women)

FEMALE SOLO TRAVEL COMMUNITIES

www.thelonetravelgirl.com

www.dametraveler.com

www.girlsthatscuba.com

FURTHER READING

- Feel The Fear And Do It Anyway by Susan Jeffers

- The Virago Book Of Women Travellers by Mary Morris

- Unsuitable for Ladies: An Anthology of Women Travellers By Jane Robinson

- Women Travel: First-hand Accounts from More Than 60 Countries by Miranda Davies and Natania Jansz

- The Art Of Travel by Alain de Botton

MONEY MATTERS

CHAPTER 2

HOW TO SAVE MONEY FOR TRAVEL

Travel, because money returns, time doesn't.
– Unknown

One of the biggest myths surrounding frequent and long-term travel is that you need lots of money to do it. This is not true. More money can buy you more luxuries and convenience while you travel, but you can still have plenty of fun on a budget. The formula for saving is simple; spend less, save more, and earn extra income. It's not always easy and for some, can mean a lot of hard work and sacrifice. Here's how to do it if you're not earning large sums of money every month.

Get your finances in order

Before you even think about putting money aside for travel, you need to know exactly what is going in and out of your bank account. You'll need to get a clear picture of all of your expenses. Split these expenses into two lists: necessities and nonessentials and cut down on the nonessentials.

There are hundreds of pre-made budgeting spreadsheets available online to download for free, as well as mobile apps and other budgeting software. Find one that works for you and begin carefully tracking all of your expenses from the previous three-six months, and every month going forward.

Once you have a better picture of where your money is going, you will know exactly how much is left after your essential costs, and what you can put aside for travel. You'll also be able to evaluate what can be cut out so you can put more money towards travel. I do not endorse making financially irresponsible decisions to finance your travels. If you are going to take out any credit to finance a trip, make sure you can pay it back, but again, this is not something I endorse and can be avoided with responsible money planning. Saving is a marathon, not a sprint, you may have to save for several months or years to have the trip of a lifetime.

Open a travel savings account

Open a savings account and give it a travel-related name. It can be as simple as "Travel Fund". Seeing your little money pot grow month by month will keep you motivated. You can also set up a direct debit, so a fixed amount of money goes into your savings account each month. Look for a high-interest rate savings account that rewards you every time you deposit money.

Make travel a priority

People assume travel is inaccessible, yet somehow find the money for other nonessentials they want; shoes, a car, luxury cosmetics, etc. You have to see travel as a priority over these other expenditures. The £30 pair of shoes you have to buy or you'll just die—that can buy you a cheap ticket to a nearby city. The designer scented candle that's now on sale—that's three days worth of food while travelling. That annual subscription to your yoga class— that can pay for your medical insurance for an entire trip. Start measuring your monthly costs against how they can be used for travel, and it becomes easier to claw back where you need to.

Get militant about saving

Setting clear rules about what you cannot buy will also help to curb your spending, so I suggest you create a 'no buy' list.

Here are some suggested items that you can stop purchasing and alternatives to replace them:

- Take out coffee—buy instant coffee or filter coffee and make it yourself.

- Bottled water—get a metal water bottle and fill up at home if you have access to safe drinking water.

- Take out food—cook at home and carry lunch.

- Clothes—create a capsule wardrobe out of what you already have. If you must buy something, it has to be for a good reason, i.e., a coat for winter. Scout charity shops or online auction sites like Ebay to see if you can get items for cheaper.

- Subscriptions—cancel any you're not using enough to justify having them. Gym membership tends to be one of the biggest money wasters. Get a gym matt and do your work out at home. There are plenty of fitness videos and resources online to help you create a fitness routine. Take a run around your block and join free outdoor gym classes during the warmer months.

- Makeup—trust me, you have enough. Wear less to cut down on the amount of product you use daily. Consider even going #makeupfree unless perhaps for special occasions. Not only will this save you money, but time off your morning routine.

- House décor—stop buying candles, wall hangings, and anything that will add to your clutter. If you're planning to travel long-term, start selling your stuff and get rid of as much as possible so you don't have to pay for storage when you leave.

- Desk items such as pretty pens and notepads. You do not need yet another unicorn sparkly notepad.

- Beauty treatments such as nails and facials—Watch YouTube tutorials and learn how to do your beauty regimens at home.

- Tobacco and alcohol—both are bad for your health anyway.

- Resist nights out with mates unless it's for a special occasions like birthdays. You can limit yourself to one night out a month if you really feel like you'll get hit with FOMO, but resist the urge to hang out every week. When you do go out, eat beforehand, so you spend less when you're out.

Make a wish list and visualisation board

Get creative and make a wish list and visualisation board full of all the places you wish to visit. Print it out and stick it somewhere you can see it every single day. This is very important because if you don't have a daily visual reference of your goals, you're likely to steer off track and lose the motivation to stick to your plan.

Make some extra income

Think of ways you can make some extra money. This can be through side-jobs, freelance work, selling your stuff, and taking extra hours at work.

The bottom line is that travel has to become a priority. Also, learning to live a more minimalist and frugal life is a very important skill to master before you ever hit the road. The lighter you travel, and the more disciplined you are with your money, the further you can go. The more you have, the more tied down you will be to one base—after all, someone has to look after all of that stuff. You'll find no shortage of frugal and minimalist living sites and forums online. Immerse yourself in these communities and learn how to pick up more financially responsible habits. This won't just benefit your travel fund—it will enhance your entire life.

HOW TO SAVE MONEY ON TRAVEL

Fill your life with experiences, not things.
Have stories to tell, not stuff to show.
—Unknown

Regardless of how long you're going to be away, track your daily spending and keep costs down where possible, especially if you're travelling long term. You can use an app such as Trail Wallet to record your daily spend. Here are some handy strategies for keeping costs low.

Stay in hostels

Let me start off by saying that no, you're not going to get kidnapped by a gang and killed. Thanks to a little movie called *Taken* starring Liam Nesson, a shocking amount of people have told me this any time I've mentioned I stay in hostels. Did that many people seriously watch the damn movie? It's amazing how a fictional narrative can overtake reality. That millions of backpackers stay in hostels every day of the year, and come home safe and sound, seems to go over people's heads.

Accommodation is going to be one of the biggest expenses on your trip, but also one of the expenses you can save a considerable amount on. You will not be spending the majority of your time in your room, so your place of stay should be comfortable and clean, but without all the extra bells and whistles that end up making staying in hotels and resorts so expensive.

Long gone are the days when you had to put up with stuffy rooms, bed bugs, and dorms that looked like an underground bunker. The travel industry has caught up with the demands of travellers and hostels are far more comfortable than what you're probably imagining. Trendy 'poshtels' fitted with modern interiors have sprung up, to cater to backpackers who want something a little more luxurious for a budget price.

Most hostels also offer single-sexed accommodations if you prefer rooms occupied only by other women. Personally, I prefer and would mostly recommend female-only dorms. That's not to say you can't stay in mixed dorms, or that they're unsafe, but my personal experience has meant this is my overall preference. If the hostel you want to stay at doesn't have single sexed dorms, ask them to put you in a mixed dorm with a higher percentage of females. I've found that many places will make an effort to meet your request in dorm rooms with less beds.

If you're feeling very adventurous, shortlisting a few places and showing up to check them out before booking allows you to scope the place before handing over your cash, and negotiate a cheaper price. You can also ring places directly as this may offset the commission they have to pay to a listing site.

Hostel essentials: Make sure to carry a sleeping eye mask and earplugs, two absolute essentials when staying in hostels. Also make sure to take locks to secure your luggage in your locker, most hostels will charge you for one if you don't have your own.

Real talk: the downsides of hostels—even the fancier ones, is that sometimes, you really just want your privacy. If you're planning on travelling for longer periods, consider getting a private room every now and again. Many hostels offer private rooms for a lot cheaper than a hotel.

Eat the local food

Where possible, avoid eating in areas too close to major tourist sites. These will usually have slightly hiked up prices, walk a few streets down instead.

Breakfast is the easiest meal to do on the cheap. When in Thailand, I often found myself walking to the local 7-Eleven grocery store to get coffee and a pastry. I also found that asking locals and tour guides was a more powerful tool than Google for finding the best and cheapest eateries. Local food is undoubtedly more authentic and delicious. Street food culture is common in many parts of the world, particularly in warmer, low-cost destinations where it is comfortable to eat outside and provides a steady stream of income for locals. Simply following common-sense advice (outlined in the Health chapter of this book) will help you avoid runny tummies and food related illnesses.

Real talk: sometimes, you will crave the comforts of home and that's fine too—just don't miss out on trying the local cuisine.

Cheap transportation

If it's efficient and safe, take whatever public transport is available. This is also a great way to infuse yourself into local life and can be quite enjoyable. Riding around in tuk tuks was one of my favourite things to do in South East Asia—just make sure to know what the locals pay in order not to get ripped off.

When travelling long distance, opt for travelling over land on buses and trains where available.

Real talk: sometimes, you just want to get somewhere as fast as possible. I skipped the twelve-hour sleeper train from Chiang Mai to Bangkok and took a one-hour flight instead. I do not regret paying the extra £30 it cost, I saved an entire day of travel. Riding apps such as Uber (available in numerous cities around the world) and Gojek and Grab (popular in South East Asia), offer fast, efficient, and affordable alternatives to taxi's that often charge hiked up prices, mainly to tourists.

Look for city tourist cards online

Depending on your planned itinerary, this may or may not be worth it, but they're worth looking into. Tourism cards are popular in many European and American cities and will usually offer free entry/heavy discounts into attractions and restaurants. Some even include public transport at a discounted rate.

Do free activities

Free walking tours are quite common, in city destinations. Look online, or ask the front-desk of your accommodation if they're running a free walking tour. This is a great way to get your bearings around a city with a knowledgeable guide. Museums, festivals, parades, street performances and installations, libraries, beaches, parks, places of worship, nature spots and national parks can also offer plenty of free fun time. A quick Google search of 'best free things to do in (name of location)', will offer up plenty of suggestions.

Book trips the weeks just before and after peak season

There are generally three things that contribute to peak season being more expensive:

1) good weather conditions
2) school holidays
3) major festivals and events

This can increase the price of flights, accommodation, tours, and entrance fees to popular sights. Booking the weeks around these time periods will ensure that you still enjoy decent weather conditions and less crowds for a lower price. Of course, if you don't mind grey clouds, rain, and colder conditions, booking at times completely off-season will save you even more money.

Settle for seconds

Every destination has smaller cities/towns. These are often cheaper to visit and can offer more unique experiences than the main tourist hotspots. They also tend to be less crowded. Take a moment to research them and see what they have to offer.

Use coupons and shop in sales

Before you book or buy anything related to your travels, always look for a discount. Most companies nowadays will offer you a first-time customer discount. If you can't find one, call up customer services and ask. The worst they will say is no. When you sign up for a service, wait a few days before paying and see if you get a reminder e-mail with a discount code, this is a popular customer acquisition technique used by e-mail marketeers.

Ask friends and family if they have referrals codes, look for coupons in travel magazines, and take note of discount codes placed on ads. This counts for every part of your travel expenditure, especially travel gear. Wait for seasonal sales to see if you can catch any promotions, and claim reward points such as air miles. It may take a while to build up enough points that are usable, but they will come in handy eventually.

Make friends on the road

Having a buddy means you'll have someone to split the costs with. If you're staying in hostels, you're bound to make friends, and you can share everything from transportation to accommodation costs to offset that dreaded single person supplement.

Real talk: Be open but be careful. I've heard many stories from travellers claiming their newfound travel friend turned into a grifter. If you start to feel uncomfortable around someone, don't feel bad about saying goodbye and going your own way. You owe them nothing for their ill behaviour, and you'll never see them again anyway.

Chase the deal, not the destination

Budapest was the first city I ever travelled to solo. I knew little about this amazing city before I started researching it. As well as being a fun, safe, and interesting, the choice to visit ultimately came down to incredibly cheap tickets and cheap accommodation. Was it my number one choice at the time? No, it wasn't, but it had plenty to do and see and was what I could afford at the time. Both my flights and accommodation came to a combined cost of £70 for a three-day trip.

Real talk: we all have a dream travel list, but be realistic. The more open you are to new adventures, the more you will see and probably a lot sooner. Sometimes it's worth travelling just for the sake of travel itself, with a curious mind-set, you can find adventure almost anywhere you go.

Pack light

The lighter you pack, the less you have to drag around, and the less you'll have to spend on baggage allowance. Budget airlines will usually give you a free cabin luggage allowance, (although some are becoming stingy with that) but will charge you for checked-in baggage.

Book accommodation with kitchen facilities

Cooking food can save you a lot of money, particularly in countries where the general cost of living is high. Pack food containers if you plan on cooking lunch as well.

Real-talk: be realistic. Consider how often you are actually likely to cook. That is time taken away from your leisure and enjoying the local cuisine is part of the travel experience. In some places, it is even cheaper to simply eat out than purchase ingredients to cook a meal.

Get travel insurance

For longer trips, travel insurance can end up being one of your highest pre-travel costs, but it will also save you money on the road should anything go wrong. Missed flights, medical costs, and travel disruptions can put a serious dent in your budget if you have to cover the costs yourself. Never leave without insurance.

HOW TO TRAVEL THE WORLD FOR FREE

If you're twenty-plus, physically fit, hungry to learn and be better,
I urge you to travel – as far and as widely as possible...
find out how other people live and eat and cook.
Learn from them – whereveryou go.
— Anthony Bourdain

I have to start with an inconvenient truth: the only thing convenient about free travel is the price. There will be trade-offs when travelling for free. This is what the numerous listicles you've probably read online about free travel have missed out. Depending on your style of travel, these trade-offs may or may not matter, but it's important you know what they are. These methods of travel are generally better for the slow-moving vagabond who is on a longer journey, and will help you stretch your budget further for longer.

House-sitting

House-sitting offers you free accommodation in return for looking after someone's home and often their pets. Sites such as Trusted House Sitters and Mind My House offer a global database of people willing to open their doors up to strangers looking for free boarding. There will be a small fee when you sign up to most of these sites.

Real talk: there are a greater number of travellers than there are places to house them. There is also little certainty you will find accommodation where and when you want it, as it is entirely dependent on when a homeowner is vacant from their property. You are also still responsible for someone's home and beloved pet, which means an extra responsibility for you. Make sure that the owner of the house has clearly communicated what they expect of you while staying in their home, before accepting an offer.

Do some volunteer work

Sites such as Work Away and WWOOF International (World Wide Opportunities on Organic Farms) offer you the opportunity to do volunteer work in exchange for basic accommodation and meals. While WWOOF focuses more on farm work, Work Away offers a much more diverse range of volunteer opportunities including; helping out at schools, yoga retreats, resorts and hostels, boat stays, general housekeeping, childcare, offering hands-on skills such as building, and tech skills like web development and online marketing. This is one of the most cost-efficient ways to extend your travels by weeks and months if you aim to stay on the road for longer.

Real talk: expect that both your food and accommodation will be basic and some positions will be in remote areas. Make sure to check the reviews and ask the host exactly what it is that is expected of you before you arrive. Typically, you are expected to work for a few hours a day anywhere from three to five days a week. Any place that asks for more than that should be avoided; you still want time to enjoy your stay. If you're not enjoying a place, or it's not what you expected, don't feel obligated to stay. Hosts have been known to take advantage and ask for more than what was agreed upon.

Become an au pair

Like children? Become an au pair and offer to care for someone's little darlings. As an au pair, you will receive boarding in your host family's home plus weekly pocket money. Aupairworld.com is one of the most trusted websites for finding opportunities.

Real talk: Consider carefully if you want the responsibility of looking after someone else's children and don't just do it because you want to save money. You will undergo a criminal back-ground check, and previous convictions may hinder your chances of getting a placement. Au pair work is generally considered a cultural exchange and not as full employment, meaning the pocket money you get is just that—pocket money. If you want an actual, liveable wage, you will have to consider getting a working visa and working as a nanny.

Apply for scholarships, grants, and competitions

You'll be surprised how many opportunities there are on offer around the world. These range from fully/partially paid international graduate degrees, to short cultural exchanges and global competitions for various disciplines. You can find a full list of places to apply for opportunities in the resources section of this book.

Study abroad

Studying abroad allows you to immerse yourself in a different country and gives you the right to stay there for an extended period of time. Some countries also offer graduate visas that allow you to extend your stay and work after you have received your degree.

If you decide to study in your home country, ask your university what exchange programmes and overseas opportunities they have. If you know you'll have to support yourself financially, ensure you have the right to work in your chosen country of study. Obtaining the right to study does not mean you have the right to work, or that you can earn enough money to live. You'll find that many countries limit the hours a week you can work if you are a student.

Reconnect with your roots

There are a small number of countries that offer 'discover your roots' programmes as a way of encouraging descendants to visit their country of cultural origin. If you are a child or descendant of immigrants, you may be eligible for one of these programmes. Countries currently offering these programs include; Greece, Hungary, Armenia, Israel and Macedonia.

Find a free place to crash

Couchsurfing.com has become the go-to place for travellers looking for a place to crash for no cost.

A fantastic alternative specifically for women, is the Facebook group Host A Sister. The private group currently boasts over 100,000 women who are willing to offer their homes—or their time as guides—to other female travellers. Although the group operates only on Facebook at the moment, it does appear that they are building an actual website.

Real talk: Cultural exchange and spending time with the host is also an important part of the experience. You become part of that household, and so, if you're not willing to give some of your time to the people you're staying with, forget it.

HOW TO MAKE MONEY WHILE TRAVELLING

"Don't live the same year 75 times and call it a life."
— Robin S. Sharma

Working on the road keeps your travel fund topped up, allowing you to travel for longer. I do however, have to throw in a word of caution; it won't always be easy to find a job, and it probably won't pay much. Having said that, stopping in one place to work for a while will give you the time to fully immerse yourself into day to day life.

Get a holiday working visa

Working Holiday Visas are designed to allow travellers to work in a country for a limited amount of time to supplement their travels funds. The general age range for a holiday working visa is eighteen to thirty, although some go up to the age of thirty-five.

The following countries currently offer Holiday Working Visas: Argentina, Australia, Austria, Belgium, Canada, Chile, China, Czech Republic, Denmark, Estonia, Finland, France, Germany, Hong Kong, Ireland, Israel, Italy, Japan, Latvia, Lithuania, Malta, The Netherlands, New Zealand, Norway, Poland, South Korea, Singapore, Slovakia, Slovenia, Spain, Sweden, Switzerland, Thailand, Turkey, UK, and Uruguay.

Some countries require that you apply for your holiday working visa before arriving and that you have a minimum amount of funds to support yourself before you can be cleared for entry.

Real talk: working holiday visas have strict limits on the hours you can work and the type of work you can do. Typically, jobs in hospitality, tourism, retail, events, corporate admin, and seasonal industries are the most common forms of work available. Holiday Visas are made as cultural exchange agreements between countries, so where you're eligible to work depends on your nationality.

Teach English

TELF (Teaching English as a Foreign Language) and CELTA (Certificate of English Language Teaching to Adults) are two of the most recognised certificates for teaching English abroad. A full-time course will typically last four weeks and take 120 hours to complete. Part-time options are also available and can be taken in a classroom or online. Once you have qualified, you have the option of teaching in a classroom at a school, or online. Teaching in a school allows for a fully immersive cultural experience while teaching online allows you to earn while you're on the move. If you want to teach English at more prestigious schools or in universities, requirements are stricter. You may be required to have a higher qualification than just a standard certificate.

Real talk: beware English teaching scams that charge enormous fees and then ask you to recruit other teachers to earn a commission. These pyramid-type schemes have become more common in recent years. The best way of finding out if a course is legit and can lead to decent work is by speaking to other travellers who have already done it. Teaching is not for everybody. It requires patients, dedication, and a genuine desire to help children develop. Do not go into teaching if you're not ready to give those children your heart and soul—they deserve the best you can give them.

Explore all your visa options

It is worth exploring different types of visa's in your country of interest. For example, perhaps you can opt for a full working visa/permit, instead of a holiday working visa. Information on visas can be found on official immigration and government websites.

In 2019, Estonia was the first country to offer the "long-stay digital nomad visa", a visa specifically catered to digital entrepreneurs and nomads looking for a place to stay long-term. As the world changes, who knows what other countries will follow suit, and what they will offer. Perhaps you have a qualification or skill that is in higher demand in another country. You'll be given much easier access to immigration if you do.

HOW TO FIND CHEAP FLIGHT TICKETS

Chase the deal, not the destination.

Following this one rule enabled me to travel to more countries in a shorter period of time. I have almost always travelled based on the price of a ticket to a destination, looking for the cheapest place to fly from my nearest airports. Although I eventually cancelled my trip, I once got a return ticket to Romania for £9.98—almost the same cost as a day travel card in London! Airfare is your biggest travel cost along with accommodation, and you can easily knock a few pennies off the price by following these small hacks.

Clear your browser

If you've ever searched for a flight ticket long enough, you'll sometimes notice that the price has slowly crept up. You're not crazy. Flight prices do increase when a particular route is repeatedly searched. Web browsers collect data as you browse, but there is a way to outsmart the system. Until you're ready to actually book a ticket, always browse in incognito/private browsing. You should find the option to do so in the top menu bar of your browser. Also, make sure to clear your browsing history after every few searches. Open up a completely different browser when looking for tickets. For example, I mostly use Google Chrome when browsing the web, but switch to Safari or Explorer when searching for flight tickets.

Skyscanner decoded

There are many flight booking sites online, but we're going to focus on Skyscanner.net as it's the one I use most frequently.

When you land on the Skyscanner homepage, select the city that you will fly out from and in the destination box type in 'Everywhere'.

There are three ways you can search for tickets:

- By cheapest month—this will throw up the cheapest airfares currently on the market

- By a selected month—this will show the cheapest airfare available for the specific month you selected

- A specific date—this will show you the cheapest airfare for a selected date

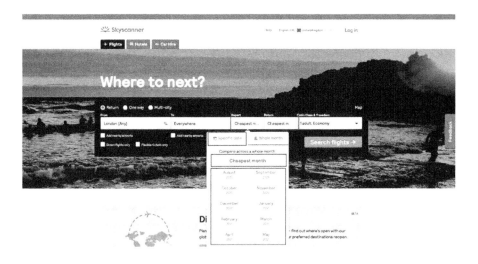

You will then be given a breakdown of each country in order of ascending price.

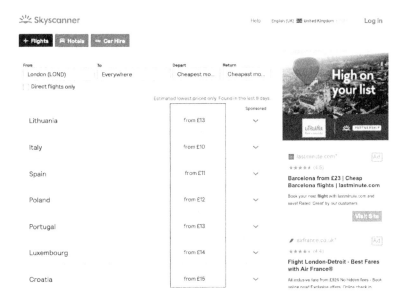

Click on your country and then city of choice.

On the next page, if you've searched by cheapest month for a return ticket, you will be asked to select your dates. When you select an outbound date, you will find that the prices on the return date suddenly change in real time. I can attest that having used Skyscanner for years, this wasn't always the case. To beat the bot, try doing two separate searches in separate windows for outgoing and incoming flights and see if it comes out cheaper.

Always end by clearing your cookies once more and going directly to the airlines website to book your final ticket.

Other flight hacks

If there is a while to go before your trip, set up a flight alert to monitor the price of your flight and watch for price drops.

Be open to longer routes and layovers as these usually come out cheaper.

Be open to flying in the early mornings and very late evening because prices tend to be cheaper.

Sometimes airlines make price mistakes and will often honour the price if you chase them up on it. Some websites specialise in spotting price mistakes and alerting you to them. They usually have a monthly subscription and can save you a lot of money if you're planning on flying to more expensive locations.

Warning, this little game of finding the cheapest ticket can be addictive once you're good at it. Search a few times a week to see what's on offer.

HOW TO AVOID BUDGET AIRLINE FEES

I would rather own a little and see the world
than own the world and see a little of it.
– Unknown

Budget airlines have revolutionised air travel, making regular trips more accessible to people that would otherwise struggle to afford them. Ryanair, EasyJet, and Wizz Air are just a few of the well-known names in the market.

Despite the low prices, budget airlines are notorious for adding fees and squeezing more pennies out of customers. Sneaky penalties and up-selling add-ons are just a few of the ways budget airlines up the price of your ticket. Here are my top tips for avoiding those pesky budget airline fees. Never pay more than what you have to again.

Print out your tickets

Making you pay a penalty if you have not printed your ticket, is one of the most common ways budget airlines force you to pay more. Make sure your tickets are printed as early as possible. Some airlines like Ryanair charge you extra for early check-in, if you don't want to pay, you usually have to wait a few days before check-in opens.

The best option is to have your ticket saved on your phone. Many airlines also have apps where your ticket will be stored and presented when you arrive at the gate.

Ignore unnecessary extras

Another way budget airlines will try to add to your bill is by tempting you with extras such as priority seating, choosing your seat and add-ons such as insurance, which you should already have. Priority seating usually allows you the privilege of getting onto your flight quicker for a slightly higher fee. The difference in boarding the time if you don't buy priority seating isn't worth it, you can simply avoid the long queue by getting there a bit early. Better still, grab a seat near the gate and wait till everybody is in and jump on the very back of the line, no need to queue!

Resist Duty Free shopping

Not a direct fee, but certainly an extra way for airlines to make money during flights.

If you wait for the sales or do a comparison search online, you can probably get whatever you wanted for even cheaper than Duty Free anyway! Duty Free being cheaper is probably one of the biggest travel myths.

Buy food before you get on the plane

As well as tasting like plastic, plane food on budget airlines is often overpriced. Eat before your flight.

Pay attention to baggage allowance

Know how much junk you're carrying in your trunk, weigh and measure your luggage.

If you're flying on multiple airlines, check the allowance for each carrier. Make sure to check every time you travel as airlines can change baggage allowance from time to time.

So there you have it, those are some of the tricks budget airlines play in order to get you to spend more than you expected. That £10 bargain ticket can end up costing you £100 if you're not careful! Never be duped again.

A FINAL NOTE ON BUDGET TRAVEL

Stuff your eyes with wonder, live as if you'd drop dead in ten seconds. see the world. It's more fantastic than any dream made or paid for in factories.
—Ray Bradbury

If you've scrolled through budget travel blogs enough, you're likely to have come across some creative, and darn right crazy methods of saving money on the road. Everything from sleeping in airports and train stations, wild camping in questionable places and hitchhiking.

I do not endorse doing anything that is potentially dangerous, or that could land you in trouble with authorities. There's an obvious line between adventurous and reckless. Wild camping for example, is perfectly fine as long as you follow local laws, respect the environment and do a proper safety assessment of your location. I also do not endorse being so tight with your pennies that you deprive yourself of magnificent experiences and basic comforts. If you have to pay an extra penny or two a night to sleep in a nicer hostel bed—do it. If you have to pay for a guide because the activity you're doing advises so for safety reasons—do it. If it's going to cost you just that little bit more to get to the next destination in one hour versus twelve—pay up.

The moments where you pull away from your set budget will inevitably happen. When you're suffering from travel burnout, want some privacy, or see a local artist painting a stunning landscape and imagine it hanging on your living room wall— your pocket will start singing. Know when to hold back and know when to treat yourself. Create a safety net in your budget where you can have these moments and re-examine which parts of your budget you can scale back from.

Whatever you do, never and I mean **never** compromise on your safety just because something is cheaper. You're better off saving for a little longer so you can travel with more funds.

Don't go all the way around the world for half the experience.

#PASSPORTREADY PROFILE
- ANNA, THE UNEXPECTED EXPAT

I remember the evening I first arrived in the UK so vividly. I remember the fresh smell of the evening rain, and the warm autumn breeze under the leafy green trees in Sheffield. As I dropped my suitcase on the pavement and the taxi drove away, I stood there looking around. It was my first taste of independence and I was frightened.

My only thought was; "Oh God, what have I done to myself".

Now reminiscing about the young me ten years ago, I wish I could place my hand steadily on her shoulder and say: "Don't worry, your rollercoaster life is only just starting, but it will be an incredible ride. And you will be fine."

The thing is, I was only meant to stay in Sheffield for six months as an exchange student in Criminology and Politics. Little did I know that a decade later, I would have a home and life I love in London. It has been and equal mix of great successes and tremendous losses, but it has been a life as raw and real as I could have ever hoped for.

I sometimes wonder if it is easier to make life-changing decisions when we are younger, and perhaps a little bit more naive. I am grateful for the courage I had to apply for the second half of my scholarship and launch myself directly to Washington DC for a summer program with The Fund for American Studies. I settled into an internship with a subgroup of The Washington Times and summer studies at Georgetown University. Following that, I was accepted to a university back in London for a masters degree in International Relations and Security, which paved the way into the very peculiar career path I was destined to take.

I remember the painting I had back at my father's home where I grew up: an image of the Palace of Westminster right above my bed back in Estonia. Who would have predicted, that I'd be heading to a meeting about counter-terrorism strategies, in the very same building years later.

After my studies and hard work, I was incredibly lucky to be accepted for an internship with NATO Counter-Terrorism Section at Emerging Security Challenges Division in Brussels. Leaving behind a dreamy flat in West London in Notting Hill, my heart heavily sank when saying goodbye to my beloved London. Like a gruelling love affair, I missed London and the home I had built with wonderful friends, as I faced the beginnings of the interesting career and incredible opportunities for learning that NATO offered.

I still wonder sometimes the parallel lives I could have lived and what my life would have looked like if I had stayed in Sheffield for only six months. But looking back, I have been privileged to live a life of travels, both with friends and solo, with extended stays in different countries, learning about so many cultures and traditions. I have had an opportunity to feel melancholic by the autumn-coloured canals in Venice, I have felt the heat of the Canary Islands, I have danced in the trendy nightclubs until morning light in Berlin with my best friends, I have sailed the blue seas in hot summery Greece. I have been deeply moved whilst witnessing life in the remote corners of West Africa in Burkina Faso, where civilisation seemed still at its very beginnings compared to the tall buildings of its bustling capital city. I will never forget the beautiful African sunrise, and the smell of wood fire, life as daring and calm as it could ever come. I felt a profound sense of peace.

The unexpected expat, I have found love and life on this incredible journey, empowered by hope and inspiration in the face of the incredible people I have had a chance to meet and know. Perhaps one day I will see myself back to where it all started, to the most beautiful country I have ever known, to the country I am proud to have roots in, the simple small nation by the Baltic Sea. Until then, I feel I have many more journeys to walk and I have no intention of stopping.

Follow Anna: @shetravelglobal

www.shetravel.co.uk

#PASSPORTREADY PROFILE
- ABENA, GOING AGAINST THE LIFE SCRIPT

When I was in university, I took the opportunity to do a study year abroad in France. It really sparked my love for travel, and I visited amazing places in the country and made a ton of international friends who told me about their diverse experiences. When I graduated, I really wanted to continue travelling—but it suddenly felt a bit rogue.

When you go on holiday as a child, it's with the safety of your family. When you travel abroad with school or university, it's seen as low risk because it seems like nothing can go wrong within an educational institution. But once you're a young adult and you want to step out alone and pursue travel—you are suddenly met with pushback, or at least, I was. Aunties and uncles telling me it would be too dangerous and the overriding message that I'm not serious about life if I'm not focusing on my career. In my opinion, it's the best time to travel because one can enjoy it freely, with fewer ties and without the life-baggage we acquire as we get older. We also have the capacity as the next generation to positively enlarge our perspectives to form a better society in the future.

With all my friends figuring out their own postgraduate lives— I've had to travel mostly solo. And last year, at twenty-one years old, I took a five-week solo trip to Southeast Asia. I was completely immersed in cultures so completely different from my own and had many special encounters with locals and other travellers that still have an impact on me today.

You might be thinking—wasn't it far for you to go alone? Weren't you scared? We all get butterflies, even the most experienced solo travellers. Inside, you're feeling nervous because you're in unfamiliar settings, you're thinking about safety, you don't want to stick out like a sore thumb. In response,

I've learned to feign confidence. It's my secret superpower. When you do this, you even forget you were nervous in the first place, and you're free to receive whatever that travel experience has instore for you.

Follow Abena: @travellingtuesdays

CHAPTER 2 RESOURCES

BUDGETING AND SAVING

www.mint.com

www.youneedabudget.com

MINIMAL LIVING

www.bemorewithless.com

www.theminimalists.com

www.becomingminimalist.com

CHEAP ACCOMMODATION

www.hostelworld.com

www.booking.com

www.couchsurfing.com

www.facebook.com/groups/hostasister

CHEAP FLIGHTS

www.skyscanner.net

www.jacksflightclub.com

www.scottscheapflights.com

HOUSE SITTING

www.housesittingmagazine.com

www.trustedhousesitters.com

www.mindmyhouse.com

www.housesitmatch.com

BECOME AN AU PAIR

www.aupairworld.com

www.findaupair.com

www.connectaupair.world

DISCOVER YOUR ROOTS PROGRAMS

Greece - www.nationalhellenicsociety.org/program-overview.html

Hungary – www.reconnecthungary.org

Armenia - www.birthrightarmenia.org/en

Israel - www.birthrightisrael.com

Macedonian – www.umdiaspora.org/cpt_services/leadership-development/#birthright-macedonia

Cuba – www.cubaone.org/aboutus/how-it-works

TEACHING ENGLISH

www.ninjateacher.com

www.theteflacademy.com

www.geovisions.org

VISA INFORMATION

www.visadb.io

www.passportindex.org

VOLUNTEERING

www.workaway.info

www.worldpackers.com

www.wwoofinternational.org

INSURANCE

www.worldnomads.co.uk

www.covermore.co.uk

GRANTS, SCHOLARSHIPS, FELLOWSHIPS AND COMPETITIONS

www.intercompetition.com

www.youthop.com

www.contestwatchers.com

www.heysuccess.com

www.scholars4dev.com

THE JOB SITUATION

CHAPTER 3

TO QUIT OR NOT TO QUIT

"And then there is the most dangerous risk of all
— the risk of spending your life not doing what you want
on the bet you can buy yourself the freedom to do it later."
– Randy Komisar

There is no one perfect way to travel.

You might choose to have a full-time career and maximise work allocated and public holidays.

You might choose to take a gap year before, during, or after your studies.

You might choose to take a career sabbatical, or several - aka mini-retirements – throughout your working life.

You might alternate between doing common service jobs to save money and travelling.

You might figure out a way of making passive income or set up your own online business and go fully nomadic.

You might work overseas and never return, going from expat to full citizen.

You might do a mixture of all of the above over time.

The spirit of being #PassportReady is that you can fit travel into your life as and when it is most convenient for you.

If you spend enough time around the travel community online, you'd think that quitting your job to travel the world is the end-all and be-all—it isn't.

I don't regret going to university, although I do wish I had studied abroad. I don't regret focusing on a career either – I value both of these experiences. I still travelled to eight countries in four years. After earning my stripes for three years at a desk job, I was able to request one month off to travel and returned with a career still in place. It was this very journey that made me realise *the dream life* often seen online, was not *my* idea of a dream life.

A popular narrative in some parts of the travel community is that you're either a worker bee stuck on a desk, seemingly ignorant to the joys that await you in some faraway land, or, you're one of the smart ones that escaped the nine to five. Some people actually do have jobs that give them meaning and purpose, or at the very least, the stability they desire.

The truth is that both of these paths have their ups and downs.

While sticking to the Life Script never guarantees happiness and stability, neither does being a permanent wanderer. The coronavirus pandemic was a harsh reminder of how fragile nomadic life can be. I believe that full-time-forever-and-always nomadic life is only for a handful of people. Some of the most popular travel influencers and other types of nomads, are settling down into more semi-nomadic lives having built their online businesses.

The reality is that long-term travel is not for everyone

When I first discovered the online travel community, endlessly travelling the world became my obsession. It took for me to do a one-month trip to realise that it definitely wasn't for me. I like the idea of going on extended trips, but I need a home base to come back to. One of my criticisms of the travel influencer community is that it has to be one or the other, that you can't find ways of meshing the two, or alternating between them.

You seldom see travellers admitting they packed it all up and went home. Physical sickness, homesickness, and even running out of cash are just a few of the reasons people go straight back to their normal lives. Again, I say this not to put anyone off long-term travelling, but rather, to ensure you go into it with a realistic outlook, and not while wearing rose-tinted glasses.

So what is one to do, how do you know what is and isn't for you?

My advice is to go with what your instincts tell you and be open to change. More than anything, don't fall into the trap of thinking that someone else's idea of *the dream* will make you happy.

HOW TO TRAVEL
WHEN YOU HAVE A FULL-TIME JOB

*"Every dreamer knows that it is entirely possible to be homesick
for a place you've never been to,
perhaps more homesick than for familiar ground."*
— Judith Thurman

It is 100% possible to travel while you have a full-time job. I've been doing it successfully for years. If you're lucky enough to live in a country where holiday leave is mandatory, congrats, you've got more days to work with. If not, do not despair. There are still a few things you can do to make your travel dreams a reality while holding down a job.

Use holiday days carefully

When booking trips, maximise weekends. Thursday through Sunday or Wednesday through Monday, giving you two extra vacation days. Not every getaway has to be a one or two week long adventure. Short breaks to nearby towns and cities can be just as fun.

On one occasion, I left work late on a Friday night and returned very early on Monday, with just enough time to get back into the office. I had to drink an extra strong coffee, but I survived.

Try and blend travel into work

If the opportunity arises for you to travel for work, take it. Book an extra couple of days in whichever location you are based in and ask if your return flight can be moved to your chosen departure date.

Use public holidays

Get an empty calendar and highlight all of the public holidays in your country and try to book trips around them. Taking your holiday leave the days just before and after public holiday days will allow you to travel longer while using less holiday leave. The obvious con with booking a trip around a public holiday is that everyone else is booking too! This means flights, accommodation, and even some attractions are busier and more expensive. Consider exploring places that are less popular to escape the crowds and if you are going to travel around public holidays, book well in advance to get ahead of the last-minute price hikes.

Negotiate unpaid leave

If you do not have enough holiday days, try and negotiate some unpaid leave from work. Make sure to speak to your HR manager well in advance. Unpaid leave costs your company nothing, and will give you a few extra days to travel.

Ask to be relocated/apply in another office

If you work for a company that has offices in different cities around the world, talk to management about a role in another location.

HOW TO QUIT YOUR JOB THE RIGHT WAY

*"The purpose of life is to live it,
to taste experience to the utmost,
to reach out eagerly and without fear
for a newer and richer experience."*
—Eleanor Roosevelt

So you've considered all the options and decided that you do want to quit your job, either for an extended period of time and then come back to normal life, or to quit forever, having solidified another source of income.

Perhaps you've seen those endless Instagram ads about quitting the grind and travelling the world…so let's start there. For those who want to quit office life completely to start a career as a travel personality, here's what many travelprenures don't often tell you: you'll still be working.

Being a successful travel blogger/influencer means being a videographer, photographer, content writer, PR person, social media manager, affiliate marketer, project pitcher, SEO expert, and more. Many travel influencers do not make money in the early phases of starting their business, and many never make a liveable wage at all. The market is more competitive than ever, and everyone wants in. It's possible, but don't expect overnight success.

Working online

If you're looking to live the nomadic dream, do not expect that success will materialise the second you land in another country. It's a good idea to have a strong business, or steady stream of clients before you make a move permanent. You'll also need some kind of skill that can be done remotely. Graphic design, video editing, copy editing and proofreading, computer programming, content marketing, digital marketing consulting, and teaching English online are the most common jobs for online nomads.

#PASSPORTREADY WORDS OF WISDOM - ALLISON, THE LAPTOP LIFE

I was in my last year of college when I realized I wasn't going to look for a nine to five job. Instead, I began searching for part-time work that I could do online and remotely. To find clients, I applied for job listings that didn't initially state they were hiring for a remote position. Once the recruiters expressed interest in me though, I would let them know that I was only taking on remote work. While not as ideal as applying for a remote position outright, I found this strategy to be effective more often than not. Other ways I've found clients is by utilizing freelancing platforms like Upwork, and networking with people in Facebook groups and in my community.

Over the last couple of years, I've travelled and worked in Indonesia, China, Vietnam, Italy, Spain, and a handful of other places. For me, this way of living is a dream, but it doesn't come without its drawbacks. Sometimes you have to say no to going out with the people you meet, or to and adventure somewhere remote where there is no wifi connection. On the flip side though, when those people you meet have to go home, you get to stay!

Follow Allison: @wolvesandwaterfalls

www.wolvesandwaterfalls.com

Make sure to have a Plan B

Think carefully about what you might do if you have to cut your plans in half. What provisions do you have in place to keep yourself afloat?

If you must apply for jobs when you come back, have an updated CV ready before you leave. Consider even sending your applications in the weeks leading up to your return so you can get a head start on job hunting.

Make sure to have at least one or two months savings cushioned into your budget so you can survive if there's no guarantee you'll have money when you return. No one wants to come crawling back to mummy and daddy, and ask for handouts when they return.

When you're ready to leave

I would avoid talking about your plans too openly. You never know who will or won't be happy for you, and some people may see your travel dreams as you being less dedicated to your job. Until you're ready to hand in your notice, keep it to yourself.

How to explain the gap in your CV

Some people will think you're awesome for taking your journey and see it as a plus to have someone who has had the experience of travel. Other people might want an explanation.

Be honest about your travels when asked. Assure your employer that you are here to stay (even if you're not) and that your travels were part of a personally enriching experience that you feel will make you a better employee. Don't brag about how much partying you did. You can even add that you have no issue travelling for work purposes if it benefits the business in any way and that you have the confidence to travel alone or work with international teams.

As well as making you look thoughtful, adding some volunteer work can boost your cv, especially if it's related to your job/studies.

Go back to the link library in the 'Money Matters' chapter to view websites where you can find volunteer work.

Affirm your commitment to your job, even if you do plan on jumping ship again in the near future. Let your employer know that you're ready to settle in permanently and have no plans of taking off anytime soon.

Anyone looking to embrace the nomadic life should still have a backup plan. Life on the road will throw you just as many spanners as normal life.

#PASSPORTREADY PROFILE
- CALLIE, THE SOLOPRENURE

Like other stories you have heard about twenty-something-year-old women fed up with their nine to five , I quit my corporate job to travel the world. It was 2017, and I was five years into a marketing position in NYC that felt so far from where I was supposed to be. After leaving, I solo travelled for four months, starting in Scandinavia and ending in Japan. The solo travelling part was easy. As many lone travellers say, travelling solo doesn't actually mean you are alone. One of my fondest memories is staying in a twenty-eight-bunk room in Bergen, Norway surrounded by people from all over the globe. The hard part was returning, and realising there was no way I could go back to my old life: a life with a job I dreaded daily, that paid well, but that left me so incredibly unhappy.

So, what next? You see, solo travel opened my eyes to something unexpected. It showed me complete freedom in a way I never experienced before. When I wanted to do something, even when it was as big as booking a flight on a whim from Europe to Asia, I just did it. Solo travel showed me I was happiest when I was fully in control of every decision in my life. I had always thought that the hate for my job and the constant dreaming of travel meant that I wanted to work in the travel industry and have freedom of location. But what I really wanted was freedom from working for other people's ideas and on other people's schedules.

And this is how solo travel led me to solopreneurship and the creation of The Lone Travel Girl; an apparel line and lifestyle brand dedicated to celebrating and educating solo female travellers. I turned my passion for travel into a business. Solo travellers tell me all the time about wanting to leave their jobs and build their own businesses. If you have ever thought the same, know that you can do it. As a solo traveller, you have it within you to leave a job that makes you unhappy. As a solo traveller, you have the resilience to achieve success.

As a solo traveller, you have innate capabilities to succeed as an entrepreneur. Life on the road makes you both strategic and fearless. If you have a dream for a different life, know that it is always one decision away. Pay attention to the things that make you the happiest and follow them. And make sure to find women who will cheer you on along the way. I am so happy that I did.

Follow Callie, Founder of The Lone Girl Travel Girl:
@thelonetravelgirl

www.thelonetravelgirl.com

#PASSPORTREADY PROFILE
- AMANDA, TALES OF AN AU PAIR

I started my career as an Early Childhood Educator at the ripe old age of nineteen. The work took a lot out of me, and at twenty-three, I was exhausted and felt like I had hit a wall in my career. I had no desire to move into a management position and I couldn't picture myself working in day-care when I turned thirty.

Looking back on how I got there, I realised that I never actually took a break for myself and one major trip aside, I had never really travelled. So I decided that I would take an Au Pair job in Ireland. I worked sixty-plus hours a week to pay off my student loan, and in a short six months, I was on the plane to Ireland! The culture shock was real, and my first few weeks in Ireland were cold, wet, and difficult. I wasn't expecting to have such a huge shock because it was an English speaking country and fairly similar to Canada. But it's true, culture shock can happen anywhere! So many things stuck out at me from the language to the mannerisms, even the radio programs and don't even get me started on driving on the left-hand side. One night I was abandoned by another au pair at a pub, although it turned out to be a blessing, because I met the man I ended up dating and falling head over heels for that night.

I met wonderful friends and people who soon became my family, tried out some new hobbies, and had some unforgettable adventures! Everyone thought I was crazy to move across the pond to live with a family I didn't know, but I somehow knew it would work out, and I would come out on the other side changed for the better.

That year I got to travel a lot of Europe, North Africa, across Ireland and Italy. I couldn't recommend it enough, and I frequently tell my young nieces and nephews not to rush into college or a job and take some time to travel by themselves and explore the world!"

Follow Amanda: @thepineapplebackpacker

www.thepineapplebackpacker.com

CHAPTER 3 RESOURCES

NOMAD TOOLS

www.nomadlist.com

Nomad List measures cities around the world on a set of 27 different categories including, wi-fi, nightlife, air quality and freedom of speech. The site also allows you to connect with other nomads and posts remote jobs.

www.everytimezone.com

Nomad life often means being in different time zones from friends, family and clients. This free web tool gives you an overview of the different time zones. Move the slider across to compare your local time against other time zones.

www.tripit.com

This free travel planner organizes all of your digital travel documents, like flight schedules and hotel bookings.

www.nordvpn.com

NordVPN is a virtual private network provider that promises to protect your privacy online. Unfortunately, the service itself has been hacked in the past, but this has not deterred users. It is a popular choice with content creators who regularly plug the product.

www.nomadprojects.org

Ready to start your new side project? Find your partner in crime that complements your skillset. Connect with nomads who want to start or collaborate on a side project.

Trail Wallet App

Designed by nomads for nomads, this handy app allows you to track your daily expenses in various currencies.

www.transferwise.com

Send money quickly and at a low cost between bank accounts in different countries. They claim to be on average 9x cheaper than leading UK high street banks.

www.xero.com

Book-keeping is often the Achilles heel of new time entrepreneurs. With Xero's intuitive online accounting software, you can see your cash flow in real-time and put business accounting tasks on autopilot.

GETTING READY

CHAPTER 4

HOW TO DECIDE WHERE TO GO

"Don't ever accept anyone else's preconceived limitations. If there's something you want to do, there isn't any reason you can't do it."
—Amy Dodson

With 195 countries around the world to choose from, and all the towns and cities in those countries to explore, simply deciding where to go can be a challenge. Here are some things to consider before making your decision.

Can you legally enter your destination?

Always check that you have the legal right to enter a country and what procedures you need to take such as acquiring a visa. As a general rule, you should ensure that your passport is at least six months in date from your time of travel. If you think your passport may expire within the time you are away, make sure to get it renewed before you leave.

What is your budget?

It is easy to find flights costing no more than a pair of shoes, but once you actually get to some places, the daily travel costs can be astronomical. Don't be fooled by a cheap plane ticket, dig deeper, and do your research. The general cost of accommodation I've found is actually a good marker for figuring out if you can afford a particular destination. If the cost of a hostel bed seems out of your reach, that's a sign other day-to-day costs will be high too. Following on from that, there are plenty of online resources that will tell you the medium costs of food, transport, attractions, and all the other things that add to your travel costs. Check out www.numbeo.com for detailed breakdowns.

Southeast Asia, Central America and South America, are some of the most favoured destinations for backpackers who want their money to stretch further for longer. Bulgaria, Hungary, Romania, Czech Republic, Slovenia and Poland are some of the more budget friendly destinations in Europe. Having said that, even pricier destinations around the world can be done on a budget if you watch the pennies and do your research.

The weather

Always check when you are likely to encounter the best and worst weather conditions in your chosen destination. You don't want to show up somewhere in the middle of rainy season, and certain countries are more prone to severe weather at certain points of the year. That said, gloomy weather is not always a reason to avoid a destination. Provided there are no major risks to your safety, if you can bear colder, wetter, and greyer conditions, low season brings with it cheaper flights, accommodation, and fewer tourists.

Ease of movement

Consider how easy it is going to be for you to get from place to place and what modes of transport are available. Are you able to get around easily via public transport, or will you have to rent a car or scooter. If you cannot drive, are you able to hire a driver, and how much will that cost?

National holidays

Depending on where you travel, national holidays can either bring new adventures and experiences such as street parades and festivals, or you can show up to your destination only to find that everything is shut down and there's nothing for you to do and see. Make sure you know what's happening when you're travelling to your destination.

Your itinerary

What is there for you to do in your chosen destination, and are you able to create a rough itinerary? Not that you have to stick to this plan, but it's good to do a little bit of research and get a feel of what there is to see and do when you get there. I have seen return flights for as little as £9, flying out from the UK to destinations around Europe. While it seems like a nice deal, upon doing some research, there wasn't a whole lot to do, and little of tourist information on the area.

Be inspired

Speak to other travellers, attend travel shows, join online groups and forums, scan the socials, read travel blogs, magazines, and all other travel media to get ideas.

HOW TO CREATE AN ITINERARY
FOR ANY DESTINATION

"Loving life is easy when you are abroad.
Where no one knows you and you hold your life in your hands all
alone, you are more master of yourself than at any other time."
—Hannah Arendt

It's a long-time debate between travellers; should you plan ahead, or should you wing it. Both options have their pros and cons and depending on the length of your trip, and where you're going, one can work better than the other. Winging it allows for an element of surprise, a chance to go with the flow and truly discover everything for the first time. Planning maximises time and gives you a solid routine, but also doesn't leave room for spontaneity. I advocate for something in the middle.

I absolutely do think that you should make a rough itinerary before you travel. What I don't think you should ever do, is be bound by it. You can take a note of activities you want to do, write listicles of recommended attractions and places to visit, and never show up when you're there. Think of your itinerary as a personal travel guide you've made for yourself based on your own interests. It is something you can refer to if needed, as opposed to wasting time searching for activities to do if you get stuck on what to do or where to go, but you don't have to follow it.

I have seen backpackers waste hours and days of their trip not knowing what to do, succumbing to chugging beers at the hostel instead. I've also seen chronic planners book things only to find something else that catches their eye, or wanting to change a route, only to find they cannot get refunds.

It is often said that over preparing can take away the mystery of travel. I, for one, agree with this, however, for nervous travellers in particular, having a plan can help relieve a lot of anxiety.

If you're not the planning type and would rather just go with the flow, one thing I absolutely urged you to always research, is anything related to safety and getting from one place to another. You don't want to arrive at a ferry port, to find out your boat only leaves at certain times of the day, or that you missed the last bus or train. When visiting places that are not regularly travelled by tourists, it is essential that you do detailed research before going.

Asides from helping you to navigate your trip, planning is a fun way to keep you occupied. I always start my trip planning some simple Google searches, and these are the phrases I commonly use:

Best places to visit in . . .

Day trips from . . .

Best restaurants in . . .

Best art markets in . . .

Best food markets in . . .

Best nightlife in . . .

Unusual things to do in . . .

Best free things to do in . . .

Best places to view the sunset in . . .

What to do when it's raining in . . .

Once you have all of these written down, pin the locations of each site on a Google map. Group points of interest together, as it will be easier to visit places that are closer. You can also go to the websites of tour operators, look at their itineraries and take some ideas from there.

Learn from the mistakes of others

A million other people have gone to the same location, and it's not just things to do that they can teach you, but also what not to do. The very next thing I search for when planning a trip is; *Things I wish I'd known before visiting (insert location).* This can help you avoid mistakes on the road.

On a final note, don't worry about seeing everything on your bucket list. You have to be realistic, loading your itinerary with too many activities will leave you disappointed if you can't see everything, and completely burnt out if you do. Learn to read the moment, it's always the most unexpected things that create the best memories.

PRE-TRAVEL CHECKLIST

"You are the one that possesses the keys to your being.
You carry the passport to your own happiness."
—Diane von Furstenberg

****PASSPORT SHOULD BE VALID FOR
SIX MONTHS UPON ARRIVAL****

The words jumped out at me on the screen. I was looking up information on visa requirements for Bali, Indonesia. My passport was expiring in four months and I risked being denied entry. I had to get a new one, and only had three weeks left to do it. I had plenty of time if I did the fast track option, but this was going to cost more. For administrative reasons, the process was delayed, and my document was to arrive only two days before I was due to take-off. Upon receiving my estimated delivery time from the courier, I sat on the balcony of my house, scanning the street like a sniper until around two p.m. I was paranoid the delivery person would fail to deliver. That's when I got an alert saying my package had arrived. The only thing I could see on the street was a bearded man on an unmarked motorcycle. I waved from the top of the balcony and yelled, "DELIVERY?" "Yes," he said, then proceeded to call out my address. I ran downstairs, showed him my ID, and retrieved the passport. Panic over.

This scenario could have easily been avoided with more pre-travel planning.

To help you avoid a similar scenario, this section is split into four parts; home prep, money prep, travel prep, and departure prep, which is done the day before. Some things should be done weeks or months beforehand, make sure to leave enough time for everything, so nothing gets missed.

TRAVEL PREP

- Check your passport expiry date and apply for a new passport if necessary. Check you have enough spare pages for stamps and visas. Make at least two photo-copies of your passport. One should be kept on you as you move around and the other should be stored away in your luggage.

- Check your visa and entry requirements of each country you intend on visiting.

- Scan/take pictures of your passport, drivers licenses, credit cards, warranties, receipts, insurance, and any other important documents. Put them in an easily accessible file.

- Check the luggage weight and dimension restrictions of the airline/s you're travelling with and weigh your luggage.

- Get your phone unlocked so you can use local sim cards, or check what options you have for roaming in your destination. Getting your phone unlocked can take up to a week, leave plenty of time to get this done.

- Get an international driving license if it's required. Anyone wishing to ride a scooter should have some kind of certified license that would entitle them to insurance in the result of an accident.

HOME PREP

- Arrange for a trusted pet sitter. Be it a family member, friend, or through a house-sitting site.

- Share your travel plans with a trusted neighbour or friend. You never know what might happen when you're away, at least one person should have keys to your house. If you don't know anyone you can trust, install a camera in your house that connects to a check-in app, so you can monitor your home remotely.

- Clean out your cupboard and fridge, you don't want to come home to rotting food and fungi. Anything that could go off while you're away should be cleaned out.

- As you leave the house, unplug appliances and switch off the electric and gas completely from the mains.

- Water your houseplants before you leave. If you're going away for a long time, fit your pots with watering globes.

MONEY PREP

- Exchange some money before you leave, so you have some at hand when you arrive. Remember that contactless and credit cards are not always commonplace in some parts of the world.

- If you have to get a visa on arrival, always assume that you have to pay in cash and have the money ready in the correct currency.

- Notify your bank of your trip. If you suddenly start using your credit card in another country, your credit cards may get blocked as part of anti-fraud protections. Either ring your bank, or most have a feature in their apps that allow you to do this.

MEDICAL PREP

- A few weeks before you leave, make sure to request and stock up on medical prescriptions. If you're travelling with any kind of prescribed medication, keep a copy of your doctors signed prescription as some substances may be considered narcotics in some countries and you will need to prove it has been prescribed to you by a doctor.

- Research whether or not you need vaccinations, and which vaccinations are required. Leave a few weeks notice to be able to get this done. If you live in a country where there is a national health service, these will either be free or cost very little. If you live in a country where you are expected to pay for healthcare, factor this into your pre-travel costs.

- Buy insurance at least a week before you travel. I highly recommend World Nomads as this can be renewed on the go, and they cover a wide range of incidences. Whichever insurer you go for, make sure to read the fine print and understand what they will and will not cover. If you cannot afford insurance, you cannot afford to travel—period!

DEPARTURE PREP

- Check the day before if there will be any disruptions to your airport route—check again just before you leave.

- Charge all of your electronic devices the night before.

- Check the weather of your destination.

- Get a good night's sleep.

- Take a deep breath—everything is going to be fine.

#PASSPORTREADY PROFILE
- EMILY, FINDING YOURSELF AFTER LOSS

Before solo travel, my life was very different. By the time I reached thirty, I was married, owned a house, and was about to take my ten-year career to the next level. I was someone who had their whole life mapped out, and navigated in the image of what society expects for a woman. I always stuck to the status quo. The very idea of travelling alone never entered my mind, mainly because there was always someone else to travel with. But then my life took an unexpected turn.

When my father died suddenly at the age of sixty-three, my life changed forever. He was the glue that held my family together. He was my compass, my confidant, my protector. Words cannot express the impact of his passing. If his loss wasn't life changing enough, a little over a month later, my husband told me he wanted a divorce. I did not see it coming, nor did I want our marriage to end, but as he had started a relationship with someone else, I had no choice.

The aftermath of these tragic events inevitably became too much to bear. I was diagnosed with severe depression, and a few months would pass before I was admitted to hospital having made an attempt to end my life. I was officially at rock bottom. I had lost all sense of identity, hope, and meaning.

Amidst all that loss and despair came my thirty-first birthday. A year before, I had turned thirty in New York City with my husband, and I was happy. I made a pact with myself that I would travel somewhere new for my birthday every year because travel was something I had always loved. Fast-forward a year, and I had a choice; either I leave my travel pact in the past, or I honour it. At this point, given the dark direction my life had taken, I made no hesitation in choosing me. All I knew was that I deserved to give myself a break, and nobody was going to stand in my way.

Not everyone liked the idea of me travelling alone given my vulnerability. I'll be the first to admit I had doubts too. Me? Alone? Abroad? Given my flaky and self-critical nature, this was as far out of my comfort zone as it gets. But things were different now. There comes a point after so much emotional trauma where fear doesn't limit you anymore. What have I got to lose? What's the worst that can happen to me now? It was time to put myself first and to stop worrying about what everyone else thought for a change.

I spent four days in the City of Amsterdam and I didn't know it at the time, but it would be the most significant point in my healing journey. I never expected to learn so much about myself over those four days. I proved to myself that I was capable, and that I could go it alone. I learnt that all those doubts in my mind were just negative thoughts, they weren't fact. Yes, I made mistakes. Yes, I found myself having to think on my feet on several occasions, but I survived, and what's more, I thrived. I was free to be unequivocally me, and it turns out I liked being in my own company. For the first time in my life, I was able to do everything I wanted on my own terms. I didn't have to make compromises. I came home with a spring in my step and knew that solo travel was something I had to do again.

One month after I was discharged from hospital, I found myself travelling solo again. I spent a week in Dubrovnik, Croatia and this trip was a game changer. This time I was more confident and better prepared. I didn't hesitate to talk to strangers. I trusted my instincts and fell in love with my newfound independence all over again. As I watched the setting sun at the top of Mount Srd overlooking the Pearl of the Adriatic, I had an awakening. As the beauty of the world unfolded before me, I knew in that moment that life had so much more in store for me. Solo travel helped me to realise that there was a whole world out there waiting for me. One with endless possibilities and new experiences that I could truly call my own. One where I could grow through grief and learn who I truly was as an independent woman. Solo travel helped me fall back in love with life, and most importantly, with myself.

Breaking out of your comfort zone and taking that bold step to solo travel for the first time can be scary, but I promise you what is waiting for you on the other side of fear is worth it.

Follow Emily: @rediscovering_emily_

www.rediscovering-emily.com

#PASSPORT READY PROFILE
- MADISON, A TWIST OF FATE

I went on my first solo trip when I was twenty years old towards the end of my study abroad semester. Up until then, I had done all my travelling with my friends and hadn't had the courage to visit a foreign country completely alone. At the time, I was nervous and disappointed that none of my friends could accompany me to Vienna. Looking back, I think it was fate that caused those scheduling conflicts.

It's now been three years since Vienna, and I have more than a handful of solo-trips under my belt. Some of my favourites include Budapest, Kraków, Lake Como, Milan, Munich and Prague. I think back to who I was before I started travelling and I've found I barely remember that girl. Travelling, especially solo-travel, has the power to give you new experiences, teach you new things and, change your life for the better. I've travelled to places I never thought I'd see, I've tasted food I never thought I would try, and I've met people who I would never have met had I not been brave enough to get out and see the world.

If there's one piece of advice I could give young women, I would tell them to travel as often as they can and start as early as possible. Let's not however, forget another reason to travel . . . it's fun!

Nowadays, life, especially life in the US, is so career-focused and goal-oriented that we forget to do things we love and truly enjoy our lives.

The days of my life when I've had the most fun were all spent travelling. These are the days that I'll look back on someday as my most precious possessions. Roaming the streets of Prague, laughing hysterically and hopelessly lost from the pub crawl; Friday nights sipping Italian wine on the steps of Piazzale

Michelangelo as the sun set; the clash of steins at Oktoberfest while we danced on the wooden tables in our colourful dirndls; my kayak cutting through water as clear as glass in the Swiss Alps; the feel of a baby elephant's trunk sifting through my pockets for stray bananas in Thailand and the pinkest sky I've ever seen setting over the Positano coastline. These moments are only a snippet of my never-ending travel slideshow, and yet, they will stay in my memories forever.

Travelling teaches you about the world and about yourself, but, most importantly, it teaches you how to be alive.

Follow Madison: @madisonsfootsteps

www.madisonsfootsteps.com

PACKING

CHAPTER 5

SUITCASE VS. BACKPACK

If you wish to travel far and fast, travel light.
Take off all your envies, jealousies, unforgiveness,
selfishness and fears.
-Cesare Pavese

Suitcase versus backpack is the traveller's version of cats versus dogs. Many swear by one over the other. Which one you carry will ultimately depends on where you're going, and what is more convenient.

Are you going to encounter loads of uneven surfaces? Are you island-hopping around the tropics and arriving on sandy beaches? Are you hiking up mountains and rocky terrains? In these incidences, a backpack is a much better option than a suitcase. If you'll be spending most of your time frolicking around resorts, hotels, and walking through well-paved cities, a suitcase is better than a backpack. Perhaps your trip encompasses both of those styles of travel, in which case, I would opt for a backpack, so at no point are you struggling with a suitcase.

Throughout your journey as a traveller you will probably purchase both, and perhaps multiple ones of each in various sizes to accommodate for different trips. We delve into the pros and cons of each and what essentials you should look for when buying either.

SUITCASES

Pros of carrying a suitcase

- Your luggage is going to be thrown around like a rag doll and hard-bodied cases in particular, can take a beating.

- Wheeling around a suitcase can be smoother than carrying a backpack provided you're moving on a flat service.

- Suitcases are easier to repack and organise than a backpack.

- Suitcases are generally more waterproof.

- Suitcases just look better.

Cons of carrying a suitcase

- Because suitcases generally allow you to pack more, it can be tempting to pack more than you actually need.

- Suitcases can be a pain to drag along dirt roads, uneven pavements, steep hills, sandy beaches, and flooded areas. I've noted on my travels that many smaller hostels do not have elevators and you often end up dragging your luggage up flights of stairs.

- Broken zippers, faulty wheels, and wobbly handles can be a pain.

Essentials when buying a suitcase

- A set of four 360-degree wheels to allow for ease of movement. You will be able to wheel your suitcase on the side and push it in front of you.

- Look for a case with a TSA lock already fitted on it, this way, you won't need luggage locks.

- A handle on the side of the case for easy lifting.

- If you're going for a hard-bodied case, opt for one made of a thinner and lighter material such as polycarbonate.
- Zipped off compartments and compression straps inside to keep your items in place.

Suitcase Sizing

- Your average cabin carry-on case should be around 55x40x20cm and weigh up to 12 kg max when packed.
- Your average medium sized, checked-in luggage case, should be around 67x46x29cm max and weigh no more than 20-25 kg when packed.

These recommendations take into account the cost of additional baggage, and general baggage restrictions, particularly on budget airlines. You can of course carry more, but it will likely cost you more.

Popular suitcase brands

Antler, Samsonite, Aerolite, American Tourister and Tripp are a handful of brands that offer budget-friendly and lightweight suitcases.

BACKPACKS

Pros of carrying a backpack

- As a backpack has less room and you will have to carry it on your back, it forces you to think carefully about what you really need to carry.
- A backpack allows for full use of your hands.
- Having your luggage strapped to you means less chance of theft.
- You can sleep, sit, and rest on your backpack more comfortably.

Cons of carrying a backpack

- Top quality backpacks can often cost more than a suitcase.
- It can take some time to find a backpack that fits your body well.
- It's a little more difficult to secure a backpack due to its numerous pockets.
- Even for the fittest person, lugging around a backpack will always be a chore and can get tiring.
- Belongings can be harder to find.

Essentials when buying a backpack

- It doesn't have to be 100% waterproof, but look for a backpack that has a relatively water-resistant material. Make sure to purchase a waterproof plastic cover for your backpack also.
- Your hips and your shoulders are going to be absorbing a lot of the weight of your backpack. Make sure the hip belt and shoulder straps have adequate padding for more comfort. The hip belt should properly align with your hips and be able to adjust to your body. The back should also be padded with and slightly contoured to allow for more even weight distribution.
- Front panel backpacks allow easier access to your belongings compared to top-loading backpacks, which only allow access from the top.
- Adjustable straps to ensure it fits onto your body well.
- Breathable mesh panels to ensure air circulation, your back is going to get hot in warmer climates carrying weight.
- Look for backpacks that have zippers that can be locked together with a padlock to keep your items secure.

- Compression straps to tighten up your bag when it's not entirely full and prevent items from rattling around when it is.

Backpack sizing

Your carry-on backpack should be around 30-40l max. while your main backpack should be around 55-70l. The less the better, but for some people, more is more, and as someone who is firmly in the middle, I know that I like to carry things that may not be essentials but add to the comfort and enjoyment of my trip.

The best thing is to either go into a shop and try several backpacks, or order them one or two at a time and try them at home. Give yourself plenty of time before your trip to test out different backpacks.

Popular backpack brands

Osprey, REI, and Kelty are some of the most popular brands that manufacture backpacks.

Choosing a day bag

A foldable backpack that can be used for day-to-day sight-seeing is a must buy. You can purchase lightweight foldable day bags that fit into your luggage without taking up room. Neekfox and ZOMAKE are two reliable brands that make lightweight foldable bags.

Other considerations when purchasing travel luggage

Don't purchase any luggage that has non-removal batteries or electrical parts. As discussed in the airport security section of this book, there is a good chance they will not be permitted on your flight.

You get what you pay for, so it's worth investing in a quality item that will last you a long time. You don't want to purchase something that breaks apart during your trip.

Avoid wheeled backpacks. They tend to be heavier and not as practical as they advertise.

Remove previous airline tags and stickers from your case.

Add luggage identifier tags to your luggage with your name, address, number and e-mail.

Using a luggage weight (and not a floor scale) weigh your luggage and repack if necessary.

SMART PACKING

On a long journey even a straw weighs heavy.
—Spanish Proverb

So you've purchased your luggage, now it's time to pack! The internet is abundant with free packing lists and recommended items for different climates and even destination specific guides. In this section, we're just going to focus on some packing essentials that will make your life easier overall.

Pack light

Packing light means more than just saving money on baggage fees. You'll also have less to lug around. Question each and every item that you want to carry. Ask yourself; do I actually *need* to carry this? Always leave room in your luggage for additional items you may purchase along the way.

Secure your luggage

If you're buying a suitcase, it is highly advisable that you buy one with a TSA lock built-in. In the event that your case does not have this, or you opt for a backpack, purchase TSA padlocks that do not require a key. Do not buy padlocks that require a key to open them—the keys will get lost.

A luggage band will also help to protect your case in the event that your zipper bursts. A brightly coloured band will also help to differentiate your case.

To protect against water damage and debris, purchase a waterproof cover for your suitcase/backpack.

Make your luggage stand out

Other people mistaking your luggage for theirs is a common occurrence. I have seen people pick up my case and have been guilty of accidentally taking someone else's also.

Simple ways of making your luggage stand out include:

- Adding some brightly coloured stickers
- Spray painting using stencils
- Adding distinct luggage tags
- Tying brightly coloured ribbons around the handle.

Use packing cubes

Packing cubes are rectangular or square-shaped containers made of light fabric.

They help to maximise space and organise all of your belongings in your luggage. Good packing cubes will have strong zippers, a stiff fabric, and a mesh top so you can see what's inside. Some packing cubes are double sided to help you separate dirty from clean clothing. Also, embrace the rolling method of packing your clothes as this saves more room also.

Carry a micro towel

A micro towel is a lightweight towel that folds easier and dries you up faster than a regular towel. Remember to pat dry with a micro towel, don't rub. Micro towels not only save your room in your suitcase, but also can be used as a sarong, beach towel, sitting mat, wrap around, and blanket.

Pack minis and solids

Do away with full-size toiletry bottles. Pack mini versions instead. You can always buy more toiletries on the road if needed. Also, where possible, use the solid alternative instead of a liquid. Pack soap instead of shower gel, a shampoo bar instead of liquid shampoo, and toothpaste tablets instead of tube paste.

If you're going to decant your cosmetics into smaller bottles, opt for squeezy bottles that sit upside down and have a no-drip valve, you'll waste less product this way.

Use shoe covers

Shoe covers keep your clothes clean of dirt and debris that your shoes pick up from the ground.

Weigh it up

Purchase a weight carrier for your luggage and carry this with you on the road too. If you're buying new items, your weight will change, and you should keep track of this as you travel.

Other essentials

- A universal travel adapter
- A rain poncho
- A large portable battery charger (preferably a solar one for charging on the go)
- A mini (lipstick-sized) portable charger for nights out
- Miniature duct tape (an easy way to fix anything that rips, pops or breaks)
- Female urinal funnel such as a Shewee

E-PACKING LIST — THE BEST TRAVEL APPS

It's not just your suitcase you have to pack, I also recommend packing your phone with some handy apps to make life easier on the road. Here are some of my most trusted travel apps, make sure to have them downloaded on your device.

Uber - share riding app that can be used in various cities around the world

All Trails - find the best hiking trails wherever you are int he world. See reviews and pictures from other hikers.

Nord VPN - protect your privacy while travelling. NordVPN encrypts your internet traffic and hides your IP and physical location. Works on 6 devices at once, on every major platform.

Google Maps - find local businesses, view maps and get directions in Google Maps.

Scout GPS - another great GPS app. I highly recommend having two GPS apps as I've had numerous situations where one did not work of sent me to the wrong place.

Priority Pass - gain lounge access to over 1300 lounges across the world.

Flush Toilet Finder - the quickest, simplest way of finding a public bathroom or restroom. Simply open the app and it will display the nearest toilets to you.

Grab and Gojek (SE Asia) - ride-sharing apps that operate around SE Asia.

Rome2Rio Trip Planner - discover how to get anywhere by searching plane, train, bus, car and ferry routes.

Google Translate – vital to communicating with locals who don't speak your native language. Will also translate signs if you hold up your camera.

Clue/Flo - either of these apps will help you track your periods.

Air Visual - check the air quality of cities and towns across the world.

Time Shifter - say goodbye to jet lag.

#PASSPORTREADY PROFILE
- PRISCILLA, SOLO BY ACCIDENT

I started travelling much later than I intended. I waited for years for my friends and family to be ready to travel too because I was always afraid of solo travelling.

About a year ago, I planned the holiday of my dreams that involved hopping through South-East Asia. When a friend of a friend said she had a similar travel goal, I immediately thought it was the perfect opportunity to do it together because of my fear of travelling alone.

After just three days of travelling in Bangkok, we fell out and went our separate ways and then I faced my biggest fear—solo travel. Solo travel can be scary at first, but, an unplanned solo trip, even scarier.

I went to Kuala Lumpur next, and the whole time I was panicked, but with each day that came, I felt more confident. I went to Singapore next and at this point, had really begun to enjoyed myself. I met interesting people (some of whom I'm still friends with), went on adventures out of my comfort zone, and had the trip of a lifetime.

Since then, I have gained enough confidence to book flights on my own and travel anywhere solo. Solo travel has been one of the most rewarding experiences for me because it has given me the confidence and freedom to just be me!

Just as with anything in life, there have been a few hiccups but don't let that deter you. No matter where you are in the world, a smile is a sign of friendship, if you are armed with a smile and good vibes, you'll never really be alone.

Follow Priscilla: @ajalaonabudget

www.ajalaonabudget.disha.page

#PASSPORTREADY PROFILE
- MICHELE, THE TIME IS NOW

As a society, we often like to think of our time on Earth as endless.

Maybe that derives from trying to avoid the elephant in the room, that in fact, life is but a mere flash in the broader scope of space and time. While this can be a hard pill to swallow, I'd argue that there is a degree of power in accepting this reality. We live with this idea that time is limitless, and so, have a tendency to put our dreams aside in the hopes that we will pursue them in the future.

The dream of travel is no exception. We wait around for different reasons. Some of us wait in the hopes that a friend will decide to come along for the journey. For others, travelling without a hand to hold, and a warm body to sleep next to, seems unbearable. The reasons to forgo travel are many. We spend so much time terrified of what could happen, that we neglect thinking about the more important question of what we could be missing out on.

Though having limited time did not concern me, the feeling of powerlessness that I felt towards my life did.

That feeling of lacking power and authority over my life spilled over into my relationships, caused self-doubt, and led to me to live a life limited by fear of all things outside of my comfort zone. I wanted to be loved, but I didn't even know how to fully love myself. I wanted to believe in myself, but couldn't shake the feeling of imposter syndrome. I wanted to experience the world, but I kept making excuses. I hid behind my fear of heights, my impressive academic transcripts and my youth.

At some point the curiosity I had towards travel, being fed up with feeling broken, and a splash of courage, led me to commit to eliminating the "what-ifs" from my life.

The first commitment I made was booking my first solo international trip, and it completely transformed the next five years of my life.

I was terrified, but one brave leap of faith led me to become the independent person that I craved to be– a person who truly lived the life of her dreams. Committing to my dreams, rather than succumbing to my fears, changed every aspect of my life for the better.

I was accepted onto a PhD program, I travelled to 39 different countries, and I moved across the world to New Zealand. I no longer allowed toxic people to swarm my life. I stopped looking for self-validation from other people. I no longer felt trapped, but felt surrounded by opportunity. I learned how to be raw and open up to the people that I care about. I learned to fight for the things I want, before the opportunity escaped me.

We get one life - just one - and it goes fast. Every decision that we make determines the trajectory of our future. Each time we choose to allow fear to guide our choices, we sacrifice all of that power that lies within each of us.

That power transforms our lives, the moment we find the strength to tap into it.

Follow Michele @gone_mishing

www.gonemishing.com

FLYING

CHAPTER 6

OVERCOMING YOUR FEAR OF FLYING

"I am willing to put myself through anything, temporary pain or discomfort means nothing to me as long as I can see that the experience will take me to a new level. I am interested in the unknown, and the only path to the unknown is through breaking barriers, an often painful process."
—Diana Nyad

I've never had a fear of flying. I would often beg my dad to go with him to the airport anytime he was dropping off, or picking up someone. Just going to the airport made me happy, and I would sit and watch the planes take off.

For some people though, no amount of excitement, even if it's going on the trip of a lifetime, can subside the fear of flying. Plane crashes are actually relatively rare, but piles of debris and a burning plane make for emotion-inducing TV, so the news cycles love to report on them, often running the story for days and weeks as investigations proceed, making it feel like it's a common occurrence. You are in fact, far more likely to die in a traffic related incident, although that hardly stops anyone from getting in a car. If you're someone who does fear flying, here are some techniques that will help put your mind at ease.

Understand how a plane works

I'm not going to give you an entire physics lesson here, but give yourself time to learn the basics of how a plane works, and the mechanisms in place to keep you safe in the air. For example, did you know that an aircraft flying at 30,000 feet can glide for miles, even if all the engines fail? Neither did I until I looked into it. Learn how such a heavy object can get enough lift to glide so effortlessly in the air, learn how air traffic control prevents air collisions, and what is actually happening to a plane during turbulence. Asides from putting your mind at ease, I'm certain you'll find it incredibly fascinating.

Book a seat in the isle

This will make you feel less claustrophobic, and you won't need to jump over anyone if you need to get up and walk around. You'll also be away from the window seat and won't have to see how far up in the clouds you are.

Avoid stimulants

Avoid drinking or eating anything high in sugars and caffeine that might make you feel more jittery and hyper alert. Instead, opt for decaffeinated hot drinks like herbal teas. In addition, practice deep breathing, controlling your breathing is vital to controlling your nerves.

Take a sleeping aid

As with all medications, discuss what options are suitable for you with a doctor before taking anything, this includes regular over the counter pills. This is particularly important if you currently take any other medications that could interact with other drugs.

Get help

There are several resources that can help you overcome your fear of flying:

Anxieties.com is a free online self-help program.

SOAR—www.fearofflying.com—provides free tips, newsletters, chats, and videos. They also provide counselling and programs, albeit for a fee.

The Founder of SOAR Tom Bunn has also written a book—*Soar: The Breakthrough Treatment for Fear of Flying* Kindle Edition

Another popular book is *The Easy Way to Enjoy Flying* (Allen Carr's Easy Way)

Download the VALK app on your smartphone. This flying app serves as an inflight therapist.

GETTING THROUGH SECURITY WITH EASE

When I was a little girl, there was a very popular television show called *Airport*. One of the most exciting things about the show was seeing if a late passenger was going to make it on time. Almost always, they'd make it just at the last minute.

In an age of heightened security, all of that seems almost mad, and it wouldn't be allowed now. Most international flights require you to be at the airport and check-in at least ninety minutes before your flight departs for baggage check-in. This is usually less if you only have cabin luggage, but always double-check for every trip and refer to the instructions from your airline. Once you've arrived, and it's time to go through security, here are some tips to pass. through with ease.

Arrive in good time

Where possible, always check-in online and make sure you leave plenty of time to get through security. Arrive earlier during peak season to avoid big crowds. Check and double check the departure times on your tickets.

Don't wear metals

This includes jewellery such as necklaces, rings, bracelets, and accessories like belts. It will only delay your time through security.

Place liquids in a clear plastic bag

Bring your own as the bags provided at the airport are often tiny and break easily. Cabin luggage restrictions permit 10 items with a maximum capacity of 100ml per bottle, per passenger.

Packing cubes aren't just for your main luggage

I also use smaller packing cubes to organise my carry-on backpack. Anything that needs to come out of your backpack before going through the scanners should go at the top and front of your backpack so you can pull them out and place them back in your bag easily.

Electricals

Place all electricals in one packing cube and where possible, take batteries out of electrical items.

Don't purchase smart luggage

From suitcases with built-in chargers and bags that roll along the floor and follow you, smart luggage seemed like the next big thing in travel. That is no longer the case. Most airlines now have heavy restrictions on smart luggage. I would advise against purchasing any type of smart luggage with electrical elements and batteries built into them.

HOW TO STAY COMFORTABLE ON LONG HAUL FLIGHTS

Most of us can only dream of flying first class. As aircraft design improves, economy class has become increasingly more comfortable over time, but it still doesn't compare to the pleasures of a higher class. There are though, ways you can make your ride in economy more comfortable.

Wear comfortable clothing

It gets cold on a plane, so make sure to wear a layer underneath your clothes, like leggings under your trousers or a camisole under your top and remove if needed. For those who are style-conscious, a black-loose fitting jumpsuit is both functional and fashionable. Also, make sure to carry a light jumper.

Stay hydrated

Dehydration is common due to the air circulation on aircrafts. Drink plenty of water, moisture your skin and use eye drops if needed to remoisten your eyes.

Put together a comfort kit including:

- A travel cushion to support your neck
- An eye mask to block light
- Earplugs to reduce cabin noise
- Compression socks to reduce thrombosis and keep your feet warm

Pick the right seat

A window seat gives you somewhere to lean, an aisle seat is better if you want to get up more often and stretch out. Decide what is a bigger priority for you. Also, being seated near the emergency exits usually offers more legroom, as there are no seats in front of you.

Ask for an upgrade

Upgrades are much harder to come by nowadays.. Now, they must be bought, or at least, earned through collecting points. There is, of course, simply no harm in asking. Simply try asking, "If this flight is overbooked and you're upgrading people to first or business class, I would like to be considered, please". Ask at the checkout desk, the boarding security gate and once you're on the flight. The worst they're going to say is *no*. Travel experts often claim that being smartly dressed and being solo (yippee) will increase your chances of getting an upgrade.

#PASSPORTREADY PROFILE
- IAYANA, YOUNG AND INTREPID

I have always had a passion for exploring new places. Although I love my friends and family, nothing really beats the exhilarating feeling of travelling alone. I am blessed that I can travel as I please, and have visited twenty-three countries in my short life.

Travelling has humbled me because it's a constant reminder to appreciate the little things. I have visited places where the locals have little to nothing to their names but, always greet you with a smile, always express the utmost gratitude and are a consistent reminder that material possessions do not equal happiness.

I have always been an outgoing individual but such a massive over-thinker. With each new adventure, I've learned to just go with the flow and trust my gut more, and becoming a more well-rounded individual, personally and professionally. Who knew booking a holiday could contribute to such transferable skills?

Don't be afraid to book that trip! I didn't quit my full-time job to travel, or wake up one day and feel a sense that something was missing. I simply decided to chase my passion. Don't let your dreams fade away through browsing Instagram accounts, reading blogs and watching travel videos of your bucket list destinations. Fight your fears, and do it yourself, create your own memories.

I appreciate how being a female travelling alone may seem daunting, start small if you must, you could go away with your friends and on that same trip venture off and do your own thing. I promise you—you will not regret it. The initial anxiety will be clouded by the feeling of fulfilment, freedom, and awesomeness of solo exploring. Get lost, find your way and allow the experience to help you grow to understand yourself more deeply.

Some of my most epic memories are from travelling and most specifically solo travelling.

I remember getting lost in Stanley Park, Vancouver. For a while, I stood in the park, feeling numb. Then I thought to myself, '*Iayana get a grip, explore whilst you are lost, you will find your way*' and I did. I didn't allow fear to cripple me, which resulted in stumbling upon some of the most beautiful sceneries I have seen to date. Remember; 'blessed are the curious, for they shall have adventures'.

Get out there and start your own adventure.

Follow Iayana: @iayanadawn

www.iayanadawn.etsy.com

SAFETY AND SOLO

FEMALE TRAVEL

CHAPTER 7

GENERAL SAFETY TIPS

"Avoiding danger is no safer in the long run than outright exposure. The fearful are caught as often as the bold."
—Helen Keller

Let's start with the obvious: as women, the number one thing we worry about when travelling solo is harassment, violence and assault from men.

Is there any other reason solo female travel is considered 'brave'?

Personally, I have experienced harassment while travelling. I've experienced the same harassment in my own city, London. This is just our reality as women as we navigate the world regardless of where we are.

Females are told from a young age that we are responsible for the actions of men, and that the onus is on us to prevent harassment from men. And so, there is actually nothing I can put in this chapter that you haven't already heard. You already know how to keep yourself safe, because you police yourself every day, but it is still my obligation to write this chapter.

TOP SAFETY TIPS

Never let your drink out of your sight and always make sure to order drinks yourself. Don't drink to the point that you are insanely out of control and helpless. Not only will you be vulnerable to assault, but a great number of tourist accidents are linked to abusing alcohol.

Always know how you're getting home if you're going to get back late and avoid walking out late at night on your own.

Always make escaping your first call of action if ever you get caught in a confrontation. Never carry a weapon if you don't know how to use it, or if possession will get you in trouble with authorities.

Walk with confidence, even if you don't feel it and try not to look lost.

Be aware that in some countries—particularly those that are incredibly conservative—reporting rape and assault can lead to harsh treatment. It may be wiser in some cases to seek assistance from your consulate first, before local authorities. Regardless, always seek help from your embassy as soon as possible to assist you. Even in more 'progressive' countries, cases of sexual assault have been known to be handled unprofessionally by authorities.

The number one way to keep yourself safe

One of the most common pieces of advice I hear and read about when it comes to travelling is 'trust your instinct'. This is sound advice, and I will reiterate it here: always trust your gut instinct, it is the most powerful weapon in your arsenal for keeping you safe.

The problem is . . . some people have terrible instincts! They can't see a lion staring them right in the face showing it's gigantic jaws. So how do you spot a toxic person?

It's not always easy. They're not always openly nasty and can often be charming, but there's a difference between confidence and arrogance. Confidence is natural and doesn't need to be put on. Arrogance is thinking you're the best person in the room and is often the sign of a narcissist.

Predators also do not respect your boundaries, will try to push them, and can't accept a no. Also, keep a distance from people who just generally have no manners and are inconsiderate to others. Being on holiday is not an excuse to act a fool, though some people seem to think so.

Carry the right safety tools

A personal alarm—this features a small pin that when pulled, makes a high-frequency noise to deter attackers and draw attention. This is also useful if you want to deter animals too.

A doorstop—this can deter an intruder attempting to get into your room. You can get alarm activated doorstops as well.

A whistle—if you need to attract attention if you're lost/trapped. Very useful if you're going out hiking or doing any adventure activities.

Safety tips you may not have considered

Always sleep fully clothed—if you have to run out in the middle of the night, clothing your body is one less thing you have to think about.

The magic iPhone button—if you press the off button on your iPhone very quickly about five times, your phone will automatically call the emergency service of the country you are in.

Have the number to your consulate saved into your phone so you're not looking for it if you need assistance.

There are bad people in good places and good people in bad places. Mostly though, you'll find most people are decent. Just follow the same common-sense safety procedures to keep you safe when out and about at home and don't lose yourself when you're abroad.

COMMON TRAVEL SCAMS

The Grand Palace is closed!

This is one of the most commonly known scams in Bangkok Thailand, so imagine how hard I laughed in the face of a con-artist who actually tried to approach me with this trick the day I visited the palace. In a way, I was almost flattered to have experienced the stuff of travel legends. I yelled the word "SCAM" while laughing and the con-man quickly scurried away.

When you're in the moment and enjoying your surroundings, it's easy to let your guard down, and if you're new to a place, there are many things you are unlikely to have an awareness of. Scammers know this and try at every opportunity to take advantage. Here are some common scams you may come across whilst on the road and how to avoid them.

I have a special price just for you

You may come across street sellers offering you items for a 'special price'. Often, they'll even say that because of your nationality you're getting this special discount. That 'special discount' is likely an over-inflated price on a cheap item, particularly if you come from a country with a stronger currency. If there are no fixed prices on items, make sure to barter the price down. Find out from locals what you should be paying for certain goods, as it's not unusual for foreigners to be charged a higher price than normal.

The (insert location) is closed

You've arrived at your destination perhaps without booking your hotel, preferring to see a few places for yourself before settling on one. Your driver tells you that your place of choice is closed/booked, and that he'll recommend you somewhere else for a 'good price'. The truth is that your place was probably never booked up, you'll be given a higher price, and your driver will get a cut of whatever you've paid.

Tell them that you'd still like to be taken to the location and that you'll look for an alternative place once you have gotten there. That way, you can see for yourself if it's closed.

A similar trick occurs with sight-seeing, like the Grand Palace scam mentioned at the beginning of this chapter. Instead of taking you to your site, you may be taken to several different vendors and pressured into buying goods.

Would you like a rose, bracelet, crystals?

The salesperson will often approach as if to give the item for free, then proceed to ask for payment. Be wary of anything suddenly thrust into your hands for free.

Having said that, it's not unusual in some countries where showing a great amount of hospitality is a norm, to be offered things like bread, or other foods—but never material items. Read the room and politely ask if you're expected to pay before taking anything if you're unsure.

Hold this animal

Street vendors holding animals and putting them around your neck or on your shoulders, and offering to take pictures is a common sight where animal welfare laws are laxed, or don't exist at all. Asides from the unethical treatment of the animals, they will also often ask you to pay for taking a picture. Anytime someone hands you an animal, give them a stern face, confident no, and keep walking.

The meter is broken

This is a common scam used by taxis. Always negotiate and agree on a price before you get in a taxi. Also research beforehand what licensed taxis commonly look like, to avoid getting into an unlicensed vehicle.

Let me wrap this for you

You've purchased a beautiful rug or, piece of clothing, and the vendor offers to wrap it for you. Without you knowing, they swap it for a cheaper item, or do not put all the items you paid for in your bag. Always make sure to watch your items if they are being wrapped and double-check just in case before you leave if you did not see the items in clear view being wrapped.

There's bird poop on your clothes

In this scam, the con artist will usually throw something that resembles a spill or dirt on your clothes and pretends to help you wipe it off. Before you know it, they've run off with your bag, phone, or purse. Kindly tell the kind stranger you're very thankful, but you'll clean it off yourself.

KEEPING YOUR BELONGINGS SAFE

The first rule of not losing things is; don't take what you don't need. There is no need to travel with expensive designer items, precious jewellery, and anything else that will attract the attention of thieves. If the thought of losing it scares you—don't take it.

In your room

Ask your accommodation if they have a safe to keep valuables in when you're out of your room unless of course, your room has a secure safe. Make sure you keep a record of anything you hand over to staff, take pictures and keep everything together in a concealed bag. You can also carry foldable portable safes, these are reinforced bags that come with a lock. PacSafe is a popular brand that makes these. You can attach these to any non-movable object such as the neck of a sink. Keep any other valuables out of sight and locked away in your suitcase/backpack.

Do not leave valuables openly in sight in your room. If you're staying in a hostel, make full use of lockers and never get too comfortable and leave valuables around your bed.

Out and about

While the market is full of antitheft backpacks that are designed with difficult to open/hidden zippers and locks, I've found that a simple padlock to clasp my backpack zips together works just as well. Alternatively, some people opt to carry their backpacks on their front too.

A retractable cable lock that can keep your bag attached to a fixed object such as a table leg when you're sitting in restaurants will also deter thieves. I found this particularly useful in countries where there is often a lot of open-air outdoor seating and there is more opportunity for someone to grab your bag.

Money belts are a good place to store cash, cards, and travel documents close to and in front of you. You can also carry your money and card in a bra wallet that attaches to your undergarment.

Snatch and grabs are a particularly common way people get their phones stolen, so get a phone case that allows you to attach a wrist band to the cover and make sure the band is around your wrist as you're walking around. Do not carry your phone, cash, or cards in your back pocket. While this is insanely obvious, I still see people do this, and it is the number one way to attract pickpockets.

If you're taking a laptop, get a portable table lock that is attached to your device if you plan on using it in public places like cafes.

Also, be mindful when in big groups of people and on public transport. Some backpacks have a smaller zippable compartment on the outside, this can be easily accessed by thieves, and I was almost pickpocketed this way on a train in Barcelona. Thankfully, I always keep any belongings in the innermost pocket of my bag and the thief took nothing.

When on the beach

Purchase a waterproof phone case with a neck strap. These are see-through and allow you to use your phone and ensure it doesn't get damaged by water and sand. You can also place other valuables in them such as money, and they'll float in the water. You may also opt to bring your portable safe to the beach and attach it to an umbrella pole or your sunbathing deck.

Cash and credit cards

Find ways of splitting where your card and cash is kept. For example, keep your money in a bra wallet, and your card in your backpack. You'll find a range of 'smart clothing' such as tank tops, scarves and socks with secret compartments to keep your belongings safe.

Have a clear idea of how much money you will need for the day and only carry that, avoid, carry large wads of cash around—there is no real purpose for this. Also, get a second credit card pre-loaded with money. If one goes missing, you can cancel it, and still have another. Invest in an RFID card that can be put next to your credit card—this will prevent your credit card details from being swiped. Avoid using ATM's that look faulty, or look tampered with, and be mindful of your surroundings and make sure no one is standing too close as you go to withdraw your money.

#PASSPORT READY PROFILE
- PELUMI, TRAVELLING IS THE KINTSUGI OF LIFE

What is your travel why? Having a why firmly enroots you in a certain belief system, and you don't find yourself changing course just because the people around you don't understand your way of life and the need to explore that is important to you. Having a why keeps you going when times get tough.

Growing up, I was bullied in primary school, and one of my many escapism activities was to go to the library and look through travel books and magazines. I would imagine myself in beautiful destinations all around the world. Fifteen years later, I am living that dream. So far, I have explored sixty-one counters. While travelling I got a little nervous because I did not know the reason why I was travelling, yes, it may have started with a need to escape, but I did not want that to be the long-term reason.

I came across the concept of Kintsugi - meaning to mend broken pottery with gold - back in 2017, and that changed everything! I was able to apply the concept to my travelling, and I've realised that travel is the Kintsugi of life. It's going to new destinations meeting people and having shared experiences that could help with the healing process of traumas you have been through. It is the mending, fixing, binding, and coming together of people who may be different but share the fundamental similarity of humanity, and are therefore connected in more ways than can be explained. Travelling allows you to experience cultural immersion and forces you out of your comfort zone.

Travelling adds more value to your life, just like when the pottery goes through the process of Kintusgi it becomes even better than it was before. The imperfection in the pottery is highlighted and not covered up.

Yes, travelling may not be perfect, but with every 'wrong' thing that may happen, a lesson can be learned.

Follow Pelumi: @black.kintsugi

www.instafeedclinic.com

#PASSPORT READY PROFILE
- PREITI, NO REGRETS

When I told people that I was quitting my job to travel, they would say 'wow that's so brave!'.

I would just smile, but in my mind, I was thinking 'is it brave?' It wasn't like I decided to suddenly turn my life upside down and take this big leap. I had done a lot of planning and self-reflection before I came to this decision.

I listed what I would gain from my trip. If I was going to cut off my source of income, halt my career and leave my loved ones, it had to be for a good reason. Some experiences in life are priceless and can't be had from within your comfort zone. When I began listing my reasons to leave, these were some of them:

I wanted to see the world with my own eyes

I wanted to experience different cultures

I wanted to learn to truly be independent

I wanted to meet unforgettable people

I wanted to try new things and challenge myself

I wanted to understand how others live

I wanted to try authentic flavours from across the world

I wanted to become adaptable and confident

I wanted to get a better perspective on life

I wanted to do all of this and so much more that can't be done if I was sitting behind a desk for 37.5 hours of the week. Lastly, I asked myself 'would I regret this for the rest of my life if I don't go?'

The simple answer was—yes!

One year later, I was on the road, and I have never regretted it since.

Follow Preiti: @bravegirltravel

STOMP STOMP

I'VE ARRIVED

CHAPTER 8

HOW TO ARRIVE LIKE A PRO

"It is not the destination where you end up,
but the mishaps and memories you create along the way!"
—Penelope Riley, Travel Absurdities

Y ou've made it - hopefully you're not too jet-lagged - and now the journey can really begin. Here are some tips to help you hit the ground running and avoid common mistakes upon arrival.

Arrive during the day

Always plan to arrive during the day, you don't want to be straddling around at night, trying to find your bearings, or somewhere to sleep if you haven't booked accommodation. Particularly in less busy and rural locations where accommodation tends to be run by locals and not giant chains. You may find that they don't have 24/7 front desks. Arriving anytime from six a.m. is fine and try to arrive by six p.m. at the latest if you have not booked accommodation, this can be stretched too much later if you have, but again, make sure check in will be open for you if you arrive late.

Purchase a local SIM card

Look for somewhere to buy a SIM card to ensure you can stay connected and don't end up with additional charges on your phone. These are usually available at airports, if not, ask a local to point you to a store where you can purchase one for a good price.

Know exactly how you're getting from the airport to your accommodation

Check beforehand what options are available to you. Most major cities will have some mode of public transport such as trains, buses, and coaches. Check timetables and when these run. Otherwise, a cab or ride-share is the most convenient way to get to the centre of town/your accommodation.

HOW TO BE A MORE ETHICAL TRAVELLER

"If we are to achieve a richer culture, rich in contrasting values,
we must recognize the whole gamut of human potentialities,
and so weave a less arbitrary social fabric,
one in which each diverse gift will find a fitting place."
—Margaret Mead

I've made mistakes.

We likely all have while travelling. The important thing is to learn from them and become more socially conscious travellers, and here are some ways you can do it.

Support local businesses

Anytime you have to choose between a small business owned by a local and a bigger operator, consider going with the local business owner. You'll generally enjoy a more authentic experience, and even if you do have to pay more, experiences run by locals have always been worth the money I've paid.

Don't engage in animal entertainment

While there is more awareness nowadays about the horrific treatment of animals in tourism, it's still a common thing to come across. Elephant riding, tiger petting, and taking photos with reptiles are just a few examples. Do not engage with any attraction that keeps animals caged/chained. In many cases, the animals are also drugged to make them more agreeable.

In response to the demand for more ethical experiences, many animal sanctuaries full of supposed rescued animals have opened up. You must still approach these places with caution. If the price is too good to be true and there are large groups of people, give it a miss.

Also do not feed wild animals as this will alter their behaviour. When the coronavirus hit and tourists had vacated the Lopburi Province in Thailand, hungry monkeys overtook the streets looking for food in a scene that looked like something from The Planet of the Apes movie. The animals had gotten so used to tourists feeding them, they didn't know where else to source their food.

Do not alter the natural environment

Don't take 'natural souvenirs' such as sand from beaches, as well as rocks and pebbles and do not pick flowers and other vegetation from fields either. Stick to marked trails and do not wander off the path and destroy healthy vegetation when exploring nature sites. Clean up after yourself and do not leave trash and waste around.

Learn some basic phrases

Not only is it courteous to learn a few common phrases, but you'll find locals will warm to you more if you do. Hello, goodbye, good morning, good evening, and thank you is the bare minimum you should know. Make the effort.

Follow local customs

While you may not personally agree with certain local customs, when you choose to visit a country, you have agreed to follow their local customs. For women, these may mean dressing in more conservative attire, not entering certain places of worship, or being excluded from certain cultural practices or parts of daily life. Remember that wherever there are limitations, there are probably brave women and activist groups doing their darned best to fight against the norm. If you feel strongly enough about an issue, by all means learn about the work local activists are doing, but do not try to make any grand social or political statements yourself.

As American author Clifton Fadiman once wrote; "When you travel, remember that a foreign country is not designed to make you comfortable. It is designed to make its own people comfortable."

Avoid giving money to children

Although it is a natural instinct to help a child in need, resist the temptation to give money to beggar children, or buy souvenirs from them. This encourages their parents to keep them out of school. It's not uncommon for children to be used as fronts for gangs and other illegal activities.

Do not volunteer at orphanages

Both UNICEF and Save the Children advise against volunteering in orphanages. UNICEF states that "many children in orphanages are not orphans. Instead, they have been separated from their families to attract fee-paying volunteers. In Nepal for example, it's estimated that 85 per cent of all children in orphanages have at least one living parent."

In addition, children do not get the attention and care they need, and a steady rotation of unqualified volunteers for vulnerable children can be damaging. Orphanages have also been known to be used as fronts for trafficking and other illegal activities.

Don't engage in sex tourism

The overwhelming majority of sex buyers are men, so I know I'm not speaking to the majority of my reading audience by adding this point to my book - female sex buyers are an absolute minority - but it has to be said. If anything, let's call out sex buyers for their behaviour, even in countries where it's legal.

Reduce your waste

Reusable items you can carry to reduce your waste include a refillable water bottle, a cotton tote for shopping, a reusable straw, and cutlery. Also opt for a toxic-free sunscreen, as sunscreens have now been found to be damaging to coral reefs and ocean water quality.

HOW TO IMMERSE YOURSELF WHILE TRAVELLING

"Travel is fatal to prejudice, bigotry, and narrow-mindedness, and many of our people need it sorely on these accounts. Broad, wholesome, charitable views of men and things cannot be acquired by vegetating in one little corner of the earth all one's lifetime."
—Mark Twain

This quote by Mark Twain is cited often in conversations about travel, and while I think it is true to some extent, the idea is not without flaws. I've met plenty of travellers who are incredibly insensitive, narrow-minded and bigoted. The saying also implies that someone who doesn't and perhaps can't travel even if they want to, can't be a culturally aware and open-minded person who sees the humanity in their fellow men and women.

I think a more accurate quote on the matter would be from Joe Abercrombie in the Last Argument of Kings that says; "Travel brings wisdom only to the wise. It renders the ignorant more ignorant than ever."

So why do so many people who travel still come home as utter twits? I believe that the lack of engagement in local life and with local people is one of the reasons. They never truly connect with their fellow human beings, often sticking to the comforts created for tourists, so they don't have to. Locals are therefore seen as just hotel staff and tour guides, i.e. people who are there to serve and not much else. Avoid this by being open to immersing yourself in as many ways as possible.

Immerse yourself in cultural experiences

Dancing, cooking, art, music and language greatly define individual cultures.

Booking an experience with a local to engage in these things can give you a great insight into a country past and present. Learn how to cook a new dish, move your feet and take a dance class, take a language lesson, or try your hand at some crafts, visit museums, art galleries and attend festivals.

Explore the markets

Markets are often the beating heart of a community. Food, clothing, arts and crafts can be found here. The food at local markets is often the best representation of the local cuisine—unchanged for the Western palette—and is often cheaper. Supporting local artists who make handmade goods, also keeps traditional arts alive and gives locals more incentive to preserve generational techniques, as opposed to buying mass produced trinkets at wholesale. Exploring markets is also a fun setting to strike up a conversation with locals. Local knowledge is the best knowledge, and they are the best sources of information on all the great things to see and do.

Look for a local guide

As well as supporting a local person, local guides are able to offer a more authentic experience, and can give you greater access to areas and experiences that bigger tours skip over. There are several websites that can facilitate finding a local guide, or visit the various travel agents that are often scattered around town centres. Air Bnb don't just offer cheap accommodation, but local day trips and activities through their 'Experiences' feature run by locals.

#PASSPORTREADY WORDS OF WISDOM
- DAAN, EMBRACE OTHER CULTURES

Something I made a tradition of doing everywhere I go is trying local dishes, things that I never imagined eating or even had any idea that you could eat.

In order to have a vast experience, I go to local markets, traditional restaurants and really fancy dinner places. This allows me to understand and appreciate the culture more fully and opens a door to let the locals know that I admire and respect their culture and allows me the opportunity to get to know them.

Practising this has greatly enriched my travelling experience. It's given me the opportunity to make friends with unfamiliar people, connecting on much deeper levels by sharing meals, music and language. Never forget to enjoy every destination you go to, marvel at its people, and soak up as much of it as you possibly can.

Follow Daan: @callmedaan_

Try the public transport at least once

As well as being cheaper, navigating public transport can turn into an adventure of its own when you travel, some countries may have modes of transport that your country does not. Stand shoulder to shoulder with the locals and experience what it's like to get around as one.

Walk and discover

I try to dedicate some time to walking around town and intentionally getting lost. Observing local life and truly immersing yourself in the moment can be incredibly enlightening. This is how you discover the hidden gems that don't show up on a Google search. Just be wary to not go so far off the main track you wander into somewhere you probably shouldn't.

Find a date/friend

Following all standard safety common sense of course, but if you find yourself charmed by the local people, start swiping on your phone app, or find ways of meet locals in sociable environments. Arrange a meal out, or ask them to take you to a cool spot. As a woman, be mindful of doing so in conservative countries where socialising alone with men may be seen as taboo.

#PASSPORT READY PROFILE:
ALICE, BREAKING OUT OF MY COMFORT ZONE

Armed with a backpack and one-way ticket to Bangkok, Thailand, I hopped on a plane across the world, leaving my cushy life in Bristol behind to embark on a six-month trip around Southeast Asia and the Far East. I've always been an outgoing character, but this was pushing me well out of my comfort zone, and the closer it got to my departure date, the more overwhelmed I became.

During the first week away I spent time in Koh Rong and Phnom Penh, my emotions were so turbulent, there were many times I contemplated going back home. I would call my mum crying, needing to pacify the anxiety I felt about being alone. My life had always been structured by education or work, and this had been replaced with a newfound freedom of being a traveller, meeting new people, and hopping from one place to another. This was both incredibly freeing, but also incredibly anxiety-inducing for a twenty year old who'd never ventured too far from home.

Two weeks into my trip, I found myself in Siem Reap, I finally managed to calm my nerves and developed a strategy of thinking in the moment, rather than planning for months ahead. I made sure I always had lots to do during the day, so negative thoughts had no room to fill my mind. After a few weeks, I became fully adjusted to the life of travelling and the time I spent away was the most exciting, fulfilling time of my life.

Travelling alone also enables selfishness. You've made the decision to come away, and it's your experience only, you have the choice of where you want to go and with whom. There are very few opportunities in life where compromise is not an option. As a woman, I found this particularly empowering. The idea of females travelling alone in a foreign country is often considered dangerous. However, I would say there was barely a moment I felt unsafe and I would urge everyone to try and have this experience at least once in life.

I am blessed to have had the opportunity to explore and learn so much more about myself than I did before I travelled. I am now more aware of which personality types bring out the best in me. I know which activities trigger my anxiety and how to deal with it. I can draw from my experiences travelling and relate them to situations back home. If I can tackle crossing the border from Cambodia to Thailand alone, on a twenty-four-hour bus, I can definitely tackle a trip to London from Bristol without breaking a sweat.

My final advice to a potential traveller is this; be prepared to feel overwhelmed at the start, but do not feel ashamed. It's a natural response to an unfamiliar situation that will soon become familiar. Just keep yourself busy and surround yourself with people who make you feel at ease.

Also, be prepared to never want to come home.

That was my only major let down – thanks corona!

Follow Alice: @alice_chubb

#PASSPORTREADY PROFILE:
KRISTIN, THE GLOBE TROTTER

The first time I moved abroad, I had accepted an assistant teaching position in a small town in France. I was both nervous and excited to move to a new country alone. But I also had barely any money saved up and wasn't sure how I would pay for hotels while looking for an apartment. I decided to do Couchsurfing instead (way before Airbnb existed).

A woman named Estelle invited me to stay with her family. She cleared out her son's bedroom for me to stay in by myself for almost two weeks.

That was only the beginning of her generosity. Estelle brought me along on family trips to different cities, drove me around apartment hunting, co-signed as a guarantor on my apartment lease, helped me open French bank account, and even lent me a bike for a year.

The warmth and kindness of both her and her family knew no bounds, and I will always remember it as a special chapter in my life. Not only did she invite me into her home without question, but she also invited me to experience the language and culture in an authentic way that still remains with me. I only hope I can pay it forward like she did when I have my own place someday.

Follow Kristin: @thefeministglobetrotter

HEALTH ON THE ROAD

CHAPTER 9

AVOIDING TRAVEL BURNOUT

"Traveling is a brutality. It forces you to trust strangers and to lose sight of all that familiar comfort of home and friends.

You are constantly off balance. Nothing is yours except the essential things: air, sleep, dreams, sea, the sky - all things tending towards the eternal or what we imagine of it."
— Cesare Pavese

Whether you're going away for one week or one year, travel burnout can really suck the fun out of your trip. Sight-seeing daily can become exhausting, and so you need to find time to rest and choose your daily activities strategically.

Stay well-nourished and hydrated

And by hydrated I don't mean chugging cheap beers at every opportunity, in fact, you must monitor the amount of alcohol you consume.

Make sure to have even a light snack for breakfast to get you going for the day and drink plenty of water, particularly if you are in a hot country.

Purchase a metal water bottle and never leave for the day without making sure it's full.

Protect yourself against the sun

Those with fairer skin in particular, should make sure to wear sunscreen every single day. Sunglasses that offer full protection against UV rays are essential in both warmer climates and colder climates where heavy snow can cause snow blindness due to reflected rays. It is also advisable to get sunglasses that feature a polarised filter and have a wrap-around shaped frame.

Wear appropriate footwear

Invest in a pair of sturdy trainers or hiking boots for those long days trekking. Soft canvas shoes are both stylish and comfortable for general sight-seeing. Dolly shoes are a stylish and comfortable alternative to heels at night. Do away with the heels altogether—your feet will thank you for it.

Spread out your activities

If you know you're getting up at two a.m. for a sunrise mountain trek, don't plan anything else heavy for the rest of that day—or for the next day even.

Try and space out more physically demanding activities and fill the days in between with activities that require less energy, or don't require an early morning start.

Also, remember to schedule resting time/resting days during your trip. This is especially important for long-term travel to reduce fatigue. If you have less time, don't pressure yourself into seeing and doing everything. Re-examine your itinerary and see what you can cut out.

Don't make every night a party night

It is incredibly easy to get sucked into the #partylife on the backpacking scene where every night is a party and alcohol is cheap. I have seen people party themselves into sickness, only to have days wiped off of their adventure because they were too worn out to do anything. It seems incredibly pointless to come all the way around the world to do the same thing you can do at home.

Stay on top of medications

Make sure you have a full supply of your medication, take it as prescribed and avoid situations that can cause interactions with other substances, such as taking medications with alcohol.

Find time for yourself

People often worry so much about being alone when they travel solo, they don't realise how often you will actually crave some alone time. I like to refer to this as 'people burn out'. You eventually grow tired of introducing yourself, asking people where they're from, where they're going, and the person snoring above your dorm bed seems to penetrate through your earplugs. You will eventually grow tired of others and want your own space. This is perfectly okay, and don't be afraid to say no when your hostel buddy asks you to go sight-seeing and you'd rather go alone. Go read a book on the beach, get a cheap massage, chill out in the hostel lounge, do whatever you like to treat yourself.

Take care of your mental health and to check in with people at home. Speaking to a familiar voice can make you feel better and reassures your loved ones that you're okay.

PERIODS DON'T HAVE TO BE A PAIN

Auntie Mildred, Aunt Flo, the P's, that time of the month, mother nature, the drips . . .

It's incredible how many code words we have to describe PERIODS!

As I've gotten older, I've come to see the beauty of this incredible part of my womanhood. We are often made to feel ashamed of what is a perfectly natural part of our biology. Because of this, we see it as an obstacle and a nuisance, instead of learning how to take control and manage it in a healthy way, and periods don't have to put a dent in your fun when you travel.

Start tracking your period before you go

Periods affect women in different ways, and while some women can power ahead without issues, others might need to take things slower.

Perhaps you decide not to do anything physically demanding on the days your flow is heavy. If you know when your period is likely to start, you can plan ahead.

Tracking apps such as Clue and Flo help you track your cycle, as well as helping you to record how your mind and body feel at different parts of your cycle. Download them onto your phone and start tracking your cycle as soon as possible so you can get the most accurate picture of when your period starts and ends when you're away.

Don't deal with it at all

There are medications available that will temporarily stop your period. Norethisterone is a common drug prescribed for this purpose. As with any medications, talk to your doctor to determine if it is suited for you.

Hormonal medication can affect your future cycles and alter your mood, among other common side effects. If you experience any uncomfortable changes, stop taking the medication immediately.

Remember that medications designed specifically to stop your period are not contraceptives or a barrier for STD's. They will not protect you from sexually transmitted diseases or prevent pregnancy. If you are having sex with a new partner and you are not aware of their status, you must always use a condom if engaging in sexual intercourse to stop the transmission of diseases.

Take a small supply of sanitary products

While in Siem Reap, Cambodia, I and accidentally purchased a brand of sanitary towels that was loaded with menthol! I don't know why anyone would think a vagina needs to smell like a breath mint. I ripped it off immediately and went back to the store to find something that didn't make my lady garden feel like it was on fire.

I highly advise taking at least one cycle supply of sanitary products with you. You can top up along the way, but remember that when travelling to more remote places, you won't always have easy access to stores.

Get a menstrual cup

The toilets in Southeast Asia lend themselves well to menstrual cup wearers as almost all of them are fitted with bidets, so you'll be able to wash your cup when needed. Test out wearing a cup until you're comfortable inserting and removing it before you travel.

Carry reusable pads or period pants

If you think you'll struggle with a menstrual cup, a good alternative is a reusable pad. Carry at least three pads so you can wash, dry and rotate. These are especially useful if you're going to remote areas where you may not have access to menstrual products. You'll also be helping the ecosystems of these remote areas as they may not have waste disposal systems.

Period pants look and feel like normal panties, but are highly absorbent without the bulky look and feel of a nappy, although they're generally not recommended for your heaviest days. Companies such as THINX and Luna Pads are the most popular brands for period panties.

Carry pain relief

Don't suffer unnecessarily with cramps, take some painkillers to help subside the pain. Heat pads can also help to relieve cramps and are more compact and convenient to carry than a hot water bottle. If you suffer consistently with severe period pains, seek advice and a closer examination from your doctor. Many women suffer when there could be a more serious underlying problem.

Periods and other cultures

As you travel, you may also encounter negative attitudes towards women's menstruation.

Don't feel offended by such attitudes. Remember that wherever in the world there are limiting ideas about womanhood, there are also women fighting for their dignity the best ways they can, so don't assume helplessness, or impose your standards on others.

SEXUAL HEALTH AND DATING

Casual hookups and short term romances are a common part of backpacker life, but don't feel pressured to do something because the people around you are. If one-night-stands aren't appealing to you at home, entertaining them on the road won't make them feel any better. What isn't for you isn't for you. If all you want is friendly company and a nice conversation over dinner, don't feel pressured into taking any further than what you want to. Putting pressure on yourself to have sex will only lead to regret and hurt feelings.

If you're using apps to meet dates, block anyone immediately asking you personal and sexually suggestive questions or requesting for, or sending illicit photos.

Even if your intentions are casual, spend time with someone over a meal, or sight-seeing during the day, so you can read signs and cues about their behaviour.

When meeting someone new, always do so in a public space and somewhere that is convenient for you and close to your accommodation. Something I often do is invite my date to hang out with my hostel friends first before going on a private date, or I insist we go out with the group together.

If you are going anywhere with someone alone, take a picture of the person's profile if you met them via an app, note the location you are going to and send it to someone.

If someone tells you who they are—believe them and stay away! It is amazing how often people pass off derogatory comments as 'banter' or 'jokes'. Take people's words seriously, especially when you're on your own. Sinister people reveal themselves in subtle ways.

Protect your heart also

Not that it isn't possible to find true love on the road, but keep in mind that a lot of people are around for a good time—not a long-time—when travelling. If you find yourself dazzled by another traveller, spend some time with them before being intimate and think long-term what the likelihood of you two seeing each other again is before getting swept away. Love can be found, but be smart and give the other person time to prove they're looking for more than just a holiday fling. Ask yourself; would they be willing to wait long enough to come and see you at a later date?

How NOT to handle contraception

If you are going to opt for any kind of method of contraception that can not be easily reversed or removed such as the coil, implant, or injection, make sure to get it a few weeks before you leave in case you have any kind of negative reaction, and it needs to be removed/treated.

Take contraception with you

If you think there's even the smallest chance you could have sex, take some condoms kids. Carrying protection doesn't make you more likely to have sex—it doesn't make you dirty either—it makes you a grown adult taking responsibility for your sexual health. Contraception around the world is not made equal, the quality (and size) may not be what you find in your home country.

Always wear protection

The only souvenirs you want to come home with are t-shirts and a fridge magnet—you do not want to come home with a sexually transmitted disease. Always wear protection when engaging in both penetrative and oral sex. If your new friend doesn't think using protection is important, that should be the end of that encounter.

Do not have sex in a dorm room

Do not be that person, okay. Putting a blanket around your hostel bed won't stop the room from hearing your booty session either. Private rooms in hostels don't often cost more than a dorm bed. For the sake of everyone; get damn room!

If anything, the showers late at night when no one is using them make for a good alternative . . . not that I'd know from experience of course, just what I've heard.

Get tested when you get home

Even if you have used protection, better safe than sorry —get tested. Asides from any possible transmission during sex, if you've gotten a tattoo, you can also ask to get tested for other infections such as hepatitis.

AVOIDING SICKNESS ON THE ROAD

Even when taking precautions, you may still get minor stomach upsets and notice changes to your excretions. If what's going into your body changes, what comes out will change too. This happens to most people when travelling and usually settles after a few days. Other illnesses may need medical attention and if you ever feel so sick that you're struggling to function, ask to be taken to the hospital immediately.

Rules for eating food

Whether you're eating at a restaurant, or eating street food, the food you eat should be served piping hot unless it's clearly meant to be a cold dish.

Street food stalls that have a lot of locals hovering around is always a good sign of food that tastes good, has been made fresh and hasn't sat around for a long time.

While it's good to indulge in the local cuisine, if you're going to try anything exotic, perhaps ask a local first. I've noted on my travels that certain foods are sold and marketed to tourists, but not eaten by locals. A good example would be the scorpions on Khaosan Road in Bangkok.

Wash your hands

One would hope you're doing this anyway, but the coronavirus pandemic revealed that many people were not, or at least, didn't know how to do it effectively enough to ward off infections. Your hands pick up bacteria and other nasties, so make sure to wash them thoroughly with soap and water for at least thirty seconds before eating your food. Where this isn't possible, use hand sanitiser.

Stick to bottled water

The sanitary standards of water varies around the world. Not all countries have drinkable tap water. Unfortunately, this contributes to plastic waste, but you will find places that offer water machines to refill your reusable water bottle.

Other things to consider

- Keep bug spray repellent handy when you're out and about in tropical locations.
- Always wear flip-flops when using communal showers to avoid bacterial infections such athletes foot.
- Where one is provided, always open out your mosquito net at night.

Carry a first aid kit

A first aid kit is essential to your travel kit. Here are the bare basics that should be inside it:

Pain relief

Thrush treatment (Fluconazole)

Antiseptic

Waterproof plasters

Gauze

Surgical tape

Tweezers

Small scissors

Antiseptic wipes

Oral rehydration salts

Anti-allergy medicine

Cold gel sheets

Travel sickness pills

Insect repellent

Mini hand sanitiser

Compressed coin tissues

To finish, I'll use this as yet another opportunity to remind you to purchase insurance! If you get sick overseas, your medical fees can be costly.

#PASSPORTREADY PROFILE
- LOUISA, POTTY ISSUES

The most interesting twenty-four hours I've experienced while travelling is definitely when I contracted severe food poisoning in Sunny Beach, Bulgaria. The day we were leaving, we had our morning buffet from the hotel and sat by the pool, waiting for our departure time. Suddenly I had the strongest queasy feeling that I couldn't shake, so I decided to make myself sick to just get it all out and hopefully feel better. As I was hunched over the toilet throwing my guts up I also suddenly felt my bowels moving, so I grabbed the toilet bin, and sat on the toilet. If you've ever seen the toilet scene in the film *Dumb and Dumber*, this is what it was like, except over a really long time, and I was also clutching a bin and puking at the same time.

By the time we had to leave to catch our transfer, it had started to settle down, but I was still dreadfully ill. Fortunately, the coach was half booked, so I could sit alone and suffer in silence with a handy cup to throw up in if needed. The puking commenced, and at one point, I actually passed out mid-puke, fell off my chair, and dropped my cup of sick all over myself to the horror of the two girls sitting adjacent to me.

"The good news is I can't possibly sink any lower than this exact moment," I told myself when I regained consciousness from my friend trying to shake me awake. But it didn't end there.

Only God knows how I made it through security at the airport as I was literally swaying on the spot. When we boarded the plane, to my horror, we found out that my plane seat was not situated beside my two friends. I was sat beside the two girls who saw me drop sick down myself on the coach! I sat on the aisle seat and threw up a couple more times in a sick bag, and handed it to the air hostess like nothing had happened. I was sick for hours still after this, and it wasn't until about the twenty-four-hour mark that I could actually start to keep down water and food.

Moral of the story;

1) Beware the cheap buffet at cheap hotels. It can potentially be a breeding ground for deadly bacteria if they're not practising proper food hygiene.

2) I later learned that if I had been ill for more than twenty-four hours, I needed to go to the hospital for a drip.

With all that said, I did actually return to Bulgaria years later, but to the quaint Varna where I gorged on some of the most delicious, fresh food I've ever had in my life.

Follow Louisa: @sillymoop

#PASSPORTREADY PROFILE
- KYLEE, EAT, PRAY . . . GET UP, AND MOVE ON

It was now day three after a heart-breaking phone call, and I was still under the covers, hair a mess, eyes swollen shut from crying over my breakup that I so didn't see coming. My ex pulled the rug out from under me. He made me believe we would end up together until . . . we didn't. How much longer could I sit here, devastated, and wonder where it all went wrong?

One month after my heartbreak, I decided that I needed to do something about it. I put my two weeks notice in at work and immediately started applying for volunteer positions that would take me anywhere from where I was. That was when I landed a volunteer job in North Macedonia.

Spring of 2017, I flew to Skopje and spent eight-weeks volunteering and travelling through Europe solo.

During those eight weeks, I had some pretty memorable moments. I ate my way through Barcelona, made friends in Ljubljana, and partied at Springfest in Munich. But looking back on my solo adventure, what stands out to me the most was the intense loneliness that I felt at times. Here I was, having this grand adventure, and I would be crying myself to sleep because I couldn't remember the last time I had a meaningful human connection. At times I felt so lonely I didn't even want to get out of bed. But despite this feeling, there is one thing that I knew was worse . . .

What was worse was sitting at home, crying over a boy, or crying over a job, or anything else that could happen to you and wondering what it might be like to see the world. What was worse was being envious of other people on social media when you want to be that person out there experiencing the world. While there were parts of my travels where I struggled, it was also incredibly life changing.

Travel is never perfect—it can be scary and messy. There may be tears, and there will be no one to turn to. Slowly, though, it takes you away from that shy and timid person who you may have been in the past. Most importantly, it proves that you are strong, and reminds you to love and cherish yourself no matter what is going on in the background of your life.

Follow Kylee: @passportsandpreemies

www.passportsandpreemies.com

DOCUMENTING

YOUR TRAVELS

CHAPTER 10

TRAVEL PHOTOGRAPHY ETHICS

"The context in which a photograph is seen,
affects the meaning the viewer draws from it."
—Stephen Shore

Documenting our travels is one of the most enjoyable parts of the journey, but this does at times, come with some ethical and safety issues. We often get the best and most natural pictures when we simply take the picture, but this can often be without the permission of the subject. It's a tough call, as travellers, we wish to be respectful, but want to capture the world around us. You could pretty much forget the idea of street photography if you had to ask every person.

So what does one do?

Simply put; use your common sense.

Do not suddenly shove a camera in someone's face, or capture them in a way that you would feel hurt by if someone did it to you. When visiting a holy place or attending a ceremony, ask a local if it's okay for you to use a camera. Keep your distance and be discreet. Usually, there will be signs to let you know where and what you can't film.

Drones

Pay careful attention to where and when you can fly a drone. Some places will clearly state that it is prohibited. This is most common in highly populated city areas, but the rules tend to be relaxed as you get further into the country. In areas where there is a heightened security, it is not advisable to fly a drone.

Don't risk your life for the shot

Influencers falling to their deaths from cliffs and bridges are just a few of the tragic incidences that have happened to travellers feverishly trying to get the best and most unique pictures. A pretty picture is not worth your life. Furthermore, publishing these pictures will encourage others to do the same.

Be respectful

Influencers and tourists acting disrespectfully while capturing images have been regularly called out in the online space. Some of their disgraceful actions include: doing yoga poses on war memorials, smiling like beauty queens at holocaust memorials and waltzing around Chernobyl wearing a bikini. Use common sense and be mindful of where you are when taking photos. You can still take photos and shoot film at sensitive sites, but do so respectfully and think about what your image is saying.

Exotifying locations and people

Avoid using words such as 'weird', 'strange' and 'outlandish' to describe locations, people and their customs. This *othering* of other cultures is dehumanising and reinforces the idea that because something is not in line with standards that define what we typically consider 'developed' countries, that they are somehow 'strange'.

CAMERA GEAR: THE BASICS

"Photography is a way of feeling, of touching, of loving.
What you have caught on film is captured forever . . .
It remembers little things,
long after you have forgotten everything."
—Aaron Siskind

If you don't have money to splash out on a camera set-up, (or would rather just not spend the money at all) your smartphone can do wonders if you learn to fully utilise its functions. It is not necessary to splash out on camera gear, but if you really want to up your game, I've stripped things down to the bare minimum.

MINIMAL TRAVEL GEAR SET-UP

The best budget vlogging cam: Canon G7x Mark iii— this is a great point and shoot camera for vlogging and taking photos, and fares pretty well in dark conditions. I filmed an entire documentary series on its predecessor the Mark ii. Considering how small this camera is, it is still able to capture incredibly cinematic footage.

Regardless of which camera you choose, I highly recommend it has the following features:

- a flip screen so you can get a live feed of what you're filming when the camera is turned towards you
- touch focus
- autofocus
- performs well in low light
- a rechargeable battery
- can be controlled via Wi-Fi

Sports Cam: GoPro Hero 7
(Or any new model after that)

I specifically recommend the Hero 7 because it was the first GoPro model to include hyper smooth to reduce shake. While there are newer models, this model will still give you clear and stable footage without the price tag of a more recent model.

Cheaper alternatives to the GoPro are; Campark Action, Camera 4K, and Crosstour Action Camera.

Pocket Cam

For super minimal vlogging, or when you want to put your bigger camera away, switch to a pocket cam like DJI Osmo Pocket which is a popular choice.

Spare batteries and portable chargers

Regardless of which camera equipment you choose, make sure to always get at least one spare battery and a portable charger for each device to charge on the go when needed. For portable battery chargers, Anker is a highly recommended brand.

Memory cards

Consider how long you're going away and how much filming and photography you plan on doing when considering how much memory storage your card should have. Once you've decided, split that in half and purchase two separate cards. This will ensure you have a backup in case one goes missing/gets damaged.

Most action cams will require a micro-card to record footage and to transfer footage from a micro-card onto your computer, which then you will need a micro-card adaptor. SanDisk memory cards are highly recommended.

Monopod/tripod

If you're going to take a tripod, I recommend a lightweight aluminium tripod that can easily fold into your backpack. These are usually no more than around 35 cm when folded.

For greater convenience, opt for a monopod. Carrying a monopod has made filming and photography on my travels so much easier. It means not having to switch between setting my camera on a tripod and putting it back on a handheld stick to continue vlogging. My camera is always on one accessory. The downside of a monopod is that it can only handle lighter cameras unless it's a heavy-duty monopod.

Other useful accessories include:

- A mini tripod
- A selfie stick
- A GoPro/action cam stick
- GoPro/action cam waterproof housing
- A 1TB external hard drive to store photos and videos
- Lens cleaner and lens wipes
- An attachable mic for enhanced sound
- Attachable cell phone camera lenses (optional but can really enhance pictures taken on your phone)
- Smartphone stabiliser/gimbal (optional)

When you're on the road, make sure to charge all of your batteries overnight, so your equipment doesn't go flat quickly. If you're on the road long-term, schedule in time to properly organsie your files into folders. This will save you a lot of hassle when you're ready to start editing projects.

Backup your footage and photos on an external hard drive and on an online cloud system to ensure you don't lose all of your precious footage.

HOW TO TAKE PICTURES OF YOURSELF

"What I like about photographs is that they capture a moment that's gone forever, impossible to reproduce."

—Karl Lagerfeld

I often say that having to take my own photos is the only downside of solo travel, but I've mastered it well over the years. Many travel influencers have professional photographers with them—or at least, a very patient and well trained Instagram husband or boyfriend. You don't need either to get high-quality photos. Here's how to do it . . .

Ask someone to take your photo

When you do ask people to take your photograph, avoid giving them a million instructions. At the most, I usually say: can you take a couple, please. That way, I have more to choose from. If someone says no it's a no, respect their answer and leave it at that. Look for someone who is already holding a camera, they're less likely to dash off with yours. Although they may be perfectly innocent, beware kind strangers who suddenly pop out of nowhere ready and willing to take your photo. Try to be the one who asks.

Use a self-timed or remote-controlled camera

A camera that can be controlled remotely is going to be the most convenient option for taking photos when you're on your own. You can either find a camera that has an app, or, purchase a camera that can be used with a wi-fi controlled remote. The advantage of purchasing a camera that can be controlled with an app is the added ability to control focus, lighting, and zoom. If your camera does not have this function, it will still likely have a delayed self-timer.

Use a selfie stick

The selfie stick was once the butt of jokes, but has become the most trusted travel companion when you're on your own. A good selfie stick should extend to at least one meter, have an adjustable joint, so you can alter the angle of your phone and an easy to grip rubber handle.

ALL ABOUT THE GRAM

"You can look at a picture for a week
and never think of it again.
You can also look at a picture for a second
and think of it all your life."
– Joan Miro

For better and for worse, Instagram has had a phenomenal effect on where we choose to travel and how we document our travels. *Doing it for the gram* has become part of the pop culture lexicon. Travellers looking aimlessly into the distance with great monuments, or natural wonders surrounding them, has become a popular style of photography on the platform. It's not clear where this trend originated from, but I'd confidently say that female travel influencers were the first to popularise it, so let's give credit where it's due, because its influence and how it has revolutionised the travel industry cannot be understated.

At best, it has encouraged people who may never have picked up a camera to take up photography, and boosted local economies by encouraging more visitors. At worst, it has contributed to FOMO culture and made certain tourist spots too popular for their own good. A good example of this would be Trolltunga, a rock formation situated about 1,100 metres above sea level in Ullensvang, Norway, that sits high above a stunning valley.

As Carrie Miller for national geographic wrote, *"Between 2009 and 2014, visitors to Trolltunga increased from 500 to 40,000 in what many consider a wave of social media-fueled tourism."* [2]

Not evident in the photos, however, are the many hikers who struggle and ultimately fail to make it up to the cliff. The ones who do often have to line up for hours, each wanting their perfect picture. Instagram versus reality has become a popular online meme showcasing crowd-free destinations versus what they look like when tourists descend upon them.

What photographers and influencers often don't tell you are the lengths they go through to get those pictures, often waking up at early hours of the morning and waiting for crowds to clear at busy places.

You'll often hear travellers talk about their love of experiences over things, but one could argue that as millennials move away from acquiring traditional symbols of wealth, i.e. cars, big houses and designer goods, travel has arguably become the shiny new object for us to show off. We have moved on from the days of pimped out rides and decked out cribs, a picture next to the blue rooftops of Santorini carries more social value. So much so, that we often become more obsessed with capturing our journey than enjoying it.

I am guilty of this too. We often feel as though if we haven't captured and shared something online, it didn't happen. While there's absolutely nothing wrong with capturing your travels, make sure you strike a healthy balance and don't become obsessed with your smartphone/camera equipment. You don't need to capture every smoothie bowl and plate of pad thai. Photography should be a fun hobby, not control your life and your trip.

How you document your travels is up to you, and perhaps you would prefer not to document them publicly at all. If you prefer to add #NoFilter to your travel photos and post as they are, that is fine too. Over the years, I have acquired a newfound love of photography, editing and storytelling, and if you want to create stunning travel photos, here are my tips for creating the perfect feed.

Add lightroom presets/in app filters

This will establish a theme and give your pictures some continuity using colour. Most photo editing apps have built-in filters. When using filters, stick to a few that create a similar effect.

If you really want to give your photos a colour boost, use presets. These are filters created specifically for use in the Adobe Lightroom app and can be applied on a desktop computer or on a mobile phone. A small cottage industry for presets has opened up online. You can find them on creative online markets for as little as a few dollars, and you will find other travel influencers often selling them as well.

Other notable photo editing apps include; Snapseed, VSCO, and Afterlight.

Planning your feed

Either Planoly or Preview are fantastic apps for planning how your feed will look before posting pictures. Both of these apps also include additional features such as in app editing tools and analytics.

Say something worthwhile

The caption of your Instagram post is where you can truly differentiate yourself from being just another Instagrammer. Make an effort to inform your followers about the picture, in a way that is meaningful or educational.

BEST PRACTICES FOR VLOGGING

So you want to be a travel vlogger, or at least, create some fun videos as souvenirs of your travels. YouTube is a great learning resource to find tutorials on how to best use your camera and editing software such as Final Cut Pro and Adobe Premiere Pro. Don't worry about being like everyone else. Vloggers that manage to push through the saturated sea of travel blogging do so because they offer something unique. Here are some other things to consider when creating travel vlogs.

Don't worry about looking strange

Vlogging and selfie-taking are common nowadays, and while some people may look at you, most people don't care. Practice vlogging around your local town and get confident before you hit the road. This will also give you a chance to try out different filming techniques.

More expensive equipment doesn't equal better videos

We're so used to slick, high definition and perfectly edited video footage, we forget it wasn't always this way. Back when vlogs were grainy, shaky and blurry, we still watched them. We watched them because we wanted to go on the journey, and because we enjoyed the personality of the person handling the camera, and how they told a story. It was not because they had the latest and greatest equipment. If you can't find a way to engage viewers, having the best camera won't make a difference.

Always do test footage

Anytime you purchase a new piece of equipment or try new settings, always shoot some test footage and play it back on your laptop to see how it looks and sounds. You don't have to know every single function, but make sure you know the basic ins and outs of whatever equipment you're using.

If in doubt, shoot on auto

The auto mode on your camera is there for a reason. It's smart enough to detect your surroundings and adapt to get you the best results possible without constantly making any manual changes.

Shoot without filters and colour effects

These can always be added afterwards in post-production, but it's difficult to edit out effects if you shot the footage with them.

Keep your lens clean

Specs of dust and smudges can ruin great footage. Make sure to clean your lens before you start shooting and check for marks throughout the day. Purchase a lens spray, similar to what you would use for spectacle glasses and a microfibre cloth to clean your lenses with.

Use image stabilisation

No one wants to get motion sickness while watching your videos. Most cameras come with a stabilisation feature that will help smooth out your footage. Test the different levels of stabilisation as putting the setting too high can alter the quality of your footage. Best to try and keep a steady hand in the first place while filming. A gimbal can help keep your camera steady if you wish to purchase one, just be aware they are not cheap and will take up space in your luggage.

Shoot on a higher fps

Shooting at a higher frame rate will allow you to slow down the video later on in post-production. Shoot in 60fps for slow motion and 120fps for super slow motion. Keep in mind that shooting on a higher frame rate will take up more room on your memory card and drain your battery faster.

Shoot plenty of B roll

The importance of b roll cannot be understated, and you need as much of it, if not more as your actual footage. B roll is the extra footage you capture to enrich a story, and it also gives you greater flexibility and more footage to work with while you're editing. B roll should include all the extra things around your main activities; getting to a from a place, getting ready, detailed closeups, local life etc. Capturing b roll will add extra depth and dimension to a story.

Film now—educate later

If you get stuck on what to say on camera, or don't know much about a place, get your footage and do some voice over going into more detail about the place later. This ensures that you're not constantly talking to the camera and gives viewers the chance to immerse in the location and not just look at you—another reason why B roll is so important.

Don't live behind the camera

Always take a moment to put the camera away and embrace your surroundings once you've got your footage and pictures. I've had trips where I was so focused on getting 'the shot' and moving onto the next thing, that I forgot to embrace the moment and later felt as though I missed it. Consider that your video will only need to be five to fifteen minutes for an average vlog, or thirty to sixty minutes for a longer docu-style video. You actually don't need as much footage as you think.

#PASSPORTREADY PROFILE
- DESI, A CURIOUS EYE

As a young girl, I dreamt of becoming a journalist. I loved the idea of interviewing people, telling their stories, and highlighting interesting places the world. Life had a different plan for me, and I never became a journalist, but thanks to technology and the growth of social media, my dream came half-true in the form of travel blogging. Every time I travel, I am humbled by all of the wonderful places and people I encounter, our similarities—much greater than our differences—as well as the warmth, love, creativity, art and philosophy. I wanted to share all this with my family and the world.

That is why I started my Instagram page @thecuriousdesi back in 2013, and for the last seven years, it served as a platform where I share photos and stories from my travels. I truly believe photography enhances our travel experience. Travel photography makes you more aware of your surroundings. I tend to notice the little nuances about a place much more, because I'm constantly looking for photos. I'm looking up at the top of the buildings, in the little cornered streets, or down on the ground because there's always something curious like an interesting tiled pavement or a beautifully decorated manhole.

There have been many times where I break off from the group I'm with to take a photo. Once you begin looking for photos, you see much more of the world than if you're just walking through it. Some places really blow you away and make you question whether you are dreaming or not. I experienced a moment like this in the Swiss Alps. I had wanted to visit Switzerland for years, but the moment became surreal as I hiked up the steep mountain trail and the beautiful view from the top revealed itself. It took my breath away. Sometimes realising how small you are can be a powerful part of your personal growth.

When it comes to travel photography (as with many things in life) patience and persistence are the keys for a great result. I can't tell you how many times I've waited for the perfect shot. I've had the most brilliant sunrises light up from the overcast, cloudy morning. I've had the most crowded squares just for myself, because I woke up earlier and waited for the perfect moment to capture it.

The best thing about travel photography is that it isn't about owning a large, expensive camera. You can do it with nothing more than a smartphone. In fact, most of my photos are taken with a smartphone. The secret is paying careful attention to your surroundings and taking the time and effort to create beautiful images. So what are you waiting for? Book that flight, pack your camera and start your journey today.

Follow Desi: @thecuriousdesi

www.thecuriousdesi.com

#PASSPORT READY PROFILE
- NASTASIA, THE DAME TRAVELLER

As a Middle Eastern girl, born in the Midwestern suburbs of Michigan and raised by strict immigrant parents from Iraq, I spent much of my younger years striving to be all that my family and community wanted me to be. That was until, I grew a little bit older and wiser. I started leaning into my intuition that constantly whispered to dig deeper. I began to seek the life I truly wanted for myself, not the path that I was expected to follow. So, in 2008, I packed my bags and moved to Chicago after getting accepted into the Marcella Niehoff School of Nursing at Loyola University Chicago. I took a leap of faith, left everyone and everything I knew to start a new life in a big city with very little support. No matter how hard it got, I persisted and never gave up.

When you commit to something and never give up, you develop a strong sense of grit, and that is the most priceless gift you could give yourself because the courage you receive from it opens one door after another.

Ever since I could remember, it had always been a dream of mine to travel to Africa and volunteer abroad. When I decided it was finally time for me to make that dream come true, I could not find a single soul to come along for the ride. And so, I fearlessly booked a ticket for two weeks on what would be my first solo adventure, and spent a few weeks volunteering with a group of other travellers. That trip completely changed my life and is the reason why I fell in love with solo travel in the first place. I was terrified on my way there, crying and asking myself what I got myself into but I cried tears of happiness and joy on my flight back because I was proud of myself for having the courage to make this dream of mine happen.

Fast-forward three years later, the Instagram page @dametraveler was born after a work-related injury that left me in bed rest for months. Little did I know, that the vision I had to celebrate and empower women to take the leaps of faith that I took, would change my life and the lives of so many others. I began posting stunning travel pictures from women all over the world, and in early 2020, released a full coloured coffee table book showcasing these amazing images.

My advice for other women thinking about travelling solo is this: be brave, take the leap, you won't regret it.

Follow Nastasia @nastasiaspassport – Founder of @dametraveler

www.dametraveler.com

COMING HOME

CHAPTER 11

DEALING WITH THE POST-TRAVEL BLUES

*"Travel does not exist without home....If we never return to the
place we started, we would just be wandering, lost.
Home is a reflecting surface, a place to measure our growth
and enrich us after being infused with the outside world."*
— Josh Gates, Destination Truth: Memoirs of a Monster Hunter.

It starts with a heavy feeling in my chest, then I get the slight
sensation to cry, although the tears never come. I get the same
feeling every time a trip is over, even when I'm ready to come
home. It's the post-travel blues. A deep sadness that wells up
inside of you once you've returned from a trip.

From my experience, the post-travel blues is worse the longer
you go away. Life moves on without you as normal, but you
change. After mind-blowing adventures, meeting so many new
people, gaining a new sense of self-confidence and pushing
yourself to new limits, there's no way you're going to come back
the same person as you left. Yet here you are, back on your grey
couch, or at your work desk, with this newfound desire to get out
and live life to the max. It can be hard to connect with people
who have not had the same experience. You also don't want to
seem like you're bragging when talking about your travels.

Intertwined with the travel blues, is what is often referred to as
'reverse culture shock'. You may begin to question things about
your own country or culture, and what seemed 'normal' isn't so
normal anymore. Some of those things can be quite comical. For
example, when in Southeast Asia, I got used to using the bum gun,
more formally referred to as a bidet shower. Coming back to the
UK where washers and bidets are not commonplace in toilets, it
was strange (and incredibly itchy) to go back to using toilet tissue.
I realised how odd it was that if we got faeces and urine on any

other part of our bodies, we wouldn't simply wipe it away, leaving remnants of it on our bodies, we'd wash it off with vigour.

Coming home can be the hardest part, but there are plenty of ways to keep the fun going once you're back at home and beat the blues!

Remember all of the things you missed when you were away

There really is nothing like the feeling of sleeping in your own bed, eating home cooked meals, and being around the people you love, know and trust. Take time to appreciate these things and catch up with the lives of your loved ones. Ask them what they were up to while you were away.

Merge your travel experiences with everyday life

The adventure doesn't have to stop when you're home. Look up recipes on meals from your trip, and try to recreate them at home, play music from the countries you visit, carry on learning the language, read books about the world, memoirs written by explorers and grab copies of travel magazines. You can also continue to explore your own hometown and look for local festivals and cultural experiences. Embrace your own back-yard—there's likely to be some hidden gems you've missed.

Document your travels

Getting to relive your adventures through the travel videos and photos you captured is truly magical. You can start editing your videos and scrapbooking your photos. Start doing this sooner rather than later, or it will drag on and before you know it, it's your next trip!

Connect with other travellers

Just as you joined groups when you first started to research for your travels, continue to connect with other travellers who can talk all day about nothing but travel, without you feeling awkward. Look for in-person events on websites like Eventbrite, to attend also so you can connect with travellers' face to face.

Start planning your next trip

After my first trip, I bought a giant map for my wall and started pinning my top desired destinations and researching new places.

Overall, embrace being home for a moment. One journey may have come to an end, but you'll have plenty more in the years to come. The world will be waiting for you when you're ready to take off again.

#PASSPORTREADY PROFILE
- MEGAN, COMING BACK HOME

Leaving a destination where you've made new lifelong friends, learned more about yourself, and submersed yourself into a culture that became like home is hard, and it never gets easier. My time spent in Monteverde, Costa Rica changed my life. I met a group of people that instantly felt like home, and two of the individuals are now close friends that I love dearly. You know when you meet someone, and the energy matches as quickly as a magnet latches onto the fridge? That's what I had with these two.

The day I left Monteverde, my heart felt heavy because I knew I'd continue my travels without them. As I arrived at my next destination, Puerto Viejo, I felt sluggish. I spent some time journaling, phoning my loved ones, and then I spent an hour crying because I missed my newfound friends. I let the tears fall down my face without shame or guilt. I allowed myself to grieve at that moment and realise how lucky I was to be meeting incredibly special people while travelling.

Boarding your flight home after a life-changing solo trip is a heavy experience. What's even harder than leaving, especially when you've spent numerous months on the road, is acclimating yourself to the culture and society that was once familiar to you, but no longer is. Reverse culture shock can provoke a. sense of anxiety that you may feel when returning to your home country after being abroad for an extended period.

It's okay to feel anxious, lost, or isolated after a solo trip. This is normal because no one can relate to the exact experience that you had while travelling solo. Protect your peace and create space to journal, blog, or vlog so you can preserve your memories that will last a lifetime.

I have personally found that the best way to combat reverse culture shock is to start planning my next trip. It's a cycle that brings with it many emotions, and I wouldn't have it any other way.

Follow Megan: @megzmccarth

www.healtharoundtheglobe.com

#PASSPORT READY PROFILE
- ANJULI, RIDE OR DIE

Travelling has been my number one priority ever since I was allowed to hop on a plane without parental consent. Some may feel rich when they wine and dine in expensive places, or from buying designer goods, then there's me; 70% of my savings go towards travelling. It's the only thing in the world that makes you richer by spending money on it. Rich in experience, rich in human connection, rich in growth, rich in heart and soul.

I had just spent two months and a half exploring parts of USA, Bali, Dubai, and Pakistan when I sadly realised I was already halfway through my five-month travel galore. So many places checked off the bucket list, with more to visit, but something was missing. I needed a wild card in the mix even though I usually only plan part of my trip and leave the rest to pure chance. That is when I found myself in the Turkish Airlines office in Islamabad, Pakistan, twenty-four hours before my flight to France, asking the lady at the counter to re-route my trip via Istanbul for a few days. It would end up costing me $102. Sometimes, you just have to take that financial hit you didn't intend for.

I arrived at my quaint little boutique hotel in the Galata neighbourhood in Turkey, grabbed my leathers, my camera and set off to explore the historic district. No map, no agenda, no data roaming, no bloody idea where North, South, East or West was. I just made sure I blended in and pretended to know where the heck I was going. Whether you find yourself in the labyrinth-like alleyways of Marrakech or the cobblestone streets of Istanbul, never appear to look like you're lost, people pick up on that, and it could leave you in a pickle. If anyone asks if you're travelling alone, (even if you are) just tell them you're with family or cousins who are waiting to join you or vice versa.

After sometime, I felt a rumbling in my tummy, and settled down in a cute little café. Five minutes in, Cemre, a sweet young Turkish girl, takes a quick glance at my leathers and the motorcycle sticker on my camera and asks in English "Do you ride?" To which I reply, "Yes". With a twinkle in her eye and the sweetest grin on her face she points to her motorcycle parked across from the café. Another five minutes in and we've exchanged numbers and plan a motorcycle ride for later that night with some of her friends. Honestly, the two-wheeled community is unlike any other. Literally every city in the world I've travelled to, I always encounter the generosity of this magical motorcycle sister and brotherhood. No matter where I end up, I kid you not, there's always a moto waiting for me to rip around on. It's truly the most liberating and unique way of discovering a city or new place and adding new friends to this incredibly passionate chosen circle of mine.

Ten p.m. couldn't have arrived sooner, the rumbling engines of their motorcycles got louder and louder as did the beating of my heart. What followed was one of the most surreal night rides of my life, whizzing through crazy city traffic under the full moon as it reflected into the Bosphorus River we rode along. Bridge after bridge, all the sights, the history, all the smells, the summer breeze seeping into the vents of my helmet. My Turkish friends did not speak English, but it did not matter. You quickly learn as you travel that language barriers are easily broken by body language, by sharing laughter, food, and just speaking heart to heart.

There is intense freedom in being alone, and being responsible for one's own happiness. In it, I found immense magic and wonderment at every corner of every street, translating all material things into poetry.

Follow Ainjul: @ainjul

www.anjuli.ai

A FINAL NOTE

"Begin doing what you want to do now.
We are not living in eternity.
We have only this moment, sparkling like a star in our hand
and melting like a snowflake."
—Marie Beyon Ray

You made it to the end, congratulations!

I hope you're feeling more confident, fired up and ready to hit the road. I fully appreciate that this is a lot to absorb, and always refer back to and reread parts of this book when necessary.

Travel has enhanced my life in so many ways. There is nothing about my travel experiences I would change. The good, the bad and everything in between. I hope your adventures will be just as fun, enlightening, challenging and eye opening as mine.

If someone comes to you and asks for advice—tell them to buy this book of course—but more than anything, encourage them to do it. I believe the ultimate traveller is one whom inspires someone else to travel.

Whoever you're waiting for, they ain't coming sis—book the ticket!

Anne.

THE START

ACKNOWLEDGEMENTS

I didn't know exactly what I wanted to be when I was a young girl, but I knew I wanted it to be something out of the ordinary. So, I want to start by thanking a young me for believing in herself, even if she wasn't quite sure where she was heading, or what she wanted to find there. I want to thank her for never following the crowd, for not caring that she wasn't in the popular clique in school, for being her weird, quirky, wonderful self always.

Thank you to my friends and family who have been so supportive throughout the entire process of me writing this book. I couldn't have done this without your encouragement. In the middle of a pandemic, as we were all dealing with uncertainty, you let me pour into you, and supported me every step of the way.

To all of the amazing new friends I've made during this writing journey, you have reminded me of the kindness of others, and how powerful we can be when we work together towards something positive.

To my brother Kevin, you're always there when I need you. Even a big girl like me still needs to turn to her elder brother sometimes. Seeing me off at the airport on one of the biggest trips I've ever taken, meant more to me than you'll ever know. I never felt alone the entire time I was away. To my younger sister Abbie, seeing your little face in the hospital the day you were born was the happiest day of my life. You remind me to always seek joy, even when the world seems to go grey. To my sister Martha, through you, I have learnt to have compassion and patience for others, especially for the most vulnerable in our communities.

To Eva, thank you for offering your voice to this book. I am truly in awe of your passion for adventure and desire to connect your audience with the places and cultures you document, and you do so with total respect and consideration for the people you meet. Thank you for inspiring me to be fearless and add more purpose to my work.

To all of the other amazing women who shared your stories in this book, you made this book so much more than I ever imagined it would become. Thank you for giving me a part of your journeys to share with others. You will surely inspire many other women to take the leap of faith and begin their own journeys. To all the incredible people I have met on my travels, especially the women, I'm proud to be part of this sisterhood of wanderlust. To all of the intrepid women who came before us, and all of those breaking barriers now, thank you for your bravery and perseverance.

To you, the reader, go forth and seek all of the beauty and chaos this world has to offer. Fill yourself with experiences and know that you are capable of stepping out on your own.

And finally, I started this book by thanking my mother, and I will end it by thanking her again. No matter where I am on this great big planet of ours, know that if you ever need me, I will always come home.

END NOTES

REFERENCES

[1] Tetteh, J., 2019. *THE RISE OF THE Sowas: INCREASE IN SOLO FEMALE TRAVEL FOR 2019*. [online] Media Centre. Available at: <https://comms.theculturetrip.com/2019/03/08/the-rise-of-the-sowas-increase-in-solo-female-travel-for-2019/> [Accessed 13 August 2020].

[2] Miller, C., 2017. *How Instagram Is Changing Travel*. [online] Nationalgeographic.com. Available at: <https://www.nationalgeographic.com/travel/travel-interests/arts-and-culture/how-instagram-is-changing-travel/> [Accessed 13 August 2020].

IMAGE VECTORS

<A href="https://www.freepik.com/vectors/travel">travel vector created by visnezh - www.freepik.com</a>

<a href='https://www.freepik.com/vectors/hand'>hand vector created by freepik - www.freepik.com</a>

<a href='https://www.freepik.com/vectors/travel'>Travel vector created by rawpixel.com - www.freepik.com</a>

Printed in Great Britain
by Amazon

25000137R00126

Foto
Lichtbild
Photo
Foto

Stempel — Stempel

Handteekening van den houder
Unterschrift des Inhabers — Signature du titulaire
Signature of bearer

Ernest H. Cassutto

en van zijn echtgenoote
und seiner Frau — et de sa femme — and of his wife

Kinderen — Kinder — enfants — children
Naam — leeftijd — geslacht
Namen — Alter — Geschlecht
Nom — âge — sexe
Christian Name — age — sex

The LAST JEW of ROTTERDAM

by Ernest Cassutto

Naomi Rose Rothstein, Editor
Dr. Benjamin H. Cassutto, Contributing Editor
Foreword by Moishe Rosen

Purple Pomegranate Productions
San Francisco, CA

Reprint Permissions
Purple Pomegranate Productions
60 Haight Street, San Francisco, CA 94102

04 03 02   10 9 8 7 6 5 4 3 2

Cassutto, Ernest 1919-1985
The Last Jew of Rotterdam by Ernest Cassutto
Library of Congress Cataloging–Publication Data
The Last Jew of Rotterdam
        p.   cm.
ISBN: 1-881022-09-9 (pbk.)
1.Holocaust.
                                        CIP

All Scripture quoted, unless otherwise noted, is from the
Holy Bible, New American Standard Version. Copyright 1995, World
Publishing, Grand Rapids, Michigan.

Purple Pomegranate Productions is a division of Jews for Jesus®

CONTENTS

FOREWORD

Every generation has had a Pharaoh, Haman or Hitler determined to exterminate every last Jew. However, Jews were never hated and hunted with such efficiency as was carried out by the Nazis. Their depraved work was fueled by a fury unmatched in history. What a perplexing context for a fun-loving, joke-telling, good-natured Jewish man like Ernest Cassutto to find meaning and hope in his life.

Ernest Cassutto was born and raised in an era when the tectonic plates of society were shifting. Early twentieth century Europe was the center of the world and the outlying nations were colonies of European power. Even little Holland had great colonies and Ernest grew up in colonial Indonesia where his father, Judge Cassutto presided. Ernest came to regard Indonesia as his home. The Dutch civil servants who governed the colonies were regarded as the elite. Characteristic of Indonesian culture was the fact that nothing was hurried. The family took time to read books. They committed themselves to learning how to play instruments, and to making their own music. Conversation was an art to be cultivated. Life was meant to be savored. Some may see Ernest's life after his departure from Indonesia as a sea that was once calm, but suddenly became ravaged by storms.

The life of Ernest Cassutto is a study of transition from the benefits of colonialism to the worst of war. His natural egalitarianism was challenged by those determined to slay him and his people. That Ernest's transition from agnosticism to belief coincided with the turbulence in the world around him is almost as remarkable as the constancy of his newfound faith during his experiences of being hated and hunted.

It was in New York, some years after the war, when I first met Ernest Cassutto. As the minister to the Beth Sar Shalom Hebrew Christian Congregation it was my duty to conduct Sunday afternoon services. One day I was told that arrangements had been made for a Dutch Jew to come and speak the following Sunday, and I was to introduce him. So I called Ernest on Thursday and asked him if he would mind coming before the service so that we could meet and coordinate the worship. At 2:00 PM that Sunday, I was in my office upstairs when the usher at the door called me. "There is some nutty Catholic priest here with a guitar who wants to see you," he said.

Curious, I went downstairs and there he was in the chapel; Ernest Cassutto, not quite a Catholic priest but wearing a black clerical collar. It was unusual. In fact I couldn't ever recall a clergyman who believed what we did dressed in anything that identified him as clergy.

He greeted me with a big grin. He didn't seem "nutty" at all. After a few words exchanged to make each other feel comfortable, I asked him about the guitar. "Oh, I thought I would sing a few songs," he explained. The person who invited him didn't tell me about any songs and we already had two soloists lined up. I explained, "Reverend Fuchs didn't tell me anything about you bringing any music; he told me that you were going to preach."

Cassutto replied, "Oh of course, I am going to do that, but I am going to sing and play also." I must have looked puzzled as I was trying to find words to ask him not to sing. Then he blurted out, "Brother Rosen, if Reverend Fuchs knew how good I am, he certainly would have told you to ask me to come and sing." I realized there wasn't the slightest trace of egotism in his expression. With a sense of bewilderment, I asked the soloists to sing next Sunday instead.

I wish I could tell you that his playing charmed the congregation. It didn't! The songs were about Jesus, but the style stunned us. I had never heard anyone play jazz guitar before, let alone at a service in our circles. He used rhythms that might have been originated by Elvis Presley a decade or so later. However, his sermon was excellent—great homiletics, great rhetoric, honoring and exalting the Messiah.

After the service, a few dozen of us proceeded upstairs to the fellowship hall for a meal. Ernie Cassutto said grace in Hebrew and English and informed me that he was going to say grace after the meal as well, which was the custom in the Netherlands. (And he did.)

He sat down next to me as we ate. "You didn't like my songs, did you?" he asked. I sputtered out something, trying to sound tactful. Then he grinned at me and said, "Someday you will; I am just ahead of my time." And the truth is that he was right! His was the kind of music called "contemporary" at the end of the millennium. Ernie was a man in transition. He was too far into the future for us to understand. I think the time has come for us to appreciate the meaning of his life.

This book is not merely about a man who survived the most difficult situations, but about a struggle to understand and rise above a wretched circumstance, a struggle toward decency in the face of deprivation. It is not merely a struggle of a person and a family to find faith, but a struggle of how to practice that faith while facing an implacable enemy of the Jewish people.

Ernest Cassutto was indeed a man ahead of his time—a tribulation saint who showed us how to transcend the worst of times and exalt the Lord. Ernest Cassutto managed to float above the troubled seas of his time, not because he was an intellectual or emotional lightweight, but rather because God gave him the spiritual buoyancy not just to survive, but also to thrive.

Moishe Rosen
Founder, Jews for Jesus
Spring 2001

vii

A WORD FROM HOLOCAUST SURVIVOR DR. VERA SCHLAMM

I was a ten-year old girl living in Berlin when Hitler rose to power. I remember my father saying that this was not good for the Jews. His statement echoed in the sound of glass shattering on "Kristallnacht," and reverberated in the cries of the Jewish people who were beaten in the streets, arrested, and sent away to places with strange names like Dachau and Mauthausen.

At the end of 1938, my family fled to Holland, but as you will read in the pages of *The Last Jew of Rotterdam*, the Nazi menace continued its pursuit there after they subdued the country in five days. Like some in the forthcoming story, I too remember spending time in the Dutch Theater in Amsterdam, and the transport to Westerbork. In February of 1944, my family and I were sent to Bergen-Belsen. I spent my twenty-first birthday in the concentration camp.

The story of *The Last Jew of Rotterdam*, like every story of Holocaust survival is a miraculous one. To live, to breathe, to laugh again after such a nightmare, and then to be able to forgive it all, is a true gift from God. The story of Ernest and Elly and their families is especially compelling. I have always felt sorry for those of my people who lost their faith in God during the Holocaust. How riveting it was to read the story of Ernest and Elly Cassutto, who found their faith during the Holocaust. Reading of their steadfast faith during their years in hiding from the Nazis reminded me of my own experiences in Bergen-Belsen. Though I did not yet know that Jesus was the Messiah,

ix

like Ernest and Elly, I never stopped praying that God would rescue my family. I felt that it was man's fault that we were where we were. God was not to blame. When people ask, "Where was God when six million Jews died?" I respond that He was where He always is, in heaven, weeping over what was done to His people.

I know God was with me during the Holocaust, even in the concentration camp. Like Ernest Cassutto, I missed transportation to Auschwitz by the slimmest of chances, and I am very thankful for all of the times God protected me. I was very thankful that we got out alive, and my desire was to please God in return. To find out what he required of me, I set out to read the Tenach, and eventually came to Isaiah 53. Through that passage and prayer, I realized that Jesus is our Messiah, and that I could have a new life in him. Nobody can tell me, or the rest of my family who also came to believe in Jesus, that he wasn't suffering with me in Bergen-Belsen.

When I was a child, my family frequently used a Yiddish phrase that translates to mean that all things work together for good. I did not know then that this is actually a verse in the New Testament: "And we know that God causes all things to work together for good to those who love God, to those who are called according to His purpose."[1] *The Last Jew of Rotterdam* is an amazing testimony to the veracity of this verse.

I trust you will find this book as moving as I did; I could not put it down.

Vera Schlamm, M.D.
Bergen-Belsen Survivor

1. Romans 8:28, New American Standard Bible

The
LAST JEW
of
ROTTERDAM

CHAPTER ONE

1941

The Hague, Holland

I awoke to the sound of someone pounding on the door. I heard shouting. More confused than frightened, I jumped out of my bed, and stumbled into the living room to see who or what was causing the commotion.

It was the Gestapo. They pushed their way into our home, and yelled for my father.

"Isaac Cassutto!" screamed Herr Fischer, the Gestapo chief. He glared at me. "Where is your father?" he bellowed.

I stood still, my legs and mouth frozen with fright. Herr Fischer was notorious in The Hague. His name meant "fisherman" and we had coined him "the fisher of Jews."

Hearing the noise, my father and mother ran into the room.

"Isaac Cassutto! You have three minutes to pack a bag and come with us," Herr Fischer barked at my father, who stared at him for a moment, and then started looking around for his belongings.

Unable to control herself, my mother shouted, "You're inhuman! How do you expect someone to pack his bags in three minutes!"

My father barely had a chance to grab his coat before Herr Fischer seized him by the arm and pushed him toward the door.

"Where are you taking him?" my mother demanded to know. The Gestapo refused to answer. They brushed past her as though she did not exist, and shoved my father out the door into a waiting police car.

1

In three minutes, my father was gone. My mother and I were left alone in the living room.

"Mother, they can't just take him like that, can they?" I asked, bewildered.

"Yes, Ernie. I guess they can," she replied, tears forming in her eyes.

For what must have been the thousandth time, I wished we had never moved to Holland.

CHAPTER TWO

1925

Bandung, Indonesia

Siesta time! Like most of the people who lived on our estate in Bandung, Indonesia, my favorite part of the day was the two-hour reprieve from work during the hottest portion of the afternoon. But while most used this time to rest and reflect, I saw it as an opportunity for adventure. I was six years old, and the island of Java was my playground.

This afternoon I managed to sneak away from home one more time. I raced to the train station. For six cents, I bought a round trip ticket to the suburbs of Bandung. I hopped on the open train car, which I shared with a throng of Indonesians as well as sheep, ducks and chickens. As the train picked up speed, I gazed at the countryside. The Dutch East Indies have to be the most beautiful place in the world, I concluded, even though I had left Indonesia only once before, when I was too young to remember.

In Indonesia, the sunshine glances off the ocean and follows the rivers as they wind their way through the mountains on their way to the sea. There are flowers everywhere, explosions of color painted on a canvas of green grass and blue sky. Lush tropical rain forests abound, and the air is always moist, warm and filled with the scent of spices.

An Indonesian native came down the aisle in the train car, a portable restaurant on his shoulders. My mouth watered at the savory aroma of the spicy foods he was selling.

Mother had told me repeatedly to stay away from these vendors and their food. Though my parents had been in the

3

islands for nearly ten years, my mother still remained distrustful of the food preparation techniques of the locals. "I'm sure they don't boil their water," she told me over and over. "Mark my words, you'll get sick if you eat that food."

Her warnings reverberated in my mind, but I couldn't resist. I gave into temptation and bought a dish of beef soaked in curry. It was hot and delightfully spicy, and I felt very grown-up and daring.

That night however, pleasure turned to remorse as I began to experience the first pangs of dysentery. I guess Mother was right, I thought as I writhed in agony for the next several days.

I did not tell my parents how I ended up with dysentery, but I avoided the train (and the food they served) for quite awhile after this episode. My taste for Indonesian cuisine did not diminish, however.

One afternoon, during siesta time, I got an idea. I headed to the seven rooms off our veranda. These were the servants' quarters. I pestered Kokkie, our native Indonesian cook, to make me some sort of native food. "Are you sure your stomach can take it, Ernie?" she asked, smiling. Recounting my earlier experience, I assured her, "That was a long time ago," and settled in my chair. Kokkie talked while she cooked, regaling me with beautiful stories of Indonesian folklore, like the tale of Sangkuriang who fell in love with his own mother, Dayang Sumbi. When his mother realized that she could not marry her son, she told him she would only marry him if he built a lake (and a boat to sail on it) by dawn. She thought that he would never be able to accomplish this task, but when it looked as though he might after all, she caused the dawn to come early. According to local folklore, her son was so angry that he tipped his boat over, and that formed the Tangkuban Parahu volcano.

"Would you and Max like to help me make the coffee?" Kokkie asked when she finished her story. I ran to get Max, my older brother. Even though he was only four and a half years older, Max seemed the epitome of sophistication. He had a knack for making people like him and a talent for mischief that impressed me far more than it impressed my father.

I found him in his room. "Max, Kokkie wants us to help her make coffee," I said eagerly, knowing that he liked helping her pour beans into the hand mill as much as I did. But he just shrugged.

"Max, what's wrong?"

"I think Father's still mad at me," he replied sulkily.

"About the cat?" I asked. Max nodded. A few days earlier, Father decided to pay a visit to our school. Not knowing Father was coming, Max had hidden a cat in his desk. Halfway through the lesson, the cat jumped out of the desk. This sent the class into an uproar. Our teacher screamed, the other children could not stop laughing, but our father was not amused. When he brought us home, he said nothing to us, but went straight to the window. When Father was really angry, it was his custom to stare out the window with his hands folded behind his back. When he was really, really mad, he began to whistle. He didn't say anything, just stood there and whistled. We knew to leave him alone during these times.

"Come on," I said to Max. "I'm sure he's gotten over it by now." So we went and helped Kokkie prepare the coffee. The beans were fresh, and as Kokkie brewed them, their rich aroma permeated the whole house.

"Here," Kokkie said to Max as she handed him a cup of the brew. "Why don't you go give your father a cup?" She smiled slightly.

Warily, Max went out on the veranda where my father was sitting, and offered him the cup. My father peered up from his book.

"Nothing is going to jump out of here, is it Max?" he inquired as he took the coffee. Then he laughed, and we knew that he was no longer angry.

My mother heard our laughter and joined us on the veranda. Her arms were full of bags of fresh roasted peanuts just purchased from one of the many Chinese merchants who traveled the roads of Bandung. For ten cents my mother purchased several pounds of peanuts. All four of us launched into the task of peeling them. It was like a ceremony commemorating the setting of the sun.

"Isaac," my mother said, in a light, cheerful tone that Max and I recognized. I leaned over and whispered to Max, "She wants something." He nodded in agreement.

"Yes, Caroline?" my father replied, oblivious to my comment.

"Let's go to the theatre this week." Max and I exchanged glances, knowing with absolute certainty the conversation that was to follow.

"Well, I don't know," Father replied noncommittally, turning another page of his book.

"Oh, come on, Isaac," Mother continued to prod, giving him reason upon reason why they should go. Finally, my father relented with a defeated grin.

"Boys, your father wants to go to the theatre this week," my mother announced, as if we had not been there the whole time to hear their conversation. From the way she said it though, had we not observed the scene, she would have convinced us all, including my father, that the theatre had been his idea. Mother was an expert at talking my father into doing something without him realizing she had done so.

My mother was a complement to my father. While he was shy and a bit reserved, she was a complete social butterfly. Whereas he had the tendency to be more withdrawn, she was warm. They were indeed a good match. Had their marriage not been as solid as it was, their transition to the Dutch East Indies from Holland would no doubt have been much more troublesome.

They had moved to the islands in 1915. While the Great War was raging around the neutral Netherlands, my mother's eyes had fallen upon an ad in the newspaper, calling for Dutch jurists to move to the Dutch East Indies and share their legal expertise.

My father was a lawyer and a law professor in The Hague. He worked hard and had many clients, but times were tough financially, and the work he did often went without compensation. Faced with pending financial crisis, Isaac and Caroline Cassutto decided to make the journey across the ocean and settle on the coast of Java. Father found work preparing Indonesian aristocrats for government service. One year later Max was born, and in 1919, I arrived.

Both of my parents were Jewish. However, when Max and I were born, the closest rabbi was in Singapore, a ten-day journey away. So neither Max nor I were circumcised.

My parents considered themselves open-minded Jews. My mother was raised Orthodox; her father was president of the Jewish community in The Hague. She, however, was not religious. My father was also from a Jewish family, but did not practice. As a young boy, my being Jewish was like the grass being green or the sky being blue; it was just a fact among many other facts that dared not claim any importance. The fact that I was a Jew made no more impression upon me than the fact that I had two hands, two legs and a nose. The idea that it would ever mean anything to anyone else never occurred to me. How inconceivable it would have seemed to me then that one day, men would look upon me and not see a man with two hands, two legs and a nose, but only that I was a Jew.

In 1929, my father was on sabbatical from teaching, and we went to Holland for a year. I met my Jewish relatives there for the first time. I realized then that being Jewish in Holland was completely different from being Jewish in Indonesia. Some of the Jewish people there looked and dressed in a way to which I was not accustomed, with long dark coats and beards. There was a sense of community among the Jewish population in Holland, and I sensed that being Jewish meant being different and distinct. This realization, though, was just one of a series of circumstances in what was a gray year for me. The flat, low land that stretched across Holland provided dramatic contrast to the picture of the high mountainous regions of Indonesia, which lay in sharp focus in my mind's eye. Much of Holland is below sea level. Man-made dikes like stalwart sentries stood militantly along the seacoast ever ready to hold back the threatening sea should it attempt to claim the land that was once its own. True, in certain seasons, fields of tulips provided a colorful backdrop for the many windmills that sat attentively upon the land, their long arms reaching out to embrace the wind. But during the long winter months, Holland lay cold and dank beneath an oppressive gray sky.

I was homesick for the constant tropical warmth of Indonesia. I felt totally out of place and strange, not at all in harmony with Holland. Even the birth of my baby brother George was not enough to excite me. I could not wait to go home.

CHAPTER THREE

1931

Upon our return, we were greeted by Kokkie, Ahmed our butler, and my father's students. I was so happy to be back at our estate instead of the apartment we rented in Holland.

Soon after we arrived, my father surprised us with a new radio! We all loved music; my mother was enchanted with American blues and swing tunes. After a bit of coaxing, she could always get my father to dance. Strains of the Charleston would fill the living room. Father had a pair of dancing shoes with black bow ties on them.

These were carefree and undemanding years; that special time in life allotted to the young, when we believe that each new day is especially for us. I had only one irritation during this time; my pesky kid brother, George. I suppose it was my turn to experience the nuisance that I must have been to Max. One day I caught George trying to climb on top of Mieke, my pet sheep. I could see that he wanted to ride her like a horse. I was appalled, and protested angrily to Ahmed. "No, no, Sinjo Ernie, that's all right! Mieke won't mind," he tried to explain. Well, I minded. Yet George prevailed.

My mother understood my need to retain a "special place" in our growing family, which is why she took me with her on special trips into the mountains. On one such foray, when I was twelve, Mrs. Nash, a friend of my mother's accompanied us. Mrs. Nash was a Dutch Jewish woman who had become a believer in Jesus. The three of us stopped for cake and tea at a sidewalk café. Suddenly, Mrs. Nash said to my mother, "Ernie is going to be a minister of the Gospel."

What a strange thing to say about any kid, let alone a twelve-year old Jewish boy. Even stranger is the fact that neither my mother nor I were shocked at her words.

CHAPTER FOUR

MOVING

"Not bad," I said to myself as I surveyed my reflection in the mirror. At fourteen, I had acquired my first set of long pants, a rite of passage usually reserved for when one reached the age of eighteen. Feeling quite manly, I went to show my mother.

I strutted into the living room. "Mother!" I called. Then I saw her standing face to face with my father, her hands on her hips. As I walked into the room, she was saying, "Well, Isaac, what are we going to do?" My father opened his mouth to respond. Then he saw me standing behind my mother.

"What's wrong?" I asked. My father looked at my mother, and my mother returned his glance. I could see they were silently debating whether or not to bring me into their conversation. My mother raised her hand toward my father, as if to say, "Go ahead, tell him." Father cleared his throat.

"Well, Ernie, you may as well know they've closed the school," he said. He took off his glasses and rubbed his eyes, then stroked his chin thoughtfully.

"You mean . . ."

"Yes, Ernie. It looks like I'm out of a job." He sighed, and then continued, "Actually, it's more like I have a big decision to make. I could go back to Holland and teach at the University of Utrecht. Or I could take a position at the school over in Mgelang."

My heart jumped. "You mean we may not have to leave Indonesia?" I asked hopefully.

"We'll see, Ernie," he replied quietly, and left the room.

We all awaited his decision with intense anticipation. I could see that my father was really wrestling with the costs and benefits of both options. "How difficult it must be to make such choices for your family," I thought, not envying him in the least. I tried to remain optimistic, hoping that he wouldn't tell us that we had to say good-bye to our friends, our servants and our home.

He chose Holland.

Until our move to Holland, I did not realize how luxurious our lifestyle was in Indonesia. We were not as prosperous in our new country. Father's salary was cut substantially, so he had to give up his car. We moved into a small apartment in Utrecht, which was like a closet in comparison to our sprawling estate in Java. I was shocked to see Dutch garbage collectors. In Indonesia, Dutchmen were usually the professionals: doctors, dentists, and businessmen.

Father was grooming me to be a lawyer just like him, so I was enrolled in the nearby Latin School. Homesick for my friends, my house and my pets, I decided to do something to ease my loneliness. Max had taught me to play the ukulele a few years earlier, so I acquired a guitar, and began to spend hours practicing my new instrument and writing my own songs. Later, I became the leader of a band, "The Jolly Rhythmicians." I also took up the saxophone, though the only one I could afford was a secondhand one that didn't even have the lowest B flat. Still, it was sufficient for a beginner like me.

I was practicing in my room one afternoon, when my mother walked in and announced, "We are going to see the Winkels tonight. Would you like to come with us?"

"Who are the Winkels?"

"Oh, you remember the Winkels, Ernie. They live in Haarlem. You met them when we were in Holland before."

"If you say so," I replied with a shrug.

I did not really want to go see the Winkels, whoever they were. I would rather have stayed home and played the guitar. But I knew it would make Mother happy if I went, and it was an opportunity to get out of Utrecht.

The Winkels greeted us warmly. I was busy taking off my coat when Mrs.Winkel addressed me, "Ernie, you remember our daughter, Hetty."

I looked up. She seemed to have appeared out of nowhere, this radiant young girl wearing a blue dress with sleeves that gathered into pert little puffs at the shoulders. She smiled at me. I was smitten.

Throughout our visit, I could not tear my eyes away from this beautiful vision called Hetty. Indeed, I had met her before, during our year in Holland, but she was only six years old at the time. Now eleven, she stirred up unfamiliar emotions inside me. The visit was over all too soon.

I began inventing any excuse I could to visit the Winkel residence. Hetty was still too young to date, but I made up my mind to wait patiently. I soon discovered that Hetty had more than just a pretty face; she also possessed a warm disposition and a beautiful singing voice. She was the bright star in my otherwise dim transition to the Netherlands. Over the next few years, I occasionally dated other girls, but my heart belonged to Hetty.

My father resigned from the University of Utrecht in 1937, and we moved west to The Hague, taking up residence in a three-story house close to the center of the city.

Many Dutch East Indies government officials relocated to The Hague after their retirement. Upon our arrival my nose caught a whiff of a familiar smell. My stomach growled at the aroma. An Indonesian restaurant! The city was dotted with Chinese and Indonesian eateries. I was home again. We were also near Scheveningen, a seaside resort town merely a fifteen minute train ride from the beauty of the North Sea. There were ice cream stands and Dutch herring stands; it was a perfect place to spend an afternoon. I had a feeling that I would have a much better relationship with The Hague than I did with Utrecht.

Our home in The Hague was a large house with three floors, located in a residential section near the streetcar connection with the main center of the city. It was quite a big house for

Mother to care for, so my father hired a housekeeper for her. Father retired from the university with a full pension. To supplement his income, he taught part-time, and started writing a book on Roman law. At the request of the Dutch government, he also sat on a committee designed to ensure fair treatment of students sitting for exams.

Mother had a new house, Father had new work, and I had a new saxophone. Seeing I had outgrown my old one, Father decided to make a proposition: If I would quit smoking for a year, he would buy me a new instrument. "Deal," I said, and as I ran my hand up and down the keys of the new sax and listened to the sweet and low note of the B flat, I knew it was worth it.

I inherited my father's shorter build, so I never was much of an athlete, but between my new band, "The Music First Boys," the occasional American film and the love of my life, Hetty (we officially started dating in 1939), I became the big man on campus. Suddenly life was so busy, too busy for schoolwork. I convinced Hetty to sing with the band, so we could spend more time together, but I could not figure out a way to combine the books with the band. This meant I often ended up leaving my studies for after band rehearsal. Many times, I fell asleep with my head on the books, as conjugated verbs danced in my head to the swinging sound of a Dixieland jazz tune. Max and George took turns waking me up. George and I had ended our careers as pesky kid brothers. The three of us boys were now close friends. George was impressed with my college band, and even Max seemed to approve.

Max was engaged to a woman we affectionately referred to as "Puck." We had known Puck as kids in Indonesia; she was the daughter of a retired Dutch Lieutenant Colonel who also moved his family back to Holland. I took my lead from him, and mustered up the nerve to propose to Hetty. She accepted. The days were filled with promise.

Yet all around us the world was in turmoil. Lines on maps were being re-drawn. A man named Adolf Hitler had risen to power in Germany. Germany annexed Austria and Czechoslovakia, and was now after Poland. Italy helped herself to Albania and Ethiopia. Japan was warring with the Chinese. We assumed that Holland's borders would be respected. After all, we were neutral in the Great War.

Gradually, however, we felt less and less secure. The shadow of the swastika grew larger and loomed closer. When Germany invaded Poland on September 1, 1939, and France and Great Britain subsequently declared war on Germany, our illusions of peace were shattered like cheap china.

I was called out of school for basic training in the Royal Dutch Army. My duty took me to Delft, just south of The Hague. The good part of this was that I was now closer to Hetty, who was living in Scheveningen. She could ride her bike to Delft each weekend and visit me at the barracks.

My musical ability proved quite useful in basic training; I became the bugle-blower. But I did not stay in Delft for long. It was decided that I would return to school to finish my last year. Upon graduation, I would be sent to officers' training school.

When I returned to The Hague, I was inspired to compose a song for Hetty. It was about a soldier, who leaves his love and goes off to fight in a war. I called it "So Long, Cherie." She loved it, and so did my family and friends, so I decided to get it published. Some of the local radio stations picked it up, and to my astonishment, it started climbing the charts. But a future as a popular composer was not to be!

Winter ran her course, spilling her palette of assorted grays upon both land and sky. Max and Puck were married two days before Christmas. Then they returned to Indonesia so Max could serve as a colonial army officer. Celebrations of the new year were dampened by the threat of war. As we hung new calendars on the walls, we wondered just what the blank days ahead held for us in a world that seemed up for grabs.

Spring arrived and my schedule was as busy as ever. No matter how I shuffled my activities, I still struggled to find time to study. Often, I bluffed my way to a passing mark on an exam. On exam days, the college tradition was to get up early in the morning, go to a herring stand, and down as many fish as possible before the exam, since herring was supposed to be brain food. Sometimes it worked; sometimes it didn't.

One night in May, I came home from grabbing a beer with some friends, and was just about to crawl into bed when I was struck with the feeling that I was forgetting something. I shrugged and turned out the light, figuring that whatever it was, it could wait until morning.

I sat up straight in bed. Morning! I had a French exam the next morning. And I was completely unprepared. I switched on the light, grabbed my textbook and started fumbling through the pages. I could not afford to fail this test. I crammed for several hours, but eventually, exhaustion overcame me, and I had to put my head down on the desk, just for a minute . . .

Thunderous noise awoke me. The windows rattled. I jumped up and ran to the front window. The sky was lit with the flashes of bombs. Holland was under attack!

I was called back to Delft, but sent home three days later. I was not trained enough to serve at the front. It was only a matter of time before Holland succumbed to her neighbor's violent advances.

German forces overran Holland in five days. The Nazis goose-stepped into Holland as if she had been theirs all along. Yet the spring sun was still warm and radiant, suspended in a clear blue sky. The tulip fields were in full bloom, and summer birds were returning home from winter havens. Nature itself seemed to be defying Hitler. If only they had known what was about to befall Holland, perhaps the flowers would have burrowed deep into the ground. Perhaps the birds would have turned back.

CHAPTER FIVE

FATHER!

At first, Nazi occupation did not seem so bad. In fact, after living under the threat of war for so many months, we were all sort of relieved. True, the Nazis were now in charge of the government, but there were very few noticeable changes at first. The most visible modification of daily life was the sudden appearance of swastikas and soldiers everywhere. Queen Wilhemina and Prince Bernard fled to England during the invasion, and Hitler appointed an Austrian Nazi fanatic, Arthur Seyss-Inquart, to be the overseer of the Dutch civil government.

In late May, Seyss-Inquart made a speech on the radio. He assured the people of Holland that life would continue as usual, that the new government had no intention of harming them. Dutch soldiers who had been captured by the Nazis were allowed to return to their homes, a gesture of good faith. He even apologized for the shambles in which the city of Rotterdam was left. The city that had played such an important role in world commerce and trade was destroyed in forty minutes. Seyss-Inquart explained that the Dutch surrender occurred after the Germans were given orders to attack the city that was home to one of the oldest and busiest seaports in the world. My family listened to the broadcast, and were thankful that I had been sent back home from the army.

After the initial relief, however, came a sense of demoralization. The unthinkable had happened. Our neutrality had counted for nothing. Despite Seyss-Inquart's promises, we remained distrustful.

In the fall, classes resumed, and I endeavored to concentrate on my studies. I had, however, lost my taste for the German language, and dreaded going to German class. Apparently, our instructor shared my sentiments. After we filed into the classroom and sat down, he turned from the chalkboard and addressed us with the words:

"Now for our Swiss class!" That pretty much said it all.

In January, all Dutch people were asked to fill out census forms. One of the questions required us to tell how many Jewish grandparents we had. We felt a pang of apprehension, but tried to ignore any sense of foreboding. When the Nazis annexed Austria and Czechoslovakia, we heard rumors that Jews were being harassed. Stories of Jews being forced to clean sidewalks with toothbrushes found their way to us. But the Nazis had been on their best behavior since the occupation. There had been no looting, no beatings of Jews in the streets, no burning of synagogues. So when the census took place, we had no concrete reason to be dishonest about our heritage. Besides, my father was a law professor, so how could we refuse to comply? We filled out the forms accurately.

It felt strange to check the boxes that indicated I was Jewish. I had scarcely considered my Judaism. I had only met one of my grandparents, my mother's father. The rest had died years ago. I was hardly involved with the Jewish community in Holland. I did not feel Jewish, or even know what being Jewish was supposed to feel like. The idea seemed foreign.

In April, the Gestapo raided our home and arrested my father. Arrests such as these were becoming more common. Herr Fischer, the Gestapo Chief, refused to tell us why my father was being taken away. But we read about him the next day in the Nazi-controlled newspapers. My father's crime? He was a Jewish professor, serving on a committee that supervised student exam procedures. Months earlier, the Nazis had dismissed all Jews in civil servant positions, but they had somehow overlooked my father. It was the Nazis' mistake, but my father had been arrested.

We were horrified to read that he had been deported to a concentration camp in Poland, but after three weeks and endless phone calls, my mother finally learned that he had really been taken to the "Orange Hotel," the jail for political prisoners in The Hague.

Mother went to work immediately. She donned her best black evening dress and hat, wrapped her mink stole around her shoulders, and set out to get her husband released. The click of her heels echoed her firm determination as she marched into Herr Fischer's office.

Herr Fischer eyed her appreciatively, but grew angry when she scolded him: "How dare you imprison a man of such high standing!"

"You have a lot of nerve, barging into my office like this, Frau Cassutto! Give me one good reason why I shouldn't throw you in jail with your husband?" he demanded.

At this, my mother was rattled, but she managed to say evenly, "Because you and I both know, Herr Fischer, that it's your fault you overlooked the fact that Isaac was appointed to that committee. Do your supervisors know this as well?"

"We meant only to use him as an example, Frau Cassutto," he said quickly, adding, "Your husband is a prominent man in The Hague. Arresting him shows we take our authority seriously. We will release him now." But even as he said these words, his eyes betrayed a silent threat, my mother said later.

She went downstairs from Herr Fischer's office to wait for her husband, and my father came home with her. But we were now afraid. We knew that trusting the Nazis' word that life would remain normal was a foolish mistake.

CHAPTER SIX

SUMMER 1941

Amsterdam

Elly Rodrigues couldn't wait for school to start again. At least then she would have something to do. Summer used to be fun, she thought. But this summer a law had been passed in Amsterdam that said that Jews could no longer enter hotels or restaurants or any other businesses owned by non-Jews. A few weeks earlier, she and her older brother Henri had begged their mother to take them to the beach.

"I'm sorry," Leah said to her children. "We can't go to the beach." She did not want to tell them why, but they persisted.

"Well, can we just go to the pool then?" Elly suggested.

"Or a movie?" Henri added, trying to be helpful.

"No!" Leah snapped. "We can't!" Seeing the look of hurt on her children's faces, she bent down and hugged them both. "I'm sorry," she told them. "It's just that ..."

"It's just that Jews aren't allowed to go to these places anymore," her husband finished for her, as he stepped into the room.

"Abe, when did you get home?" Leah stood and went to hug him.

"Just now," he replied. "You should have seen the lines."

All of the residents in Amsterdam had been ordered to turn in their radios to the Nazis. Elly's family lived in the southern part of the city. Their father had left very early in the morning to try to beat the crowds. Elly remembered the sadness in her father's eyes as he listed the places where they were no longer allowed because they were Jewish.

Now, she and Henri and her mother sat in the living room. Her mother was sewing. Henri was playing a game of solitaire. Elly was restless. She longed to go and play on the beach. She was daydreaming about sand between her toes when her father came downstairs.

"So," he said, attempting to be jovial, "How are my children on such a beautiful summer day?"

"Bored," Henri answered flatly.

"Me too! Papa, how long until school starts?" Elly asked. "I miss my friends. The only ones I ever see anymore are the ones who go to synagogue."

Abraham put his hand on his daughter's head, smoothing back her dark curls. "You may not see them for quite some time, Elly."

"Why not?" she asked, surprised at his words and the sadness in his voice.

Abraham Rodrigues paused and looked at his wife, hoping that she would answer for him.

"What's wrong?" Henri demanded. "Is it something about the business?" Elly and Henri knew that finances were tight; their father owned a textile business and had lost several clients. Their parents had explained to them that they would have less money to spend. Elly and Henri understood that they would not be able to afford as many new clothes or toys, and that they had to conserve food. Both children had taken the news well. Their parents were proud of them. Perhaps the mournful look in their father's eyes had something to do with that, Elly thought.

"Elly, Henri, we need to have a talk," Abraham said solemnly. A few years ago, he would have sat his children on his lap, but now they were too old for that. Elly was eleven and Henri was thirteen. They sat at his feet.

"I'm not sure how to tell you this," Abe began. "You two

won't be allowed back in your school."

They looked at him, startled. Surely going to school could not be against the law!

"From now on, you will go to school with all the other Jewish children," Abe finished.

"I don't understand, Papa. What did we do wrong?" Elly's lower lip quivered.

"Nothing, nothing," Leah said, and hugged her. "Things are just changing, that's all."

"Will I still have to go to synagogue for Hebrew school, or will I get ready for my Bar Mitzvah at the new school?" Henri wanted to know.

Again, that look of uneasiness passed between Abe and Leah. "Son," Abe said, "You may as well know that they're closing the synagogue."

"What!" Henri cried. "But how ..."

"I will tutor you here, Henri. Private lessons from the rabbi's son, eh? What do you think?" Abe tried to sound cheerful.

Elly looked at her brother, and could see he was trying to be brave, trying to accept all of this. Synagogue was their life! How could the Nazis just erase such a large part of their lives? It seemed cruel.

Now Elly couldn't even look forward to school.

CHAPTER SEVEN

GOD?

I could not believe what my father was saying. I had finally graduated from Latin School (due to some intense cramming), and now my father was telling me I would not be able to go on to law school after all. The Nazis had barred all Jews from the universities. It was another in a series of laws that were creeping into our lives, making the simplest things difficult.

"But we're not really Jewish!" I exclaimed in my frustration.

"Bite your tongue!" my mother said firmly. "Your grandfather is turning in his grave right now!"

"I'm sorry, Mother."

But though I was quiet, my mind was racing. I had been in synagogue maybe once or twice in my life. I looked at myself in the mirror. Was I really Jewish? Was this a Jewish face? And why did it matter so much?

In autumn, my father started to tutor me in the study of law. I tried to mask my growing disinterest in the subject. In times that were becoming more and more desperate, studying law seemed like a waste of time.

Hetty and I were taking a walk. We did not have long before the curfew the Nazis had set. I was in an irritable mood and felt it better to walk silently and let Hetty talk, but I found it difficult to concentrate on her words. As we traversed the streets, a memory flashed into my consciousness . . .

I was a small boy in Bandung, playing outside as usual. Feeling a little adventurous, I decided to walk to the center of town. Turning a corner, I saw the main church in Bandung.

Curious, I tried the heavy door, and found it open.

Inside, the empty church was silent. The sanctuary was beautiful, but distant. It felt cold to me. Though the air was warm, I shivered. I did not stay long.

What I remembered most was feeling like I was on the hunt. I fully expected to find something or someone inside those walls. When I did not, I felt hollow.

That was how I was feeling now; like I was still looking for something that eluded me . . .

Hetty interrupted my moment of reflection. "Ernie?" she said, sounding somewhat impatient.

"I'm sorry, Hetty, what did you say?"

"I was saying how I missed hearing our song on the radio since the Nazis banned the broadcast of songs by Jews." She studied my face for a moment. "Ernie, what's on your mind?"

I hesitated for a minute, and then blurted, "Hetty, people are being arrested for no good reason. Our freedom is vanishing. All because we are Jewish. But I don't even know what it means to be Jewish. And it's not like I can go to a synagogue anymore to find out. And I can't escape this feeling that if I don't find out what it means to be Jewish, then all this"— I waved my hand towards a shop on which the words "DIRTY JEW STORE" had been scrawled— "all this will be in vain." The look on Hetty's face registered shock, then compassion.

"I'm not sure what to tell you. I wasn't brought up in a religious family either," she said quietly. We walked on a little farther in silence.

I stopped at the corner and turned to her, "Hetty, do you believe in God?"

"I was about to ask you the same question," she said.

"I don't know what I believe," I said.

"Well, Ernie, you certainly have interesting timing," my mother said that night when I asked her what she could tell me about the Jewish faith. "Of all times to want to be more Jewish!"

"I'm not saying I want to become Orthodox or anything,

Mother. I just want to know what this 'chosen people' business is all about," I tried to explain.

"Like I said, what an interesting time to want to be 'chosen,'" she smiled wryly. She got up from the table and went to her room. I could hear faint sounds of drawers being opened and shut. Several minutes later, she returned with an old copy of the Tenach.

"I haven't touched this since my Hebrew school days," she said, wiping dust from the cover. "If you want to know about being Jewish, Ernie, I suppose this will give you a better explanation than I can."

So I, Ernie Cassutto, who had up to this point picked music and beer over books, began to read the Bible.

CHAPTER EIGHT

NEW SCHOOL

The first day of school. Jewish school. Elly was nervous, and yet relieved to finally have somewhere to go. When she arrived, she was pleased to see some of her friends. They had a few minutes before class began, so they spent the time in the hall, talking about what they had done over the summer. While they were busy chattering, Elly noticed a pretty girl on the other side of the hall watching them.

"Who's that girl over there?" she whispered to a friend.

"She and her family are the ones who moved here from Germany. Her sister goes here, too," Elly was told.

"Oh, right, I remember seeing her at our old school," Elly said.

Elly left her friends and approached the girl, not knowing if the latter would be able to communicate in Dutch.

"Hello," Elly said in Dutch, then motioned to herself. "I'm Elly Rodrigues."

"Hello," the girl replied in Dutch, with a thick German accent. "My name is Anne. Anne Frank."

"It's nice to meet you," Elly said. "Are you really from Germany?"

The bell rang. Time for class. They would have to continue their conversation later.

CHAPTER NINE

QUESTIONS

December in Holland! Other than tulip season, there is no more festive or joyous time of year for the country. Beginning in October, the Centrum (downtown) of all the cities and towns are adorned in bright and beautiful lights. Holiday shopping in Holland begins early, because the Christmas gift giving to Dutch children actually occurs on Sinterklaasdag (Santa Claus' Day), December 6. On the evening before, children are to leave their wooden shoes outside the house. If they have been well behaved that year, Sinterklaas puts chocolate and other candy in their shoes. The following morning, Sinterklaas enters the town and children sit on his lap while he gives out presents. In Amsterdam, there is a huge parade as Sinterklaas enters the Centrum.

In the Netherlands, for Christians, Christmas is also a religious holiday, a time to celebrate the birth of Jesus. For the Jewish population, Christmas is significant only because it provides another day off of work. Hanukkah, on the other hand, delights the Jewish children. Usually, one could easily distinguish which households in the neighborhood were Jewish, and which were not, by the holiday decor. Until now, that distinction carried no consequences.

By December 1941, we knew that efforts to stop Hitler were escalating. When America finally entered the war after Japan attacked Pearl Harbor, we were excited. Perhaps they would join in the war against the Axis powers and take some of the burden from weary Great Britain, which was reeling beneath air raids, and expecting invasion any moment. Our enthusiasm was held in check, however, by the fact that without a radio, we were never really sure what was going on in the world. The latest news we had heard was that Germany was attempting to invade Russia.

We relied on good friends in The Hague to keep us up to date. One such source of information was my close friend from school, Martin Kwint. He always seemed to know the latest news. We got together frequently.

Knowing that Martin's father was a minister in the Dutch Reformed Church, I decided to tell him that I had been reading the Bible. "But just the Jewish part," I clarified.

He seemed happy to hear that. "What does Hetty think about this?" he asked.

"She's being supportive," I said. "Though I think she thinks I'm a little crazy," I added. "The other day we were talking about the sacrifices commanded in Leviticus. I asked her if they slaughtered a lamb the last time she was in synagogue. She was horrified."

Martin smiled. Then he invited us to attend services at his father's church in Scheveningen the following Sunday. I was hesitant, but told him I would seriously consider his offer, and mention it to Hetty.

"I'm not sure how going to church will help you figure out what it means to be Jewish," Hetty said when I asked her if she would come with me to Reverend Kwint's congregation.

"To tell you the truth, I'm not either," I confessed. "But Martin is a good friend who wants to help. Plus, I'd kind of like to meet his father." I did not add that Martin had mentioned that there was a friend of his father's he would like me to meet. I avoided telling her this because I was not sure who this friend was, and I knew that she would ask questions. Hetty agreed to go with me.

Reverend Kwint's congregation was called the "Congregation of the Dunes" because of its location in the seaside resort town of Scheveningen. Hetty and I visited the church on a cold Sunday morning a few weeks before Hanukkah. When we walked into the congregation, I had no idea what to expect. Reverend Kwint began the service with prayer. "Dear Father in Heaven," he said. "We ask for your help and guidance in this time. We pray that you will keep our

Queen Wilhemina safe and give her and Prince Bernard wisdom in the protection of our nation. Let the Dutch people not ignore our Jewish brothers and sisters. We pray for them, and hope that they will be able to persevere in this time. Give us strength to be able to help our Jewish neighbors however we can, despite the persecution it may bring us . . ." He continued after that, but I was stuck on those words, "despite the persecution it may bring us." What did he mean by that?

After the service, Hetty and I were invited to join Martin and his father for coffee. Naturally, the conversation centered around the subject of war. I kept looking for an opportunity to interject with my question, but no such chance arose. Finally, I could not keep from asking, "Reverend Kwint, what did you mean when you prayed that the church would help the Jews?" That stopped the conversation dead in its tracks. Reverend Kwint set his coffee down on the table.

"Ernie," he said, gazing at me directly. "It is very likely that things will only get worse for your people."

His statement was uttered with such gravity that even though I suspected that what he said was true, it still resonated in my mind as a new revelation. "How do you know?" I asked, having nothing better to say at that moment.

"Many of us in the Dutch Reformed Church have been in touch with the underground resistance movement. We've heard rumors that the Nazis are going to start deporting Jews from Holland, as they have already begun to do in other occupied countries."

"But what can you really do about that?" I asked.

He lowered his voice to a whisper, even though we were in his home. "It may be necessary to start hiding Jews. We can certainly help that way."

I recalled my father's recent stay in the Orange Hotel. He had committed no crime and had still been taken into custody. How much more would the Nazis do to Reverend Kwint and his friends if they knew what he was up to?

"What on earth would make you put yourselves at such a

risk?" I asked in disbelief. Hetty squeezed my hand, a signal that I was raising my voice too much.

"The way I see it, we don't have much of a choice," Reverend Kwint answered. Then he asked, "How much do you know about Jesus?"

Jesus? What did Jesus have to do with any of this? "I don't know," I replied. "My father always said he was a good man, but that's it, I guess. My butler back in Indonesia was a believer in Jesus, which I thought was kind of strange since I thought he was supposed to be a Muslim," I added, hoping to lighten the mood a bit.

Reverend Kwint smiled slightly. "What are you and Hetty doing tonight?" he asked.

"Not much, why?"

"Well, I'm hosting a service here tonight. My good friend, Reverend John Rottenberg, is coming to speak."

"A service here? Why not meet at the church?" Hetty inquired.

"Reverend Rottenberg isn't allowed in the pulpit anymore," Martin said.

"Why not?"

"Because," Martin said. "He's Jewish."

"Great. A converted Jew. I'm just barely starting to understand what it means to be Jewish and already you want me to become a Christian," I said, only half-joking.

"No, Ernie. I'm inviting you because Reverend Rottenberg has been very outspoken about the Nazis' treatment of the Jews. Martin tells me you have been trying to figure out why the Jews are being persecuted. I think he can help you answer that question."

"Can he tell me what it means to be Jewish?" I asked, a bit tongue-in-cheek.

"Yes, I think he can offer you a new perspective on that, too." Reverend Kwint said.

That night, the Kwint house was packed with members of the Congregation of the Dunes, who collectively clung to the words of Reverend Rottenberg. Hetty and I were engrossed as well.

He began by saying, "Thank you Reverend Kwint for asking me here tonight. I come to speak to you as a Jew and as a believer in Jesus. I see what is going on in our country right now. There are many Dutch who are aligning themselves with the Nazis and their hatred of the Jews. Many seem to have forgotten about the Jews here in Holland. Some feel that they deserve whatever happens to them, for one reason or another. That's exactly how the Nazis want you to feel. But God has not forsaken his people. The New Testament says that there will come a time when 'all Israel will be saved.' God has a future for the Jewish people."

As I listened, I realized that Reverend Kwint was taking a huge risk by inviting Reverend Rottenberg to speak in his home. Then I realized that even having Hetty and me there could be dangerous for our friends. I looked around at the faces rapt with attention at Reverend Rottenberg's words. What could possibly make them care so much about us?

Hetty and I met Reverend Rottenberg after the service. He greeted us enthusiastically. "I hear you have been reading the Tenach for the first time, Ernie. What do you think?"

"I'm not sure," I admitted. "It seems that yes, we are the chosen people, but chosen for what? Does that have anything to do with what you were talking about tonight, when you said that 'all Israel would be saved' or something like that?" I figured I would take the opportunity to hit him with a difficult question right off, since who knew when I would see him again?

"Tell you what, Ernie," he responded. "Why don't we discuss this when we have more time? Would you and Hetty join me at my house for dinner the day after Christmas? We can talk more seriously then."

Hetty and I accepted his invitation without hesitation. "In the meantime, why don't you take this, and begin reading?" he said. He handed me a pocket-size Bible. The cover read, "The Bible: Old and New Testaments." I slipped the book in my pocket before Hetty saw it.

That night, as we journeyed home, we were quiet. It had been a mentally exhausting day. I was tossing one particular idea around in my head, though, one that I could not leave alone. It seemed so crazy, and yet . . .

"What are you thinking about?" Hetty asked.

I did not answer at first, fearing that she would tell me I was indeed insane. After a few sighs and false starts, I finally said, "I think I should start reading the New Testament."

She looked away from me.

"You think I'm out of my mind, don't you," I asked.

"I don't know what to think, Ernie," she said, still averting her eyes. "I can understand you wanting to know what it means to be more Jewish. But I don't see what reading the New Testament has to do with that."

"Hetty, did you see all those people tonight? Did you hear Reverend Kwint? They are all willing to stand up to the Nazis on our behalf. My question is why? What could make them take such a stand? I think maybe if I read the New Testament it will help me understand that."

"Fine," she said, turning to face me at last. "But don't tell your mother."

CHAPTER TEN

BARRY

"The King Who Couldn't Laugh" read the sign, and underneath the title, in large lettering were the words, "AUDITIONS TOMORROW." The drama teacher's solution to the boredom caused by racial laws, was to put on a play. Elly had never been in a play before, and she thought it had to be more fun than studying all the time. She asked her parents if she could try out and they said yes.

Her stomach was churning with nervousness when she showed up for the auditions after school. She noticed a very engaging boy on stage. He was singing in a most animated fashion. It seemed he was born for theatre. Watching him distracted her from her own uneasiness.

After he finished, it was Elly's turn. Oh no, I have to follow him, she thought. But he was so good! She was suddenly convinced that she would forget the words to the song she had prepared. However, once she started to sing, it all just came out exactly as she had hoped. When she finished, the boy who preceded her was applauding loudly. Elly blushed and sat down. The boy got up from his chair and took the seat next to her.

"Nice song," he said, grinning.

"Thank you," she said, and fought to keep from smiling back.

"My name's Barry." He extended his hand towards hers. She shook it briefly.

"That applause was a little much, wasn't it?" responded

37

...tending to be slightly miffed.

Well, come on, I certainly wasn't going to applaud for any of my male competition!" They both laughed.

"My name's Elly. Elly Rodrigues."

"Nice to meet you. Don't you have a brother named Henri who's always joking around in the hall?"

"Yes, that's him. What's your last name?" Elly inquired.

"Spaanjaard." replied Barry.

"Wait, are you the kid from America that everyone's been talking about?"

"Yes, I was born there, but I don't remember it. I was only two when we left for Holland."

Barry's parents were Dutch immigrants to the United States, who moved back to the Netherlands due to financial troubles. The fact that Barry was an American citizen gave him special status with the Nazis. All the kids in school, including Elly, suspected that, but it didn't matter to her. She liked him. They watched the rest of the auditions together. When they were over, she picked up her books and started to the door of the auditorium.

"Hey, you're not going to walk home by yourself?" Barry asked her.

"Why not?" Elly inquired.

"Because it's not safe out there anymore. Let's make a deal."

"A deal?" she asked, slightly suspicious.

"Yes. I'll walk you home from now on, and if we get in the play together, we can use the time to study our lines. Do we have a deal?"

"Deal!" Elly agreed.

The following day, the cast list for the play was posted on the school bulletin board. As soon as class was over, Barry and Elly rushed to see the results.

"Hey, I'm the king!" Barry shouted.

"And I'm the queen!" exclaimed Elly. They smiled at each other.

Maybe this school isn't so bad after all, Elly thought.

CHAPTER ELEVEN

INVITATION

Hetty and I were in a kind of holiday no-man's land. Our families had not celebrated Hanukkah since we were children, and they certainly were not going to risk it this year. However, we certainly had never celebrated Christmas either. How depressing it was not to have a holiday to anticipate. Hetty and I were very grateful when the Kwints invited us to spend Christmas Eve with them. We did not receive any such offers from our other Gentile friends; most of them acted as though we didn't exist anymore.

When I went to pick up Hetty so we could go to the Kwints, she was still putting on her make-up. "I'll be down in a minute," she called.

"Come on, Hetty. We'll be late!" I said impatiently, grabbing her nice coat and gloves from the closet.

"All right, I'm ready," she said, hurrying into the entryway. She went to the closet to get her coat and gloves. Seeing they weren't there, she turned and laughed as she saw me holding them out to her.

"Ernie, look at you. I've never seen you in such a hurry for anything."

I helped her put on her coat. "I'm just really anxious to see Martin; that's all," I told her. We stepped out into the chilly twilight.

We kept silent for a few minutes, as we adjusted to the winter wind. Hetty's breathing seemed heavy, and I noticed that I was walking at a faster pace than usual, and that she was struggling to keep up with me. I slowed down and apologized to her. "I'm sorry, sweetheart. I guess I just have a lot of questions for Martin and his father, and I'm anxious to get there so I can ask them."

"So much for a lighthearted social evening," she replied. But she grinned as she took my arm and we quickened our pace once again.

"Ernie, Hetty! Merry Christmas!" Martin said as he opened the door. "Come on in, you two. The coffee is just brewing."

Hetty and I exchanged excited glances as our noses detected the smell of real coffee! What a treat in times like these! And as if that weren't enough, as soon as we settled in our chairs, Martin offered us a plate of Boterboek; authentic Dutch butter almond cake!

"That must have cost you a fortune in ration coupons, Martin. You didn't have to go to such trouble for us," Hetty remarked with concern. Delicacies like almonds and vanilla were getting scarce in Holland. All the high-priced items that were usually shipped into the Netherlands were being directed to the Nazis serving at the Russian front. Even staples like butter, sugar and flour were rationed to support the Nazi troops.

"Don't worry," Martin replied. "Just make yourselves at home."

I thoroughly enjoyed looking around the Kwints' living room. A wood fire was burning and the Christmas tree shimmered with candles. Mrs. Kwint joined us for cake and coffee, and a few minutes later, Reverend Kwint arrived home from church. I had not been in such a cozy place in months.

The conversation gravitated toward a discussion of the Allied war effort against Germany. The subject inevitably cast a shadow over the festivities. As we speculated about the future, the mood gradually became less cheerful. Looking downcast, Hetty remarked, "What a shame to have to spend our first Christmas Eve talking about Nazis."

Mrs. Kwint reached over and patted Hetty's hand. "Yes, let's change the subject," she agreed. "We want Hetty and Ernie to remember their first Christmas fondly," she said to her husband.

"True," he agreed. "After all, without Ernie and Hetty's people, we would not even have a reason to celebrate Christmas!" He helped himself to another piece of butter cake and smiled.

"Excuse me?" Hetty looked up from her coffee with a baffled expression on her face.

"What do you mean?" I asked.

"Well, the Jewish people brought Jesus into the world," he stated.

"Oh, Ernie can tell you much more about Jesus than I can. He's been reading the New Testament, you know." I blushed at Hetty's words.

"Have you really, Ernie?" Reverend Kwint asked.

"Well, just a little," I replied. "I started reading the Tenach first, because I wanted to try to understand what it means to be Jewish. I realized that this isn't the first time we've been singled out and discriminated against, which I've got to say isn't much of a comfort in these times. I've heard people talk about us being chosen people, but from what I can tell, that status hasn't really done us much good. Is this the thanks we get for giving you Jesus?"

"Ernie, you shouldn't be so sarcastic," Hetty scolded.

"That's alright," Reverend Kwint said. "It's obvious you've given quite a bit of thought to these matters, Ernie. Let me ask you something now."

"Go ahead," I said.

"Have you ever considered the idea that Jesus could be the Jewish Messiah?"

"The Messiah? Reverend Kwint, with all due respect, if you lined up ten rabbis in this room and asked each of them who they thought the Messiah was, you would get ten different answers. At least," I said.

"I thought the Messiah was supposed to bring world peace

or something, and give Israel back to the Jews," Hetty said, looking confused.

"Right," I said. "Don't get me wrong. It's not like Jesus didn't do some great things, but how could he possibly have been the Messiah?" I waited for an explanation, but all Reverend Kwint said was, "Have you had a chance to read Isaiah 53 yet?"

"No, I haven't," I replied. "Why do you ask?"

"Well, I could try to explain the part of the picture that you're missing, but I think the Lord does it better in the fifty-third chapter of Isaiah."

"So you're giving me homework, I take it?" I said, amused.

"Yes," he replied. "But it would be unfair of me to give you homework without a new copy of the textbook. He arose from his chair and went to his bookshelf. He pulled out a Bible with a gold-embossed cover. He handed the Bible to me, and said, "I can't think of a better Christmas gift for you and Hetty."

"Thank you very much," I said. I looked at my watch. "I had no idea how late it was. Forgive us for staying so long."

"Not at all," Martin said. "It was our pleasure. Don't forget the Bible."

"Are you kidding," Hetty said, as she took my arm. "I'm sure he'll be up all night reading it."

"Well, that was an interesting evening," Hetty said as soon as we were outside. "What do you make of it?"

"I don't know," I said. "I guess I don't know enough about Jesus to know where he fits into the picture. It's like you said, Hetty. Jesus can't be the Messiah, because from what I've been reading about him, peace and deliverance never happened when he was around. In fact, according to what I've read, the reason the Jews didn't accept him was because he didn't save them from the Romans. How could he be the deliverer?"

CHAPTER TWELVE

ANSWERS

I found it strange that instead of directing me to more of the New Testament, Martin's father suggested that I read something from the Hebrew Scriptures.

As Hetty predicted, after seeing her safely home, I went into the house and immediately went to my room. I took the Bible, turned to Isaiah 53, and started reading.

Who has believed our message? And to whom has the arm of the LORD been revealed?

For He grew up before Him like a tender shoot, and like a root out of parched ground; He has no stately form or majesty that we should look upon Him, nor appearance that we should be attracted to Him.

He was despised and forsaken of men, a man of sorrows, and acquainted with grief; and like one from whom men hide their face, He was despised, and we did not esteem Him.

Surely our griefs He Himself bore, and our sorrows He carried; yet we ourselves esteemed Him stricken, smitten of God, and afflicted.

But He was pierced through for our transgressions, He was crushed for our iniquities; the chastening for our well-being fell upon Him, and by His scourging we are healed.

All of us like sheep have gone astray, each of us has turned to his own way; but the Lord has caused the iniquity of us all to fall on Him.

He was oppressed and He was afflicted, yet He did not

open His mouth; like a lamb that is led to slaughter, and like a sheep that is silent before its shearers, so He did not open His mouth.

By oppression and judgment He was taken away; and as for His generation, who considered that He was cut off out of the land of the living, for the transgression of my people to whom the stroke was due?

His grave was assigned with wicked men, yet He was with a rich man in His death, because He had done no violence, nor was there any deceit in His mouth.

But the Lord was pleased to crush Him, putting Him to grief; if He would render Himself as a guilt offering, He will see His offspring, He will prolong His days, and the good pleasure of the Lord will prosper in His hand.

As a result of the anguish of His soul, He will see it and be satisfied; by His knowledge the Righteous One, My Servant, will justify the many, as He will bear their iniquities.

I was astounded. I flipped over in the Bible to the gospel of Matthew. Then my shaking fingers turned back to Isaiah. The passage seemed to describe . . . Jesus? Could it be? I could not wait for the next day to pass. I was so glad we had arranged to meet with Reverend Rottenberg the day after Christmas. We needed to have a serious talk.

Hetty and I were seated with Reverend Rottenberg in his home. Before we could venture forth into small talk, I decided to tell him, "Reverend Rottenberg, I was at Martin's on Christmas Eve, and Reverend Kwint suggested I read Isaiah 53."

"Why did he want you to read Isaiah 53?" Reverend Rottenberg asked.

"I think it was because I had said that Jesus' life on earth didn't fulfill the Jewish requirements of the Messiah."

"And did reading Isaiah 53 change your mind?"

"Well, it was pretty compelling to compare what Isaiah

described to what happened to Jesus. And I read some other prophecies in Zechariah that seem like they could also be talking about Jesus. The question is, do these prophecies pertain to the Messiah?"

"That's a good question, Ernie. The writers of the New Testament certainly thought so. And all of them were Jewish. For centuries, rabbis thought that those passages referred to the Messiah. Now, put it together with what you've read in the New Testament. Joseph was instructed by an angel to name the child in Mary's womb 'Yeshua' because he would save his people Israel from their sins, and the name is a kind of Hebrew slang for 'Yehoshua,' or 'salvation.' The angel doesn't say how, but the Torah teaches us that the only acceptable method of atonement is through the shedding of blood. That is exactly what happened; Jesus was crucified in order to atone for our sins."

"He was pierced through for our transgressions," I said thoughtfully.

"Yes, Ernie. God chose Abraham from among the heathen because Abraham feared and obeyed him. He chose Israel over all the other nations to worship him and show them that there is only one God. But we repeatedly sinned against God. Many Jews think that the Messiah was supposed to come and establish world peace. The sacrifice Jesus made for us allows us to have true peace with God."

He paused and looked at us. "I know it's a lot to take in."

"I'm with you, Reverend. I am. Jesus blatantly says he's the Messiah and that he came to die for our sins. But what's all this stuff about him being God's son? As Jews, aren't we supposed to believe in one God?"

Reverend Rottenberg nodded. "First of all, let's remember that the same prophet who predicted the Messiah's death, also predicted his birth in Isaiah 9:6. Not only that, he calls the child to be born 'the Mighty God' and 'the Eternal Father.'

"There are other verses in the Tenach which refer to the Son of God. In Psalm 2, David is prophesying about a king whom the Lord shall set up. In verse seven, he quotes the Lord's words regarding this king:'He said to Me,"You are My Son, today I have begotten You."'

"Proverbs 30:4 says, 'Who has ascended into heaven and descended? Who has gathered the wind in His fists? Who has wrapped the waters in His garment? Who has established all the ends of the earth? What is His name or His son's name? Surely you know!'"

I may have looked calm on the outside, but inside I was reeling. My heart was pounding and my mind was racing. I knew there was a God; the continued existence of our people for thousands of years despite endless persecution was proof of that. And if God existed, and he was holy like the Torah says, then how could I possibly stand before him? What if I died during the course of the war? Was I ready to meet my God?

"But you're still Jewish, even though you believe in Jesus?" Hetty was asking.

"Yes, Hetty. A Jew who has found his Messiah," he said. "And I know that even through all this I am safe in his hands."

"Hetty, I think I'm beginning to understand how the Kwints and all our other Christian friends can be so defiant of the Nazis. If they have this same faith that Reverend Rottenberg has, then they aren't concerned about what the Nazis will do to them," I said.

"I think you're right," Hetty agreed.

So that night, Hetty and I prayed with Reverend Rottenberg. We asked God to forgive our sins. We told him we accepted Jesus' death on a cross as a sacrifice for our sins, and that we believed that Jesus was indeed our Messiah.

My inner conflict was resolved. I not only knew what it meant to be Jewish; I knew what it meant to have a relationship with the God of the universe.

This does not mean that I stopped having questions. That Sunday, Hetty and I started attending the Congregation of the Dunes. After the service, I met with Reverend Kwint.

"Reverend Kwint, I truly believe that Jesus was my atonement and that he is my redeemer, but I'm not quite sure how he's pulling it off. I mean, how can he help us now, considering that he died two thousand years ago?"

Reverend Kwint replied, "Are you sure Ernie, that Jesus died for your sins?"

"Yes," I answered.

"Then you should be just as sure that the Lord God raised Jesus from the dead."

"Yes, that's what the gospels say. But I'm still trying to put this all together. Am I to believe that just as God raised Jesus from the dead, he will do the same for me?"

"Absolutely, Ernie. Jesus was raised from the dead to show us that we have that hope, as long as we trust in him."

So no matter what lay ahead of me, I knew that I would spend eternity in heaven with God. I turned that idea over and over in my mind, basking in the peace this brought me. I had no idea then, as 1941 became 1942, just how much I would cling to that hope during the years to come.

CHAPTER THIRTEEN

THE STAR

It's just so bright, Elly thought as she looked at herself in the mirror. She put her hand over the yellow star on her jacket pocket, but she could still see the top of the star poking out above the tips of her fingers. She drew her hand away, and her eyes focused immediately on the word printed in mock-Hebrew lettering:JOOD. The star seemed to shout at her. "You don't have a name anymore! You're just a Jew!" It was just so bright ...

"C'mon, Elly, you'll be late for school," Leah called to her daughter. Elly entered the living room, and saw her mother sitting among heaps of her family's clothing. A stack of yellow stars lay next to her on the couch. Leah looked up and saw her daughter's pale face, and noticed that she had pulled her hair over her shoulder to cover up the yellow star. Leah could still see it gleaming underneath her curls.

"You'll get used to it, sweetheart," she said, trying to comfort her daughter.

"I don't want to get used to it!" Elly cried, and slammed the front door behind her.

"I can't believe they made us pay for these things," my mother said as she walked into the house. She had just been to the local Nazi food office to purchase enough yellow stars to be sewn into all our clothes. The stars were sixteen cents apiece. Mother's face looked worn and tired. George and I were in the living room, taking a sort of inventory. Along with the edict making it law for us to wear the yellow star at all times, all Jews had been ordered to turn in their valuables, things like jewelry and artwork. My mother watched us take down paintings for a couple of minutes. I imagine she was trying to get used to the idea that they were not hers anymore. Then she bit her lip and went straight to work at her sewing machine. I heard her fiercely humming a big band tune. Within a few minutes and one chorus of a Glenn Miller song, she had the first star sewn into my jacket, right over the left breast pocket. She handed it to me. I did not take it from her.

"Ernie, I know it's difficult, but you must wear this." Strange how the sight of that piece of yellow fabric made my own jacket suddenly look unfamiliar to me, like it belonged to someone else. I finally took it from her reluctantly.

The thought flashed through my mind: What if I just didn't wear it? What if I refused? The punishment for not wearing the star was six months in jail or a thousand guilder fine, or both, depending on the Gestapo's discretion. But I did not have distinctive Jewish features. If the police stopped and searched me, I could very easily pass for a non-Jew. I wasn't even circumcised! What if I just ripped this piece of cloth off right now?

Then I looked at it. This little piece of cloth would identify me as a Jew for the world to see. I thought of the sign that hung over Jesus' head while he was nailed to a cross: "King of the Jews" it read. I was sure that if Jesus stood in my shoes at that moment, he would wear the yellow star. So would I.

When I went out on the street, I felt like I was on display. The star definitely illuminated people's true feelings about us. Some, seeing the star, were quite congenial, offering me sympathetic smiles. But I noticed that other people who used to tip their hat to me no longer looked at me when I passed them. As for my fellow Jewish people, we found it difficult to look at each other.

The star made enacting restrictions against us easier than before. We were officially prohibited from visiting the homes of Gentiles. Jews could only shop in non-Jewish businesses from

3:00 to 5:00 (a time when nearly everything was sold out). Jews could no longer make use of non-Jewish barbers and hairdressers. Also, the Germans prohibited Jews from riding trains or any kind of public transportation. Exceptions were made only for people working directly for the Germans. Finally, Jews were prohibited from using public phones.

As the months passed and the stars ceased to be so bright, rumors filtered down to us that kept us from sleeping at night. A Jewish Council had been formed as a sort of liaison between the Nazi government and the Jewish community. They informed us that Jewish males between the ages of 16 and 41 would be deported from Holland. The council members told us that there was a labor shortage in Germany, and that we were going to make up for the deficit.

"Slave labor!" my mother cried when I told her what I had heard.

"Caroline, shouting won't make matters better," my father said in an effort to calm her down. "I've heard David Cohen has protested. He told the Nazis that deportation violated international law. (David Cohen was co-chairman of the Jewish council.) He told them that forcing civilians in occupied territories to serve as slaves was a violation of . . ."

"A lot of good that will do!" my mother interrupted. "The Nazis are playing the council like fiddles. Most of the members are out to save their own necks! It's like every man for himself!" She looked at my father and sighed. "I know you're used to putting faith in the law, Isaac, but you can't. Not anymore. For once I'm glad Max is so far away."

There was a moment of silence while we all considered Max and Puck. Inwardly I prayed for them; that God would watch over them and keep them safe. Safer than we were here. My mother was right; we could not afford to put our trust in the law. But I knew I could entrust my brother and sister-in-law to God.

I had not told my parents the rest of the rumors I had heard. Rumors that were too dark to be believed during the day, but at night they took on a reality that kept me awake for hours. There were tales of countless Jews herded into cattle cars and taken on journeys that lasted several days. I could not stand the thought of being trapped inside a dark, airless transport while it jerked forward to ... where? Perhaps that uncertainty was the most fearful part of the image. What we really suspected was that the words "German labor" were a veil disguising something much more sinister, but who could guess what?

My father was pacing the living room. I remembered how tall he seemed to me when I was younger. Now I was 23, and my father was no longer the giant of my childhood. "What are you thinking, Father?" George asked.

"I was just thinking that maybe we will be spared yet. It's been seven months since America entered the war. It can't be much longer before they defeat Germany."

Perhaps he's right, I thought. But I knew that when the deportations started, I would most certainly be one of the first to go. The yellow star would make it easy for me to be arrested on the street and taken away. Not only that, but the census we had filled out back in 1941 assured us that they could find us easily. The Nazis had imposed a curfew on Jews. We had to be in our homes from 8:00 PM until 6:00 in the morning. We were sitting ducks.

The Nazis turned the theatre in Amsterdam into a deportation center. Their plans to get rid of us were meticulously organized. On July 5, the first 4,000 deportation notices were sent out to Dutch Jews. They went by special delivery, and people were told that they were to report for "labor service" within the week. Enclosed was a list of clothing items each person was to bring. Failure to comply with this notice would result in arrest.

We kept informed of these events by reading *Het Joodche Weekblad* (The Jewish Weekly), the newspaper published by the Jewish Council, the only one we were allowed to read. After the initial notices were sent out, we read that many Jewish people refused to come forward for deportation. The Nazis announced that if the 4,000 Jews did not come forward by July

15, they would take 700 other Jews as hostages. I became intensely worried about Hetty. She lived much closer to the deportation center.

On July 12, a big yellow envelope arrived at my house. My father gave it to me without a word. I opened it, even though I already knew what it said. I had three days to report to the "Dutch Theatre" in Amsterdam.

Until that moment I had tried to keep thoughts of leaving Hetty from my mind. They caused so much pain I could not cope with them. But as I stared at the letter, her face was before me, as was the reality that in three days we would be separated. And who knew when I would come back? I loved her fiercely; just thinking of saying good-bye to her made me feel sick, dead even. "I cannot leave her," I thought. "Lord, I can't do it."

I must have said these words aloud. My father put his hand on my shoulder. "Call her," he said.

I went to the phone. My hand was numb as I dialed, and I could barely make my lips move.

"Can you come over right away?" I said when she answered the phone. "The letter came."

"Oh, Ernie," she said, and I heard her swallow hard. "How can I come? We aren't allowed on trains anymore. I can't even leave my house now, or I'll get arrested."

"I have to see you," I said, almost begging.

"I'm sorry, Ernie. I'm so sorry. I love you so much . . ." she broke off, sobbing.

"I know, darling. I love you, too. Please know that."

I did not want to prolong the conversation; I knew I could not keep from crying. So we hung up. I was miserable for the rest of the day. I tried to start packing; a vain attempt to stave off thoughts of leaving, but it was all too real now. I looked at our house, the street, my mother and father and George. In three days they would all vanish.

At 6:30 that night, the doorbell rang. I went to open it, wondering who could possibly be visiting us at that time.

Hetty's arms were around me almost before I could get the

door open. I buried my face in her neck. "How on earth . . ." I stuttered. I was too overjoyed for words.

"I couldn't bear not seeing you again. I tore off the star and hid it in my shoe on the train."

"Hetty! That was very dangerous! What if the Gestapo had caught you? What if. . . . Oh, I don't care." I hugged her again. "How long can you stay?"

"I'll stay here until you go," she answered.

Having Hetty stay with us was bittersweet. Each time I looked at her, I was at once overcome with happiness and a tremendous sense of impending emptiness. We had planned on spending our lives together. How were we to fit a lifetime into three days?

Three days became two, and then one. The night before I was to report for deportation, a friend of ours from the congregation paid us a visit. We invited him to stay for coffee.

"I have something important I want to say to you both," he said as Hetty was pouring the coffee, or at least what passed for coffee these days. His tone was serious and sad.

Hetty set down the coffee pot. "Yes?" she asked hesitantly.

"This 'labor service' that Ernie's been called to . . ." He stopped and lowered his head.

"What is it?" I asked.

His eyes met mine. "First of all," he began, "It's only a matter of time before Hetty is summoned for deportation as well."

"Me? Do you really suppose there is that much work in Germany for all of us to be sent there?"

Our friend raised his cup to his mouth. Then he set it down deliberately. "I've heard from underground sources that the Nazis mean to rid Holland of its Jews for good."

"But where would they send us?" Hetty asked. "They can't just make us disappear." Silence.

"If you and Ernie report for labor service—if you do as the Nazis say—I am certain that you will not live to return to Holland." His words hung in the air, ominous as storm clouds.

Hetty shivered. I too, felt cold. It was the middle of the

twentieth century. Surely, they did not mean to kill us! They would never get away with it. But as I considered his words, I knew that it was entirely possible.

"What choice do we have?" I asked when I had recovered my voice.

"Hide," he said.

Hide? Where? How? "Lord, what can he mean?" I prayed silently. Then I remembered Reverend Kwint and his words about being ready to help the Jews no matter what the cost.

After our friend left, I telephoned Martin Kwint. "Martin, it's Ernie. I received a letter a couple of days ago. I'm to report for labor service . . ." Before I could say what I wanted, he promised to come over right away and hung up the phone rather abruptly.

While we waited for him, Hetty and I prayed. "Lord, is this what you want us to do? Can we put ourselves and others at such a risk?" We were lost. We needed guidance.

When we finished praying, there was a knock at the door. I let Martin in; he was out of breath. "Sorry to rush off the phone like that," he apologized. "Our phones may be tapped. We don't want to run the risk of someone overhearing our conversation."

I nodded. My adrenaline was soaring. I told Martin what we were thinking of doing.

"Praise God!" he said, but he kept his voice to a whisper. I began to wonder how involved with the underground Martin was. "I have a friend in the Dutch Reformed Church who can get a list of people willing to hide you two right away," he said. "You will have to pack quickly. Take only one bag with you, one that you can carry on your back. Hetty, I'm afraid you won't be able to go home first. You will have to bring whatever you brought to the Cassuttos with you." Hetty nodded. So much to take in, and so quickly. We were quiet as he continued to give us instructions. He bid us a hasty good-bye, and rushed off to contact his friend. Just as he left, my father and mother came downstairs. "Who was here, Ernie?" Mother asked.

"That was Martin," I replied. I told my parents our plans. My mother was skeptical. "These people will just hide you out of the goodness of their hearts? I find that hard to believe."

"They're Christians, Mother."

"There are 'Christians' everywhere, Ernie. More of them are too busy goose-stepping and wearing swastikas to hide Jews."

"There's a difference between real Christians and Gentiles who just call themselves Christians because that's what their parents are, Mother. The people at the congregation would do anything for us, even risk their own lives, because they believe that's what the Bible tells them to do," I tried my best to explain.

My family had taken the news of my new faith in Jesus in stride. There was so much else to be concerned about, and they were never very closed-minded to anything. Though they did not agree with me, they remained supportive. They were not going to let my new beliefs keep them from loving me. For this, I was grateful. My younger brother George was quite curious about my faith. He even asked me to write down some of the messianic prophecies in the Tenach so he could look at them.

My parents were afraid for me and Hetty, but I eventually convinced them that hiding was a better option than submitting to deportation. At least in hiding we could avoid slave labor. At least in hiding, we would be together. That was all that mattered.

We discarded our yellow stars, and assumed new roles. False identity cards and ration cards were procured for us. New words entered our vocabulary. We spoke of hiding as going "under water." An address or contact that was suspected by the Gestapo was called "hot." People who took us in were called "hosts."

The first person to "host" Hetty and me was a chemistry teacher in The Hague. I struggled to convey my gratitude to him for allowing two complete strangers into his home. No amount of money in the world could repay him and his eighteen-year-old son, who worked feverishly in the Dutch underground effort.

We managed to stay at this man's home for several weeks, until one day we received word that the Gestapo was trailing the activities of the teacher's son. The address was "hot." We would have to leave immediately.

Our next "home" was in the attic of a house that belonged to a Dutch Indonesian woman. Many underground workers sealed off basements or attics as hiding places, camouflaged by curtain panels or matching wallpaper. I could scarcely believe the trouble they took to ensure that we would be safe. Such goodness seemed out of place in such a world.

We stayed in that attic for a few weeks. It was difficult being there alone with Hetty. We shared the same food, the same room and the same bed. We were each other's constant and only companions. Day after day, and night after night, the possibility of sudden separation covered us like a blanket. We were so much in love and so alone. With each day possibly being our last together, we were excruciatingly tempted to make love.

I'm not sure how we managed to keep from doing so. We spent our days praying and studying the Bible together. We desperately clung to the verse: "Blessed are the pure in heart, for they shall see God" (Matthew 5:8). God restrained us, I believe. I have never regretted it, not for one moment.

After a few weeks, our host informed us that we had to flee; the Gestapo were getting suspicious of the address. We tried to deny it, but it was obvious that hiding two people was riskier than hiding one. We had to split up. The speed with which we made the decision to part did nothing to lessen the agony. "Just one more minute," I whispered as I held her close to me and felt her head against my neck.

Martin Kwint arrived shortly before dusk. Hetty would stay with his family until they found a better place for her.

I must have kissed her good-bye. I must have told her I loved her and promised to pray for her every day, every minute. I don't really remember. I just remember feeling lost—the kind of lost where even the familiar is bewildering and frightening.

CHAPTER FOURTEEN

NOVEMBER 1942

Elly buried her head under her pillow, but she could still hear the sirens. Every night the family could hear the blaring of police car sirens as they came through the neighborhood and stopped in front of homes where Jews lived. Each night the horns seemed to get louder, as more and more Jews were arrested and driven from their homes. Elly noticed dark crescents forming under her eyes, and struggled to remember what it was like to sleep through a night.

She lay in the dark and tried to forbid her mind from thinking of the arrests and the sirens. Conjuring up an image of Barry, she smiled as she remembered a joke he told her that afternoon on their walk home from school. Weeks earlier, after the play had ended, Barry had asked her to be his "girlfriend." His manner as he asked was so awkward and shy in contrast with his usual confidence, and it touched Elly so much that she almost said yes before he was done asking! Maybe I'll marry him when I grow up, she thought.

Saturday morning. Her mother made breakfast, meager though it was. Abraham Rodrigues had almost no clients now, and food was dwindling. Elly noticed her father was quieter than usual, which made her nervous. Four or five times, it looked as if he was opening his mouth to speak, but changed his mind. Finally, as her mother began to clear the table, he uttered a few words.

"Children, Leah," he began, his voice barely louder than a whisper, "I think it's time for us to hide."

"Are you serious?" Leah stared at her husband. Elly and Henri said nothing, but Elly was certain her own face mirrored her mother's wide-eyed, ashen and confused stare.

"Very serious. I wish we had left before all this started. But leaving Amsterdam now seems impossible."

One horrible thought crept into Elly's mind. "Why doesn't someone ask the question?" she shouted inwardly. She wanted to scream, "Why doesn't someone ask it?" Unable to control herself, she finally blurted out the words, "Papa, who would hide all four of us? Will we have to separate?"

Henri turned swiftly to his father. Leah too, sat down, still holding the two coffee cups she had started to clear from the table. "Where would we hide, Abe?" she asked, her voice quaking with the effort to sound normal.

Abraham lowered his voice to a whisper.

"Do you remember the Bochoves in Woubrugge? Apparently, their brother Bert has been taking Jews into hiding for a while now. He has a huge house and pharmacy in Huizen. Jan assured me that we would all be safe there. Together."

Elly knew her father went to Woubrugge frequently since Jan Bochove was one of the few people who would still buy from him. For a minute, she was almost happy. Just hearing that they would get to stay together was like receiving a surprise party.

"I guess we should start getting ready to go right away," Leah said.

"Yes," Abraham replied. "And Elly, Henri, I need you to listen very carefully. It is going to be very difficult for you. You won't be able to go outside at all. You won't be allowed to play like you do here, because we'll be found out. We will probably be hiding in an attic, maybe with other people, and it will be very cramped. We must share bedrooms and bathrooms. Please, you must be on your best behavior. Also, you must not under any circumstances tell anyone that we are leaving." His voice was stern. Elly knew that he was trying to get her

and Henri to see how much danger they were in.

"Yes, Papa," she answered.

"Henri, do you understand?" Abraham asked.

Henri nodded. "Yes, Papa."

"What can we take with us?" Leah asked.

"As little as possible. We will wear layers of clothes, no suitcases. We must be ready to go at a moment's notice."

"What about the rest of our things?" Leah asked.

"We must leave them."

"Everything?"

"Yes, everything. The most important thing is that we get out of here. Nothing else matters, Leah."

"Children, go start picking out clothes," Leah said. "I'll come help you in a minute."

Elly almost leapt from the table. She could not stand the look of sorrow on her mother's face. Leah had spent years fixing up their house, making it comfortable. Elly was aware that her mother's heart was torn at the thought of leaving. As she and Henri left the dining room, she heard her mother choke back a sob.

"Leah . . ." Abraham began, but he had no idea how to continue.

"I knew this was coming, Abe. I knew it. I thought if I just didn't want it to come badly enough, then maybe it wouldn't. I don't know . . . What am I saying?" Her crying became muffled. She must have her head in Papa's shoulder now, Elly thought. He must be patting her hair.

"And the children . . ." Her mother implored. "How will they manage this?"

"I don't know, Leah. They will have to grow up much sooner than we planned."

Elly turned to Henri, who had also stopped in the hall to eavesdrop on their parents' words.

"I don't know about you," Henri whispered. "But I feel old already."

"What's wrong?" Barry asked, squeezing Elly's hand. It was Monday. They were on their way home from school, and Elly had been silent for most of the walk.

"Nothing," Elly replied, trying to sound cheerful.

"What is it? Tell me," Barry insisted, his face registering increased concern.

Elly didn't know what to do. She wanted to tell Barry that her family was going into hiding, but she remembered her father's sober warning. Could she trust Barry to keep their secret?

At any rate, he was looking at her expectantly. She had to say something.

"If I don't show up for school one day, I don't want you to be scared, alright?"

"What are you talking about?" he asked, looking distraught.

"I'm sorry, Barry. I didn't mean to startle you like that." Elly looked around. There was no one in sight. Still, she lowered her voice to a whisper. "I want to tell you something, but you have to swear you won't tell anyone, alright?"

"Of course," he said.

"Do you know what it means to go 'under water?'" she asked him.

Barry cupped his hand to his mouth to keep from speaking too loudly. "You're going to start hiding? When? Where?"

"I can't tell you that, Barry. I want to, but I can't."

"I know," he said. "I'm sorry. I don't want you to tell me. The less I know, the better."

"Right."

They stood silently for a moment, not knowing what to say, not wanting to move. "If I stand really still, maybe I can freeze time," Elly thought. On the other hand, it was risky to just stand out in the open air like this. Barry did not have to wear the yellow star, since he was an American citizen, but Elly was conscious of hers. Suddenly, Barry grabbed her and hugged her tightly.

"I will miss you so much. But I'm sure you know that," he whispered.

"I know," she said. "We'll have to make the most of the next few days. But no one can know that my family is leaving. Just try to act normal, alright?"

"I understand."

"Promise?"

"I promise. Not a word."

Elly lingered in that hug for a few more seconds. Then she turned and ran up the steps to her house. She did not want Barry to notice the tears that were forming behind her eyes.

As she shut the door behind her, she saw her father and mother standing in the living room, and she knew something must be wrong. "What is it?" she asked.

"Elly, you need to go put on the layers of clothing we picked out, and come downstairs as soon as you can," her mother told her.

"What? Why?" Elly asked, perplexed.

"Bert came to see me today. He heard that arrests are starting in our neighborhood. He feels we should leave right away, as soon as he can arrange it. So we may have to go as early as tonight," her father explained.

"But I thought . . ." Elly stammered.

"I know, Elly. I know," her mother said gently. "But we don't have time to discuss what we 'thought' was going to happen. Go get ready."

Elly stormed into her room. As she added layer upon layer of clothing to her body, her resentment and anger grew. "Why?" she wanted to scream. It was so unfair. All she wanted to do was live a normal life. Was this too much to ask?

Her anger gave way to numbness and she finished dressing methodically. Her tears dried and she squared her shoulders and looked in the mirror. The sight was almost comical; so many layers of clothing indoors! "At least I'll be warm. At least we'll be together."

That night, as expected, a hearse picked up the Rodrigues

family. Henri remarked that being driven in a hearse was a bit morbid, but Abraham explained that hearses and ambulances were the only vehicles that the Gestapo wouldn't inspect. It was a twenty-minute ride in the hearse to the train station in Amsterdam. The Rodrigues family had taken off their yellow stars, and each of them held a false identity card under his or her clothes.

The train ride to Huizen was nerve-wracking. They tried to appear as a normal family taking a trip. Elly was conscious of all the clothing she was wearing, and huddled inside her coat to make it look like she was cold and needed all those layers. All of them did their best not to call any attention to themselves.

They were exhausted when they arrived in Huizen. Bert met them at the train station and escorted them to their new "home."

Bert's building shared a wall with the house next door. The brick firewall dividing the two structures was actually behind the place where the two rooflines met, under what appeared from the outside to be the neighbor's roof. At the point where the two roofs met in his attic, Bert built a new wall, creating a large triangular room behind it, under the neighbor's roof. He camouflaged the new wall by impeccably matching its wood and joinery to that of the rest of the attic. The hanging door he built swung open from the bottom. To conceal the seam, he added shelves along the top edge of the door that he filled with drugstore goods. A beam placed all the way across the floor hid the bottom edge. On the inside of the new wall, Bert stapled old packing paper so that to someone knocking on it, the sound was the same as the other attic walls. Elly and Henri marveled at the intricacy of the construction.

Bert showed them the part of the attic in which they would spend all day. There was a large bed in the center of the room. "The pharmacy downstairs is open from 8:00 in the morning to 5:00 at night, so you will all have to stay on the bed and not make a sound until then. Right now the reward for turning in fugitive Jews is one loaf of bread, one pack of cigarettes, and five guilders, and there are four of you. I know several families in our neighborhood that could do very well with that, so not a sound until 5:00 PM. All it would take is someone hearing a small creak in the floorboard, and that's the end. At 5:00, I'll come up and give you the all clear sign and dinner," Bert explained. His voice was firm and authoritative. Elly got the feeling that his business-like tone was a mask to hide his concern for them. That would explain his detached air.

"Children, do you understand?" Abraham asked. Henri and Elly nodded. Bert turned and went downstairs. As if on cue, all of the members of the Rodrigues family climbed on the big bed. "We may as well try it out," Abraham said.

They sat there, all on one bed, looking at each other for about ten minutes. Finally, Henri couldn't take it anymore. He clapped his hand over his mouth, and his face was red from laughter.

"Henri!" his father hissed. "You aren't going to start behaving like that or this isn't going to work!"

"I'm sorry," he whispered, fighting his giggles. "It's just so ludicrous! We live on a bed!"

"Seriously," Elly said when Henri had finally calmed down. "What are we supposed to do all day? We can't possibly just sit here."

"You will if you want to keep from getting caught." Bert had re-appeared. He gave them each a piece of bread. "I've just heard that the Gestapo are starting to make arrests on your street. Looks like we got you out just in time," he said, and then departed.

Elly felt a lump in her throat. She thought of her bed at home, her warm blankets and soft pillow. She squelched the tears that came to her eyes when she thought of Barry. Then she looked around, at the faces of each of her family members. It occurred to her how lucky she was to have them all so close to her.

How long would they be able to stay together, she wondered.

CHAPTER FIFTEEN

VISIT

A few weeks after we parted, I learned that Hetty had been taken in by a divorced woman living in The Hague who wanted some company. The underground contact assured me that this was one of the safest places for Hetty. Hetty could easily assume the identity of this woman's niece or housekeeper.

As for me, I spent the next several months migrating from place to place. Through an intricate underground network, I managed to keep in touch with my parents, always letting them know when I moved to yet another home, another hiding place.

The Nazis continued to liquidate Holland of its Jews. They were no longer arresting and deporting just the working-age men and women. The Gestapo began to raid the homes of the older Jewish population. My father and mother were increasingly worried that their home would be next. I began to pray to God that they would soon decide to hide as well. My younger brother George, was also still at home. I prayed fervently that God would keep him safe.

After my departure, my parents rented my room to a Jewish woman who had left Germany a few years before the war to seek refuge in Holland. Miss Kaufman persuaded my father to take the family into hiding. She told them that from what she had witnessed in Germany, hiding was their only hope. My father told me this one day when he had managed to meet me in the home where I was hiding.

"She's right," I said. "I'm glad you are taking her advice."

"We should have done it long ago," he confessed. "I'm just

hoping that someone will help us."

"Father, why don't you call Reverend Kwint? He's been so helpful to Hetty and me, and he knows exactly whom to contact."

"Your mother is still distrustful of these Christians."

"Are you?" I asked.

"Well, Ernie, I don't know that we have much choice really." And then he said something that took me completely by surprise.

"Actually, I've been looking into the New Testament myself. I've been considering some of the things you've said about Jesus. I haven't made up my mind yet, but I can't really see refusing help from Christians."

I was speechless for about three minutes. I couldn't decide what to say first. "Father, I wish I could be with you as you study," I said. "Personally, I don't know what I would do without Jesus right now. The Scriptures have been my only solace." I paused to take a deep breath, signaling to my father that what I was about to say was going to come as a shock, "When the war is over, assuming I make it out of here, I'm thinking of becoming a minister."

My father studied me intently, as though he were trying to memorize my features. "I can't believe how much you've changed, Ernie. Who would have thought that my son would become so interested in theology?"

"Well, Father, a lot of things have come to pass that we never thought were possible." He grimaced. "Yes, that's true."

"One thing is for sure. What is happening now has certainly strengthened my faith in God, and erased my faith in humanity without God," I said, reveling in the freedom I felt to share these thoughts with my father.

"Well, the trick will be getting your mother to study with me," he said. "But she actually said the other day that she has been pleasantly surprised at the changes in you since you . . . since you . . . ah . . ."

"Became a believer in Jesus," I finished for him. "Thank you,

Father, for coming to see me. I will be praying for you and Mother and George. I pray for you every day."

"Pray for Max and Puck and little Robert, too," he replied earnestly. "We haven't heard from them in so long; your mother and I are starting to worry." News from Indonesia was scarce, and the threat of Japanese forces capturing my brother, a colonial officer, was very real. Touched at my father's insistence that I remember them in my prayers, I assured him that I would pray for them. Then he left to begin packing a bag to take with him as he began his journey "under water."

"Lord," I prayed when he left, "Show him that you are real, and that Jesus is the Messiah. I know you can do this. Please, show him the truth."

CHAPTER SIXTEEN

LOSS

Every day, Elly counted the moments until 5:00 PM, when the "all clear" sign would come from downstairs. Elly and Henri then climbed off the bed and scurried to the upper level of the attic where a quilt was laid out on the floor for them. Not much of a playground, but it sure felt good to exercise and do gymnastics across the quilt.

Once a week, the underground brought news concerning the status of the war. Things were going poorly for the American forces in the Pacific. In Europe, Hitler was trying desperately to capture the Soviet Union. For the Dutch citizens, this relentless pursuit of the Russians made their once plentiful food supply practically non-existent. A country that once had an abundant supply of dairy products, vegetables and grains, had been stripped bare, and the land of plenty had become a land of want. Most of the Dutch agricultural products were being sent to the German front.

The Rodrigues family had become completely dependent on their benefactors for food, clothes and news about the war. It was through this contact that Elly learned that two days after they came to the pharmacy, their house had been raided. Had they stayed just a little longer, they would have been arrested.

For Elly, hiding was becoming increasingly difficult. Outside, the windmills turned, sifting the wind through each new season. As much as she wanted to hide and be safe, the desire to run and play outdoors like before remained. Her *mother tried to tutor her and Henri during those long hours spent on the bed, but the constant threat of discovery made it almost impossible to concentrate. Elly was disturbed by the constant feeling that it was just a matter of time before the Nazis found them.*

I had lived through four seasons in hiding. As the summer of 1943 approached, I began to lose count of the number of places where I had sought shelter. It is amazing how quickly one can adapt to circumstances. I hardly remembered a time when I was not on the run. I began to feel like an expert; it was almost as if I had mastered the game. If I could just keep two steps ahead of the Gestapo, perhaps I would make it.

I spent much of my time studying Hebrew and the Bible. I frequently talked to God. I prayed for safety, for the safety of my parents, my brothers and Hetty.

Hetty and I were occasionally able to pass messages to each other through the help of our friends in the underground. One day in spring, I received a package from her. It was her personal diary and her New Testament. She wanted me to see what had taken place in her mind and heart during our separation. In the back of the diary were penned these words: "Ernest, we must pray for the Germans. They need our prayers so badly!"

What a notion! Pray for the Germans? But as I continued in my personal Bible reading, I had to admit that the Jesus with whom I fell in love came to die as a sacrifice for all of our sins. And that included even the sins of the Nazis. What a work God had done in Hetty. I began to pray that God would give me a heart attitude like hers.

Usually around once a week, I would receive news about the war from an underground worker who would call on people in hiding. One early summer day, while I was hiding in the home of a Salvation Army officer in The Hague, my informant showed up earlier than usual.

"Ernie, I have some bad news. Hetty has been arrested."

I could not process what he was saying. I didn't want to. To do so would mean accepting what he was saying was the truth. "What?" I gasped. I covered my face with my hands. "I can't believe it! Where is she?" The worker had no more information. I slumped to the floor and looked up at him, horrified. "I'm all alone!" I cried.

"No you're not," he said in an even, consoling tone. "Remember, you have Jesus; you have everything." He turned silently and left me to my own hell.

For the next six weeks, I wallowed in a personal abyss. I wanted to die. I could not even talk to God. Shut up in one small room crowded with fugitive strangers, I had no place to run from the sorrow and grief that ripped through my soul. Spells of uncontrollable weeping shook my body, and I thought I would go mad. "We had so many plans for the future," I protested silently. I'd clutched these plans in the lonely night hours. Now I would never hold her again, never even look at her. God, what I would give for just another look at her! My dreams were torn from me. No marriage, no children, we would never even consummate our love for each other. I sank deeper and deeper into depression. Why try to survive, I thought. Why bother?

One night, my anger and despair caused me to hurl caution as far away from me as possible. In my rage and frustration, I grabbed my guitar, which had been smuggled to me by my parents, and climbed up on the roof. I began playing and singing with all my might, loving the feeling of the night air on my face. Horrified, the man who owned the house where I was staying yanked me back into the attic before the neighbors realized what was going on.

My host tried to console me. Over and over he urged me to pray, to turn to God. Finally, I did. I was ready to be soothed. I told God of my grief. I asked him to comfort me. I held Hetty's New Testament in my hand, and turned to a verse I had heard many times. But reading it again seemed to shine light into the black pit where I was living. "For God so loved the world, that

He gave His only begotten Son, that whoever believes in Him shall not perish, but have eternal life" (John 3:16).

The words of Reverend Kwint came back to me: "Jesus was raised from the dead to show us that we have that hope, as long as we trust in him."

My wounds still hurt, but in that moment, they began to heal. I realized that I still had hope. I would see Hetty again someday, and even if I had to wait until heaven, well then, that was still hope. I wished my family could know this hope, too!

Over the next few weeks, I prayed, and one thought kept surfacing in my mind. I remembered the words of my mother's friend back in Indonesia: "Ernie is going to be a minister of the gospel." The words reverberated in my head until I thought that others must hear them, too.

"Lord," I prayed. "I promise, if you allow me to survive, you've got yourself a minister." I was not bargaining with God, I was making him a promise. I would tell others of the hope that was within me, the hope that carried me through the darkest hours of my life.

CHAPTER SEVENTEEN

BIRTHDAY

"Happy Birthday, Elly!" Her mother gave her a hug, as she awoke. "We have a special surprise planned for tonight."

"Where's Father?" Elly whispered groggily.

"That's the surprise. He actually went 'above water.' We're completely out of food, so he is going to the countryside to sell some fabric in return for some food. He'll be back with a surprise for your birthday."

"That's a surprise? That's terrible. What if he gets caught?"

"Don't worry sweetheart. He took off his star, and he has his false identity card. He'll be alright." Elly knew her mother was not as certain of her father's safety as she pretended to be.

For the past few months, all there had been to eat was a potato for the four of them or a few slices of bread each day. Conditions in the pharmacy became more crowded. Bert hired a woman, Jopie, who used to live near the German border, to work in the pharmacy. To Elly and Henri, she seemed a little strange and unfriendly. But for some reason, she had taken a liking to Leah Rodrigues. The children were more comfortable with Diet Van Roosendaal, from Woubrugge. She worked in the store as kind of a manager. She was bright and dependable, and always willing to help the Rodrigues family. Annie also worked in the store, and the children liked her as well. Also, soon after they came to the attic, another Jewish family, the Ickershams—Peter, his wife and three children—moved into the other side of the attic. They were from The Hague, and Elly always got a kick out of hearing Peter's Haagse accent. He was bald and blue-eyed, so one could hardly tell he was Jewish. Initially, Elly, Henri and her parents were in one triangular room, but when the Ickershams moved in, Bert built two large bedrooms in the attic, with the Rodrigues family on one side, and the Ickershams on the other. It was still imperative that the children get on the bed at 8:00 am, even though it was Elly's birthday. Soon after they did so, Diet came up to the attic.

"I have a job for you and Henri today."

"Yes, Ms. Van Roosendaal?"

"Annie has brought up five bushels of fresh cherries that need to be pitted, and the stems need to be pulled off. Do you think you two can do that quietly?"

"Yes, Ms. Van Roosendaal." Grateful for the activity, Elly and Henri sat on the bed, and took the cherries from one basket, removed the stems, pitted them, and put them in another basket. The problem was that Elly was hungry. Her stomach growled. There was no food for breakfast that morning. Elly fought the urge to eat the ripe, plump fruit, but temptation soon overcame her. For every cherry that she pitted, another went in her mouth.

Suddenly Elly froze. There was a commotion downstairs in the pharmacy; men were shouting angrily.

"Heil Hitler! We are searching the neighborhood for Jews. We got a tip from an SS officer that there were two families of Jews here! Where are they hiding? Tell us now, or you will be arrested!" the Gestapo officer screamed at Annie.

"Jews? I don't know what you're talking about. There aren't any Jews, here," Annie protested.

Elly, Henri and Leah huddled on the bed behind the wall, trying with all their might not to move or breathe. Elly heard the men pace all throughout the first and second floors. Finding nothing, one of them asked impatiently, "What's on the third floor?"

"It's just the attic. We never go up there," Annie said matter-of-factly. Ignoring her, they raced up to the third floor.

All they saw was a wall with shelves stocked with drugstore items. The Nazis strolled around the room, looked in between the shelves, and stood in the middle of the room for several minutes, waiting to hear a suspicious sound. Elly was sure they could hear her heart pounding. She bit her lip and held her breath.

"Well, I'm not convinced," one of the officers said to Annie. "But let me assure you, we'll be back, and if we find what we are looking for, you and your family will be on the next train to a concentration camp. That I can promise you."

He stormed out of the attic, his accomplices behind him.

Thinking they might return, it was several minutes before Leah and the children felt the liberty to speak. Elly started to cry. Her mother held her and Henri close. All three were shaking. "They're gone now," Leah said, but she did not speak the words of comfort she wanted to say. She could not look at her children and tell them that it was fine, that everything was going to be all right. She knew that this meant that they would probably have to move from the pharmacy; they were still in severe danger. She would not lie to them.

"Get back to work with the cherries," she told them. Elly and Henri obeyed, welcoming the distraction. As Elly continued to work on the cherries, she had lost her appetite, but due to her terror, more cherries were going in her mouth than into the basket.

As the sun began to set, Elly began to get nervous. Where was her father? Why wasn't he back yet? Had the Nazis caught him? She continued to pit the cherries, but now her stomach started to feel queasy. The queasiness gave way to a dull ache, which was soon usurped by sharper pains.

"Mother, I don't feel well," she groaned.

Leah looked in the basket of pitted cherries. There seemed to be far less than the original amount. "Children, how many cherries did you eat?"

"Don't look at me," Henri exclaimed. "I'm not the one who is sick."

Meanwhile, Elly doubled over with cramps.

"Oh, Elly," her mother sighed as Elly whimpered. Then her voice became firm. "You need to sit up and try to act normal. Your father risked his life to go out and get you something for your birthday. We don't want him to find you sick from eating too many cherries that you weren't supposed to eat in the first place!"

Elly sat up just as Abraham came upstairs.

"I just heard what happened. Are you alright?" Abe rushed to his family and tried to hug them all at once.

"We're fine, Papa. Well, most of us are anyway," Henri smirked as he threw a knowing grin at Elly, who glared at him in return. This went unnoticed by Abraham, who grabbed Elly and swung her around, not knowing that her stomach was doing more somersaults than she could ever do on the quilt.

"Abe, shhhh. Keep your voice down. We need to talk," Leah said.

"I know we do, and we will," Abraham replied. "But not right now. Tonight is Elly's birthday. And to celebrate, guess what I've brought?"

"What?" Elly said, trying to sound excited, and not wince with pain.

"Beef sausage! Your favorite! I had to trade some very fine fabric for it, but it was worth it. Bert's having it cooked right now!" Abraham was extraordinarily pleased with himself.

Elly did not dare tell her father that she was sick. He had risked life and limb for her, and she was going to eat dinner, no matter how sick it made her. "I'll never eat cherries again," she vowed to herself.

After dinner, Bert cleared his throat, and began speaking in a low, serious tone. "I don't want to dampen the mood, but I need to tell you something very serious."

"What is it?" Abraham asked.

"It looks as though we are going to have to find a new hiding place for all of you," Bert said.

"We figured as much," Leah said. "After what happened today ..."

"Yes," Bert interrupted. "What happened today was no accident."

"What do you mean, Bert?" Abe asked.

"When I got home today, Annie told me about what happened. And she showed me something else. After the Gestapo left, she and Diet were talking, trying to figure out how they would have known to come search here. Who has access to the pharmacy?"

"You and Annie and Diet and ..." Leah began, and then her voice trailed off, as the conclusion became obvious.

"And Jopie," Bert finished for Leah. "We've had problems tracking our inventory lately. Diet's numbers keep coming up short. Jopie left to go out of town a few days ago. Annie remembered this afternoon that Jopie asked us to mail a package for her while she was gone. Getting suspicious, she opened the package and found quite a bit of merchandise. Jopie was stealing from us."

"My God!" Leah exclaimed.

"That's not all," Bert continued. "Diet went through her other things and found this." He reached into his pocket and pulled out a piece of paper. It looked like a letter. He placed it in front of the Rodrigues family so they could read it:

"Dear Jopie: When you go on vacation, we'll get the Jews out of the house."

Leah's face turned white as she read. "She claimed to be my friend," she stammered.

"She is engaged to a Nazi, Leah," Bert told her gently. "She is no friend. We made a huge mistake trusting her, and now we have to get you out of here right away."

"Leave?" Elly thought. "But where will we go?" she said out loud, suddenly loving the attic that had provided them shelter for almost a year.

"Diet has a sister in Garderen. She will go there with Elly and Henri. On the way, we will drop Abe and Leah off with

Diet's aunt in Utrecht," Bert said.

"You mean we have to split up?" Elly asked, even though she knew the obvious answer already.

"I'm afraid so, at least for a little while," Bert said. "Diet's sister's place is way out in the country, so it will be difficult for the Gestapo to find you there, but the place isn't big enough for all four of you. Plus, the local people will be less suspicious of two children. Diet can always say they are cousins or something."

He continued, "We must act quickly. We shouldn't even wait until tomorrow, but since it's Elly's birthday, I thought we might delay for the night."

"No," Abraham said. "If it's really that dangerous, we will leave tonight. The sooner the better."

"I hoped you would say that," Bert said, his face registering relief. "I will arrange it while you get dressed."

Elly was still feeling ill, and the sudden activity was too much for her; she thought she would faint. It was all so surreal, to finally be leaving the attic to which she had become accustomed, and to think that in a few hours her parents would probably disappear. She was weak and delirious, but hurried as fast as she could.

They were instructed to wait on a street corner near the pharmacy at 10:00 pm for a hearse to come and pick them up. The night was pitch dark, and there was no moon or stars. The air tasted delicious to Elly as the family huddled on the street corner. She wished she could bottle it and save it for later.

A hearse screeched to a halt in front of them, the back door opened and a hand reached for Elly and pulled her inside. She scooted in as far as she could to make room for the rest of her family, who climbed in after her. Then the door slammed shut, and the hearse sped away. Her eyes slowly adjusted to the gloom inside the hearse. At first, she could barely make out the faces of her family members. The underground worker driving the hearse assured them that everything would be fine. The ride to Utrecht would be about one half-hour.

"Listen, you two," Abraham Rodrigues warned his children. I want you to listen to what Diet says and do what you're told, understand?"

"Yes, Father. But how will we know what has happened to you and Mother?"

"Don't worry, honey," Abraham answered. I will try to come once a week to visit you two and see how you're doing. Don't make any trouble for Diet or her sister." He put his hand on his daughter's cheek. "At least you will be out in the country, not cramped up in an attic," he consoled her. "And you will have clothes and food, more than you had at the pharmacy."

Elly didn't care about that; she was afraid to leave her parents. She would have gladly stayed in the attic if only to have them near her.

When the hearse arrived in Utrecht, Abraham and Leah quickly hugged their children good-bye, and then the burial transport made its way to the Dutch countryside. As they pulled away, Elly wondered if she would ever see her mother and father again. This was the worst birthday ever, she thought.

CHAPTER EIGHTEEN

FRIENDS

Following the news of Hetty's capture, I spent the next few months in what had become a familiar routine of journeying from hiding place to hiding place. One day, I stopped and counted and realized that I had hidden in over forty separate locations in one and a half years.

In March of 1944, I was housed with a garbage collector in Leiden, when my host's son was called up for labor service in a munitions factory in Germany. Apparently, the Germans were desperate for hands at that point. My host decided that they would flee rather than risk sending his son to Germany, so that meant that it was time for me to go as well.

However, this time I had no place to run. I was alone, virtually out on the street with only one lead, an address of a pharmacy in Leiden passed on to me by the garbage collector. All he knew was that the pharmacist was a Christian. Beyond that, I was on my own.

As I opened the door to the pharmacy, I was filled with fear. Perhaps this man would turn me in; I had no way of knowing what was ahead. I would just have to trust God.

"I have no place to go," I whispered to the man who greeted me. "I heard you are a Christian. Tell me where can I go and be safe?" I did not have to tell the man I was Jewish; I suppose he knew already by the desperation in my voice.

"Why don't you go to the Rescue Mission?" he said gently. He gave me the address. The mission was within walking distance. I set off immediately. With each step I grew more and more anxious. What if they turned me away?

When I arrived, I rang the bell at the front door. I dared not think of the possibility of rejection. The door opened and I spoke to the man in the doorway.

"I'm Ernie Cassutto," I said. "I'm a Jew who loves Jesus." I could think of no other introduction.

"Come in, Brother," he greeted me warmly. "You have shelter here."

CHAPTER NINETEEN

GRIETJE

Elly and Henri spent a safe summer in Garderen, with Diet and her sister. Their father was able to come and visit, like he promised. On one such visit, as autumn was approaching, he gave Elly and Henri some news.

"It looks like you'll be moving again," he told them.

"Where?" Henri asked.

"Why?" Elly asked at the same time. The last time they had to move, it was because things had become dangerous. What was the trouble this time?

"Diet is needed back at the pharmacy," Abraham said, to Elly's relief. "She mentioned that it would be better if you were closer to Utrecht. So I thought of the Keitel family in Alphen A/D Rijn. They were always very generous to me. I contacted Aardje. She said that Henri could stay with her, and Elly, you will go live with her sister Grietje. She's a home economics teacher, so she is used to being around children your age, Elly."

"Where does she live?" Elly asked.

"In Hazersvoude, which is just a few miles away," Abraham answered. Again, Elly was overcome with relief.

Two weeks before the school year was to start, Abraham took Elly to Grietje's house. The door was opened by a smiling woman, dressed very primly. She looks like a country schoolteacher, Elly thought.

"Oh, welcome!" Grietje gushed. "I've got your room all set up. You must be starving, you poor thing. Here, have some rolls and cheese." She gestured to a plate full of food.

85

Abraham and Elly were speechless. They hadn't seen any kind of cheese for almost six months.

"Where did you get cheese like this?" Abraham asked.

"Oh don't worry," Grietje replied. "Between my sister and myself, we are doing alright. I also get provisions in exchange for sewing clothes for children. Don't worry Elly, you'll get enough to eat here. Mark my words."

"But still, things might get worse," Abraham replied.

"Oh, I'm not worried. God will take care of us," Grietje said resolutely, her bright eyes shining behind her glasses.

"Don't get me wrong. My wife and I are so thankful for your willingness to house Elly, but are you sure you want to take the risk?" Abraham persisted. "It can't be easy to share what little food you have and risk your life for one twelve-year-old Jewish girl."

"Mr. Rodrigues, I'm a Christian. When Jesus was on earth, he said that what we did for even the least among us, it was the same as doing it for him. And since Elly is Jewish and Jesus was a Jew, well, that just makes me want to help her even more."

Her explanation made no sense to Elly, who was busy devouring a roll from the plate on the table. She had never heard the name of Jesus in her house. Abraham did not press the issue, so Elly could tell that her father did not really care what religion her hostess practiced; he was just happy that Elly would be fed and cared for properly. Abraham thanked Grietje Bogaarts, kissed Elly good-bye and left. For the first time in her life, Elly was on her own.

After dinner, Grietje showed Elly her bedroom. "I know you're used to indoor plumbing, but in this house there isn't any. Each room has a pot that you can use during the night, and then tomorrow, we will empty it out back."

"This really is country living," Elly thought.

When it was time to say good-night, Elly was not sure how to behave. Neither her parents nor Henri were there to give her any cues. Timidly, Elly kissed her new hostess goodnight. Grietje smiled, and Elly got into bed. "Good, I didn't make a mistake," she thought.

In the middle of the night, Elly had to go to the bathroom, so she remembered about the pot, and tried to use it. It wasn't like sitting on a toilet, and much of the urine went on the floor. Elly could find nothing to use to wipe up the mess. Finally, she gave up, and climbed back into bed. But she was deathly afraid that her new hostess, upon finding the mess, would call her father, and send her away.

The next morning, Grietje Bogaarts got up very early and went into Elly's room to wake her up. "Good morning, Elly!" she said brightly. Then Grietje saw the urine on the floor. Elly thought that Grietje would yell at her, or maybe even beat her. But all Grietje said was, "Well, you should have just gone on the floor!" There was no malice in her voice, only amusement.

Grietje then prepared breakfast for herself and Elly. After breakfast, Grietje said, "Well, Elly, it's time for your lessons. You must get ready. School starts in two weeks."

Elly was confused. "Lessons? Father didn't say you would be tutoring me."

"No, I won't be tutoring you. You are going to school like all the other children. You can't stay here all day while I'm at school. People would get suspicious. No, I have a plan. We're going to give you a different last name. And instead of 'hiding' you, we'll tell everyone that you're a distant family member; let's say my sister's niece. But you'll have to go to the school where I teach."

"You mean I actually get to go to school? Great! I really like school, especially music class!" Elly exclaimed.

"It's not that simple, dear. You see, this is a Christian school. We have Bible class every day, we sing hymns and we pray and recite things that you definitely won't know. You will have to make everyone believe you are a Christian girl, or they will begin to suspect us."

"That's no problem," Elly said. "I know all about the Bible. I can even recite the Ten Commandments. Number one . . ."

"That's very good, Elly," Grietje chuckled. *"But there's a whole other part of the Bible that you don't know about. It's called the New Testament. There are certain things you will have to know about it or you'll call attention to yourself."*

"What's this other part about?" Elly asked, perplexed.

"It's about Jesus of Nazareth," Grietje answered. *"You see, we Christians believe that he is the Messiah. Did you learn about the Messiah in Hebrew school?"*

Elly had to think for a minute. *"A little bit. We learned that whoever the Messiah is, he hasn't come yet. And when he does, the Jews will return to the land of Israel."*

"Well, I know this is going to be difficult for you to understand, but you have to learn about Jesus of Nazareth and what the Gospels say about him. You'll have to celebrate all the important Christian holidays and be able to recite parts of the New Testament. You mentioned that you like music?"

"Yes, I do," Elly answered eagerly. *"I was taking piano lessons before ... before ..."* Elly faltered, but she could see that Grietje knew what she was trying to communicate.

"Well, there's an organ in the study, so you can start learning hymns. You'll have to sing them in school and church."

"You mean I have to go to a church? Do my parents know about this?" She did not want to sound ungrateful, but she was a little nervous and suspicious.

"Your father said that whatever I had to do to keep you safe, to go ahead and do it," Grietje said gently.

So, for the next few weeks, a routine was established. Grietje woke Elly up at 6:30 AM. Elly accompanied Grietje to the shed outside the back of the farmhouse and helped her with the daily chores. While they worked, Grietje Bogaarts prepared Elly for her new role. *"Your new name is Elly Van Toll,"* Grietje told her.

Each morning, they studied the New Testament together, following the life of Jesus as he healed the sick and did many other miracles. Elly read the Sermon on the Mount, the Lord's Prayer and the story of how Jesus died on a cross. She was *struck by his words, "Father, forgive them; for they do not know what they are doing" (Luke 23:34).*

After they read the gospels of Matthew, Mark, Luke and John, they read about Paul, who journeyed to Damascus, threatening the disciples of Jesus. She was fascinated by the story of how the light and thunder from heaven caused him to stop and cry out, "What shall I do, Lord?"(Acts 22:10). Elly was surprised to learn that all of Jesus' disciples were Jewish. So was Paul. This is a very Jewish book, she thought to herself.

Elly was a good student; she learned quickly. Grietje drilled her again and again on what she was reading, and decided that as long as Elly was cautious, she would do fine. She was enrolled in the sixth grade.

When she started school, Elly fit in well, blending her voice with the others in hymns of praise to Jesus, and reciting Christian prayers. "It's like a game," she told herself. "Like acting in a play." She knew she was a Jew, and that when the war was over and she was back with her family, she could forget about this Jesus business. She was not going to let it get to her.

Ernest Cassutto as a boy, 1926

Isaac Cassuto with his son, Ernest, 1929

Ernest's brothers Max (left) and George Cassuto, 1935

Elly's parents, Abraham and Lea Rodrigues, who died in Auschwitz

Ernest in his Dutch Army uniform, 1935

Engagement photo- Hetty Winkel and Ernest, 1938

Background image: the city of Rotterdam after bombing by Germany in 1940

Tante Grietje and Elly

*Elly and Ernest on their wedding
day, April 22, 1949*

*Family picture circa 1958, back row, left to right:
Albert Cassuto, Ernest Cassutto, Elisabeth Cassutto,
George Cassuto, Max Cassuto; front row: Hetty
Cassutto, Grietje Bogaarts, Carolyn Cassutto,
Caroline Cassutto, Puck Cassuto, Marilyn Cassutto,
Robert Cassuto; seated on floor: Irene Cassuto*

*Ernest Cassutto as
the pastor of
Emmanuel Hebrew
Christian
Presbyterian
Congregation,
circa 1974*

CHAPTER TWENTY

WESTERBORK

Meanwhile back in Amsterdam, Barry thought about Elly all the time. He kept his promise, and did not reveal her whereabouts when the rumors at school began to circulate about her disappearance. When his classmates asked, he shrugged that he didn't know, and sometimes even faked irritation that she had not told him.

He was beginning to wonder if his family should hide as well. So far they had evaded fourteen attempts at deportation by leaning on their American connections. But Barry had a growing sense of uneasiness as more and more Jews started disappearing, and the Nazis showed no signs of being discriminatory in whom they arrested anymore. "It's almost as if they want to rid Amsterdam of all Jews," he thought as he walked home. He still missed Elly, especially on the way home from school. He figured the loneliness would pass with time, but thoughts of Elly consumed his mind as he opened the door to his house.

His father was sitting on the couch with his head in his hands. "Father, what is it?" Barry asked, alarmed. His father, looking like a scared child, gazed up at his son. "They've taken my mother away," his father said in a flat, almost mechanical voice.

"What?" Barry could not believe it. What could the Nazis want with an old woman like his grandmother?

For the next few days, Barry walked around in a daze. When the Gestapo arrived at the door of his home, he was not surprised. "It was only a matter of time," he thought as the Nazis gave his family ten minutes to pack before marching them off to an air raid shelter. Barry hardly noticed the cold bitter air as they arrived with 500 other Jews. There they received word that they would be transported to Westerbork. Barry overheard one of the Nazi guards tell another prisoner that they should be "thankful." "Westerbork is heaven compared to some of the places your friends have gone," the guard smirked.

Westerbork was in the Northeast Netherlands. The journey there took three days. When they arrived, weary from the journey, Barry's father asked him to go to the registration area and inquire after Barry's grandmother.

The SS guard Barry asked searched the incredibly long list of names in front of him. "Sobibor," he said without even looking at Barry, "They took her away about five hours ago."

"What's Sobibor?"

The guard did not answer him. But another prisoner behind him did. "Sobibor? You don't want to know," he said. Barry relayed that message to his father, who considered the information his mother's death sentence.

Although still a prison, life at Westerbork could have been worse. The barracks had heat, and there was medical care. Barry learned that this was because Westerbork was designated as a "showcase" camp that the Nazis used for Geneva Convention inspections. Barry sometimes received packages from his Jewish classmates back in Amsterdam. He immediately took them to the barracks to share the contents with his father. With each package that arrived, he was reminded of his life in Amsterdam, and of Elly. All he could do was hope that she and her family were still safe.

CHAPTER TWENTY-ONE

MISTAKE

Bible class. It was here that Elly's nerves were tested the most. One false move and she would be discovered. Every day, the teacher selected a student to read a portion of the Bible aloud. It was Elly's turn.

"Elly Van Toll, would you please read us a portion from the prophet Isaiah?"

Elly stood up and started to read. Someone snickered and then the entire class started to laugh at her. Wondering what she had done wrong, Elly stopped reading, and she could feel her face burning. What was her mistake?

"Don't you know how to pronounce 'Isaiah?'" one of her classmates, a particularly obnoxious boy, sneered at her.

With sudden horror, Elly realized what she had done. Grietje had worked furiously to teach her about the New Testament. It did not occur to Grietje to go over the prophets with Elly since Elly had been to Hebrew school. But when Elly stood up to read, she had pronounced Isaiah's name in Hebrew!

Not knowing what else to do, Elly tried to laugh off her mistake, and finished reading the passage from the prophet. Keeping her voice from shaking was the hardest thing she ever had to do.

When she finished, she sat down, struggling to fight the urge to bolt from the classroom. She saw her teacher staring at her, and she knew that the charade was over.

Grietje trembled as she opened the door to the principal's office the next day. "You wanted to see me?" she asked, trying to sound nonchalant.

"Yes, Grietje. Close the door," the principal responded curtly. Grietje did so. "Have a seat," he commanded.

Again, Grietje complied with his order. She waited, hoping he would say something soon, before her heart collapsed from beating so rapidly. Ever since Elly told her what happened in class the day before, Grietje had been praying feverishly that the incident would go unnoticed. It did not look as if her prayers were going to be answered.

"Grietje," the principal said slowly, "The little girl staying with you isn't your niece, is she?"

Was this a test? Should she lie? "What do you mean?" she asked, stalling, hoping the right words to say would land in her mouth.

"Grietje, what do you take me for? I'm told she pronounced Isaiah in Hebrew. She's Jewish, isn't she?"

Grietje bowed her head, but made no response. The silence seemed to roar in her ears. Could this really be happening? They were discovered!

Before she could say anything, the principal spoke again, but this time he lowered his voice to a whisper. "I can help you," he said.

Grietje raised her head and stared at him. "What?" she asked with trepidation and incredulity.

"Surely it is difficult having another mouth to feed, Grietje. I know you could use some extra food."

Was he serious? Grietje stared at him in astonishment. "Yes," he answered her surprised gaze. "I know people who can help you find food and clothes for Elly. And I will let you know if I hear you are in danger of discovery. It's hard to know who to trust these days, eh?" Now he was smiling at her. She smiled back weakly, her fright giving way to exhaustion.

"One thing, Grietje," he said.

"Yes?" she asked.

*"You may want to go over the rest of the prophets with her,"
he said, still smiling. She nodded, and almost laughed. "I
believe I will," she agreed.*

*They heard voices in the hallway. He raised his voice again,
"That will be all, Miss Bogaarts. Good day."*

*"Thank you, God," Grietje said in a silent prayer as she
closed the door behind her.*

*That night, when she went home, Elly greeted her. "Look
what was on the back step!" she exclaimed, as she took Grietje
by the hand and led her to the porch.*

*There was a sack of potatoes and a sack of beans. "Who
could they be from?" Elly wondered aloud.*

*"I have to tell you what happened today," Grietje answered,
beaming.*

*Elly knew that her father came to see her at a great risk to
his own well-being. But she looked forward to his weekly
visit, whereupon he brought a precious ration card and
money for Grietje, and then spent some time with his
daughter.*

*Today, she had something particular she wanted to discuss
with him. They settled in two chairs by the window that
looked out onto the farmland in the back of Grietje's home.
Except for the occasional Allied plane that flew overhead, they
could almost ignore the existence of the ugly war as they
looked out on the serene beauty of the farm.*

*"Father, when is the Messiah supposed to come," Elly asked
abruptly. Abraham looked at her in surprise. "What makes
you ask that, Elly?"*

*"Tante Grietje has a Messiah she believes in. I just
wondered when ours was coming."*

*"And what 'messiah' does Tante Grietje believe in?"
Abraham asked warily.*

*"She says his name is Jesus. She says the Tenach talks
about him, but I don't think I've seen him there." Elly's brow*

furrowed.

"We don't believe what Tante Grietje believes about Jesus,"
Abraham said, putting his arm around his daughter.

"Why not?" Elly asked, feeling safe in her father's embrace.
She leaned her head on his shoulder, and looked up at him
with earnest, questioning eyes.

"There are several reasons why, Elly. Now listen to me. I do
want you to learn all the things that Grietje is teaching you,
so you will be safe. But always remember this: We are Jews.
When the war is over, and we are together again, you will be
able to forget about all of these Christian teachings. Alright?"

"I understand, Father," said Elly, feeling reassured that Jesus
was not for her.

CHAPTER TWENTY-TWO

ARREST

Christmas Eve. Elly could not believe that Tante Grietje was making her go to church. But Grietje reminded her that the people of Hazersvoude would be quite suspicious if Grietje showed up without her. "It's a small village. People talk, Elly." So Elly got dressed. She would not have admitted it aloud, but part of her was a little excited to attend services, just to see what they were like.

My first Christmas, Elly thought with some amusement. As she and Grietje walked to the church, Barry's face flashed through her mind. She wondered what he would think of her attending church. She wondered where he was, if he was safe, still cracking jokes somewhere in Amsterdam. She felt a twinge in her stomach as she realized that she missed him and her life back home. She drew a deep breath of the cold night air and tried to smile. She did not want Tante Grietje to see her upset. Elly knew that this was a special holiday for Tante Grietje. Grietje had been so good to her. She deserves a night to celebrate, a time to forget about the war even for a little bit, Elly thought.

When they settled in a pew in the Reformed church, Elly repeated inwardly over and over, "I do this every year. This is nothing new for me. My name is Elly Van Toll. I celebrate Christmas every year."

"The scripture reading for tonight's service comes from the Gospel of Luke, the second chapter, verses 8 through 14," announced the minister.

Then he read, "In the same region there were some shepherds staying out in the fields and keeping watch over their flock by night. And an angel of the Lord suddenly stood before them, and the glory of the Lord shone around them; and they were terribly frightened.

And the angel said to them, 'Do not be afraid; for behold, I bring you good news of a great joy which shall be for all the people; for today in the city of David there has been born for you a Savior, who is Christ the Lord.

'And this will be a sign for you: you will find a baby wrapped in cloths and lying in a manger.'

And suddenly there appeared with the angel a multitude of the heavenly host praising God and saying—"

Suddenly, the church choir stood up and started to sing, "Glory to God in the highest, and peace on earth, goodwill toward men!"

Elly watched and listened in amazement. The holiday music and the words are beautiful, she thought. Yet she reminded herself that she did not really believe what was being spoken. "When the Messiah comes, he won't be born in a stable. He'll be born in a palace," she said to herself.

After the service, while they were walking home, Grietje asked Elly what she thought of the service. Elly's inclination was to tell her that she liked it fine, but upon further consideration, she decided to ask Grietje some questions.

"Tante Grietje, if Jesus was born in Bethlehem, why do you call him Jesus of Nazareth?"

"Because he lived in Nazareth as an adult," Grietje replied. "But the fact that he was born in Bethlehem is extremely important."

"Why?" Elly asked.

"Because the prophets foretold that the Messiah would be born in Bethlehem."

"Really?" Elly asked. "I didn't know that. What else do the prophets say about the Messiah?"

"*They also say that he had to be from the lineage of King David.*"

"*Is that true?*" Elly wondered. "*Because if it is, it would be impossible for the Messiah to be born now. How would we trace that?*"

"*That's a good question, dear,*" Grietje replied.

A few days later, Elly was doing dishes when she heard Grietje let someone into the house. Not wanting to interrupt, Elly finished drying the dishes. Just as she was hanging up the towel she had used, she heard Grietje call her.

"*Elly, darling, come here please!*" Elly detected urgency in Grietje's voice, so she hurried into the living room. Grietje was alone, and Elly could see tears in her eyes. Grietje kept trying to blink them back.

"*What is it?*" Elly asked, afraid.

"*Your parents have been betrayed,*" Grietje said.

Elly stood motionless. "*What? How?*"

"*Apparently, their host got into an argument with the man who delivers their coal. During the fight, the deliveryman yelled something like, 'I know you have Jews in your house!' They dismissed it as an idle threat, but it wasn't.*" Grietje wiped her eyes, and stood up. "*Elly, I know you are devastated, but we must move quickly. We have to leave Hazersvoude right away.*"

Elly could not make sense of what Grietje was saying. All she could do was ask, "*Why?*"

"*Your father had pictures of you and Henri in his wallet. If the Nazis find those pictures, they will force your father to tell where you are hiding. We have to get out of here.*"

Elly noticed that Grietje kept saying "we." She was afraid to ask, but she went ahead anyway, "*You mean you aren't going to send me away?*"

Grietje hugged her. "*No, Elly, I couldn't do that. I'll take care of you from now on. Whatever is mine, is yours. If I have one slice of bread, then you'll have half. But we have to start packing right away."*

"Where will we go?" Elly asked.

"We are going to a small village up north in Dronthe. And your brother is going north also, to Freisland."

Elly went to her room. Somehow she found the strength to pack a suitcase. It seemed like only minutes before they boarded a train to the northern part of the Netherlands.

The train was crowded. Elly observed the other passengers. "I wonder if anyone else is running away like me," she inquired silently. "I wonder if any of these people know how I feel right now."

Elly was trying not to cry, but she was too frightened to really exercise much control over her actions. She huddled close to Grietje, who looked down at her with pity in her eyes. "Maybe we'll be able to come back here after things calm down," she said, but Elly could tell that her hopes were hollow.

The scenery outside began to look familiar. Elly knew the train would soon be stopping at the station in Utrecht, where her parents had been hiding. Elly still thought of them as if they were in Utrecht instead of—no, she would not think of it.

Then the train doors opened and five Gestapo agents stormed into the car.

"Everyone take out your identity cards and have them ready for inspection, NOW!" one of them shouted.

Elly was terrified. She huddled even closer to Tante Grietje, who pushed her gently away.

"Sit up straight and act naturally!" Grietje whispered.

She did as Grietje said and watched as the Nazis began scrutinizing everyone's identity card. I feel like a hunted animal, she thought. She knew they would arrest her. She thought of her parents in a concentration camp. Why did they have to be separated? Why was she traveling across the country with a woman who was not related to her at all? It was so unfair! What had they done?

Before Elly and Grietje boarded the train, Grietje had prayed to Jesus for their protection. Elly had stood silently as she prayed. Now she wondered if this Jesus she had pretended to worship could really protect them. Grietje said Jesus was the Son of God. If that was true, could he not help her? In that train car, for the first time ever, she prayed earnestly to Jesus.

"Jesus, if you really do exist, if what Tante Grietje has been telling me for the past six months is true, if you truly are the Messiah, and the Son of God, then please help me!"

Amid the noise in the train car, she heard a gentle voice say to her, "Do not fear. I'll be more to you than a mother and a father."

"Alright, woman, let's see your identity card!" the Gestapo man bellowed at Grietje. He looked at Grietje's card, and saw Elly sitting next to her.

"And who is this girl sitting next to you?"

"She's my niece," Grietje replied.

"Let's see her card," he insisted impatiently.

Elly took out her identity card and gave it to him. He looked at it and then looked at her for a few seconds. He gave the card back to Elly and continued on to the next passenger. Not another word came out of his mouth. The Nazis stayed in the car until the next stop and then they moved on. She was safe! Jesus had heard her prayer!

Peace washed over Elly. Something had happened! She had cried out to Jesus, and he had answered her. He was real! The train was still pushing onward, and there would be more running and hiding, but it was different now. Elly knew God would take care of her. He told her so.

Elly did not tell Grietje what had happened right away. She decided to wait for an appropriate time, and she wanted to be sure that she really believed in Jesus.

After arriving in Dronthe, Elly and Grietje spent the next six weeks hiding in an attic. Grietje brought a Bible with them so they could continue Elly's studies in the hopes of finding a school she could attend in Dronthe.

The day of her first lesson in the attic, Elly decided that it would be a good time to tell Grietje that she believed in Jesus.

As Grietje opened the Bible, Elly took a deep breath, as if she were about to make a startling confession. "Tante Grietje, I have something to tell you."

"Yes, dear?"

"I'm not Jewish anymore."

"Elly, what do you mean," Grietje said, shocked.

"When we were on the train ride up here, I was so scared. I was sure that the Nazis were going to arrest me. So I prayed to Jesus to keep me safe. And he did. So now I believe in him."

"That's wonderful! I was praying the same thing while we were on the train. But what do you mean, you aren't Jewish anymore?"

"Well, I can't be Jewish and believe in Jesus, can I?" Elly asked, perplexed. "Besides, I thought you wanted me to not be Jewish anymore."

"No, Elly I was praying that one day you wouldn't just be memorizing verses or reciting prayers because you had to, but because you really believed in Jesus. But that doesn't mean you aren't Jewish anymore."

"It doesn't?"

"No. After all, Jesus is Jewish. Do you believe that Jesus died so that you could be forgiven for any bad things you do?"

"Yes."

"Do you believe that he rose from the dead, like the Bible says?"

"Yes, otherwise he could not have helped me in the train."

"Well, then Elly, you have found your Messiah. What could be more Jewish?"

Elly thought for a moment and then she smiled broadly. "That's true," she said. "So why don't most Jews believe in him?"

"That's a good question, Elly."

"Tante Grietje, you have to teach me everything you know about Jesus, and the Bible, so when the war is over, I can tell Henri and Mother and Father about him!" Elly was almost begging now.

"Of course, Elly," Grietje said, and hugged her. "Of course."

CHAPTER TWENTY-THREE

AMERSFOORT

Barry no longer received packages from his friends back home. He did not have to guess why they stopped coming. They were not so sheltered at Westerbork that they did not realize that Hitler was aiming to rid Holland of all its Jews. There were rumors circulating in the camp that all of the prisoners with foreign papers were going to be transported to a concentration camp at Amersfoort, near Utrecht. Apparently, Westerbork was going to be used as a deportation center for large transports of Jews headed for a place in Poland called Auschwitz.

Barry was told that conditions at Amersfoort would be much worse than at Westerbork, but he could sense that leaving Westerbork would be far better than staying.

The day the transport to Amersfoort occurred, Barry and his family and the other Jews selected were forced to stand for three hours on the drill field while they waited for the train. It took two hours to get to Amersfoort. An armed SS guard then led the weary and freezing group on a march through the town of Amersfoort to the camp. They had eaten nothing since the night before, and many passed out on the way from exhaustion. As they marched through the town, Barry ached, knowing that the people who resided in the houses they passed were free and he was a prisoner. So close to freedom and yet so far away.

The camp entrance processing was tedious and draining. Barry could not wait to get to sleep. Conditions in Amersfoort appeared worse indeed. The food was scarce and barely edible.

Diarrhea was rampant and sanitary provisions were nonexistent. The stench of the place was excruciating.

That was not the worst of it. In the woods, about 500 yards away from the camp, was a gully. Anyone caught violating any of the camp's rules, such as curfew, was forced to stand at the edge of the gully. Then he was shot in the back of the head. Barry heard the shots of the firing squad often. He knew that the Nazis had dug the gully close enough to the camp so the other prisoners could hear the shooting.

A month after their arrival, the foreign Jews were ordered to return to Westerbork. The mass deportations to Auschwitz staged there were completed. Once again, Barry and his family were marched through Amersfoort. Once again they boarded the train. Arriving in Westerbork, they were assigned to a special barracks reserved for foreign Jews and Jews married to Gentiles.

About 10,000 Jews had passed through Westerbork on their way to Auschwitz. When Barry and his family returned to the camp, there were still approximately 1,000 Jews waiting to be "processed" and deported. They were housed in Barracks S, which became notorious. Any slip-up, and it was Barracks S for the guilty prisoners.

The Nazis had done a thorough job of rounding up most of the Jews in the major cities of Holland. Barry wondered frantically about Elly. Was there any chance she was in the camp? What if she were in Barracks S? Or had she passed through already?

He could not stand not knowing. "There must be a way to find out," he figured.

His only option was to ask a guard, like he did for his grandmother, and see if the Rodrigues family was there. He barely stopped to consider that the guard had only to be annoyed to send him off to Barracks S.

"Excuse me," he said to the man at the desk in the administration barracks. "I was wondering if you could tell me . . ." He faltered. "I was wondering . . ."

"What is it?" the guard said gruffly.

"May I see the list of deportees?" Barry asked as politely as he could.

The guard was obviously annoyed. "Are you serious, kid? No way. Now get out of here, I'm very busy."

"I know that, sir. I just . . . well, I'm wondering if the name of a friend of mine is on that list."

The guard looked at him, disgusted at having to interrupt his business for this boy.

"Please," Barry said. "The name is Rodrigues."

Sighing with boredom and irritation, the guard flipped through the list. "There are several Rodrigues families here. Could you be more specific?"

Barry thought for a moment. "I think they were Rodrigues Lopes," he added. His stomach churned as the man ran his pointer finger down the list of names, then stopped abruptly. He looked up at Barry, but refused to meet his eyes.

"Well, I shouldn't tell you this, because you're not family, but yes, the name is there, and they've come and gone."

Barry said nothing in response to the guard, but he was devastated. He had until that moment believed that Elly was still safe in hiding. "Why?" he wondered to himself. "Why would I think that they wouldn't have found her? They've found everyone else." Still he was shocked, almost too shocked to cry.

CHAPTER TWENTY-FOUR

HAZERSVOUDE

Elly and Tante Grietje climbed aboard the train and settled in for their return trip to Hazersvoude. Elly recalled how scared she had been six weeks before, on their journey to Dronthe. She was not nearly as frightened now. "If Jesus protected me once, surely he can do it again," she reasoned.

Elly and Grietje had spent the past month and a half studying the Bible together. Study time transformed into a time of meaning for Elly. The words were alive and exciting, not just verses to be memorized for the sake of pretending she believed in Jesus.

Their time in Dronthe had to come to an end, as people back in Hazersvoude were beginning to talk. The school principal back home sent word that the villagers were asking questions. "Where is the schoolteacher? Christmas vacation is long over." Grietje and Elly had better return home. "We'll just have to trust that we've been gone long enough for the Nazis to forget about us," Grietje said to Elly.

Arriving in Hazersvoude, Elly resumed her role as Elly Van Toll. Grietje concocted a story, saying that she and Elly had been away on "family business." Elly returned to school.

The winter of 1943-1944 was harsh. There was hardly any food, even in the rural community of Hazersvoude. Grietje's skills as a home economics teacher proved invaluable. Not only did she share every morsel of food she had with Elly, she unraveled her own sweaters and re-knit them for her young charge. When the temperatures became too icy for the child to bear, Grietje fashioned her own good coat into one that would fit Elly and keep her warm.

Elly could not find words to express her gratitude to Grietje. She came to depend on Grietje as she had depended upon her mother. Thoughts such as these troubled her as she lay in bed at night, praying for her parents. "Lord, keep them safe. Protect them," she whispered into her pillow. "Don't let me forget about them," she added.

One Sunday, while Grietje was cooking dinner, she noticed Elly was quieter than usual. "What's on your mind," Grietje inquired of the pensive girl.

"Tante Grietje, if God is so loving, then why does he allow us to suffer so much?"

Grietje stopped peeling the potatoes, and stood silently for a moment. "I don't know, dear," she replied. Then she said, "Actually, I think what's happening to you and your family and all the other Jews doesn't say so much about God. I think it says more about humanity."

Before Elly had a chance to reply, there was a loud knock on the door. "I'll get it," Elly said, sliding off her chair. She reached for the doorknob and pulled open the door.

Standing there in front of her was a Nazi SS officer. Elly's lower jaw dropped in surprise, which quickly turned to fear at the sight of his gun.

"Let me in this house, right away!" he shouted in German to the frightened thirteen-year-old girl. Elly was too terrified to speak or move. The SS officer barged into the house, as Tante Grietje heard the commotion, and ran to the front entrance.

"What are you doing, barging into my home like this?" Grietje demanded in a volume that almost matched his shouting.

"An American pilot has been shot down somewhere around here. We are searching every house until we find him!"

"What on earth makes you think he would be here?" Grietje inquired, as if she were aghast at the thought of being suspected. Elly realized Tante Grietje was stalling, to give Elly

enough time to get out of the officer's sight. As she moved quietly to the kitchen, she heard the officer speaking to Grietje as if she had no brains.

"Because," he replied in a mocking tone. "We all know you Dutch are Allied sympathizers."

"Well, you still have no right to storm in here and scare us to death!" she replied. "But search away."

The officer shrugged off Tante Grietje's comments, and began to search throughout the house. Elly remained in the kitchen, pretending to wash dishes. "Please, God, don't let him suspect! Help me be calm. Help me be calm!" she prayed. She poured more soap into the sudsy water and methodically washed a perfectly clean plate.

When the SS officer searched and found no one, he left as suddenly as he had come, without another word. The slam of the front door behind him was the most welcome sound Grietje and Elly had ever heard.

Grietje went to Elly, who continued to wash the same plate over and over. "He's gone, dear," Grietje whispered. Only then did Elly start to tremble.

"Tante Grietje, I thought he was coming to take me away!" Grietje wrapped her arms around Elly. "So did I. But he didn't even suspect you! Oh, God is good!" She pulled Elly closer to her.

Elly instantly felt safe. God was looking after her. "Jesus loves me," she whispered into Tante Grietje's shoulder.

"Of course he does. He loved you enough to die, remember? As difficult as it may be to realize, he understands our sufferings, Elly. Think how much he suffered himself."

Elly and Grietje put away the dishes. Neither one was hungry after their encounter, and they decided to go to bed early. Elly was exhausted from her earlier struggle against fear. As she drifted off to sleep that night, she thought to herself once more, "God loves me." That night, for the first time in over a year, she felt safe as she slept.

CHAPTER TWENTY-FIVE

GUEST

The rescue mission consisted of three floors, with a chapel on the first floor, living quarters on the second, and an attic on the third. "Pa" and "Ma" Henri ran the rescue mission, and lived on the second floor with their seven children. Pa Henri was the one who invited me into the rescue mission the night I fled there when I had nowhere else to turn. After I had stayed with them a few months, Ma and Pa Henri took me into their hearts as well as their home, and I was treated like a family member rather than a fugitive. We read the Bible together, and they helped me fill the idle hours by playing unending games of chess and checkers with me.

Food was becoming increasingly scarce, and the typical daily diet consisted of fake tea made with cherry leaves, fake bread made with ground peas and potato starch, and fake meat made with barley, oats or turnips. Ma Henri always made sure there was enough to feed all of us. One morning, as we sat down to breakfast, Pa Henri made an announcement: "I've been in touch with the underground, and it seems that there's a Jewish family hiding in The Hague, and they need to be split up. The youngest son is coming to stay here," he said.

"Really?" I asked. "When is he coming?" I was excited at the prospect of having some new company, though I wondered how Ma and Pa would manage to feed all of us.

Just then the doorbell rang, and Pa Henri jumped to his feet. "That must be him," he said. I was amazed at the excitement this dear man displayed over having another "houseguest." He sprinted down to the first floor. Ma Henri and I followed him.

He opened the front door, and suddenly I was looking at the face of my younger brother George.

"George!" I shouted.

"Ernie!" We embraced, and I turned to Pa Henri. "You knew?" I asked. He smiled broadly. "Word came that the address where your family was staying was getting hot. So my contact asked me if we could hide one more person. Then I found out it was George," he replied.

"George, you must be hungry. We haven't finished breakfast yet. Come upstairs," Ma Henri urged.

As we climbed the steps to the dining room, I found it difficult to absorb the reality that my brother was walking beside me. "How are Mother and Father?" I asked.

"They're doing as well as can be expected, but they had to separate, too."

We sat down together at the table. Ma Henri poured George a cup of tea. I continued to stare at my younger brother. "I have to admit part of me thought I might never see you again, George. Seeing you makes me realize how much I'm aching to see Mother and Father," I said.

Pa Henri spoke up, "Actually, you may have an opportunity to see them in a few weeks."

"You're kidding. How?" I asked eagerly.

"Your mother needs some dental work. I'm going to try to find an underground dentist who would be willing to do the work. I think I know a fellow in the area who can help."

"Pa, you and Ma have been so good to us. I don't know how we could ever repay you. I thank God for you both," I said. They bowed their heads and humbly accepted my gratitude. I knew that George would also see the love of Jesus in them. Together, we anxiously awaited the reunion with my parents.

CHAPTER TWENTY-SIX

SEPTEMBER 1944

It took a few more weeks than expected to find a dentist for my mother. The plan was for my mother and father to meet at a secret location "above water," travel to Leiden to visit the dentist and then come to the rescue mission. The day they were to arrive, George and I spent the morning helping Ma Henri with the chores, changing linens and cleaning the second floor. We expected them for lunch. Ma Henri even managed to obtain some real bread for the occasion.

I tried to keep as busy as possible. Now that their arrival was so soon, waiting was agony. That morning seemed to stretch out longer than the previous two years.

Twelve o'clock came and so did my parents. I was immediately in their loving embrace. The four of us hugged each other tightly for several moments.

"Ernie, we've missed you so much," my mother said as she stood back and looked at me. Her mouth was a bit swollen from the dental work she had undergone, but she smiled broadly.

"I know. I've missed you terribly, too. It's wonderful to see you. If only Max were here, then it would be a true family reunion," I said.

During lunch, I told my family about my last two years in hiding. "I've hidden at forty-four different addresses in the past two years," I said at one point. Astonishment appeared on all of their faces. "I know," I said. "I can hardly believe it myself. I really believe that God has guided me every step of the way."

"I have to admit I've been incredibly touched by the

Christians who have chosen to hide us, Ernie," my mother interjected. "They are good people. They have risked their own lives to protect us," she said, looking at Ma Henri, who was busy slicing bread.

After lunch, we settled in the living room. It had been two years since we had simply sat together in one room, and we savored every moment, trying to stave off the inevitable separation for as long as we could.

The ring of the doorbell interrupted our conversation. Pa Henri was on an errand. Ma Henri was doing the dishes. "Are you expecting anyone?" I called to her.

"I don't think so," was her answer. The doorbell rang again. She wiped her hands and went downstairs to the chapel to see who was there.

We heard shouting. "Open, this door, immediately!" a man's voice yelled.

Ma Henri opened the door, and an SS officer and three Gestapo agents pushed past her and stomped up the stairs! "Where are the Jews?" one of them screamed.

Ma Henri's face blanched. "I don't know what you're talking about!" she protested indignantly after them. They ignored her and started their hunt.

If only there had been some warning when the doorbell rang. How could it possibly sound the same as it did when rung by the laundry man or the mailman or the newspaper boy? Should there not have been some variation from its normal tone? No, there had been nothing. We were caught completely off guard. I made a beeline for the attic just as the Nazis were coming up the stairs. I motioned for my family to follow me, but they were scrambling, trying to find close places to conceal themselves.

I crouched behind a curtain in the attic, holding my breath. I knew the curtain was a meager shield between me and the Nazis, but I had no other choice. My world was caving in around me. I heard the Nazis start towards the stairs that led to the attic. Fear churned in my mouth, and I longed to spit it out. I listened to the sound of footsteps as they reached the top of the stairs and moved steadily towards me.

Abruptly, the footsteps stopped. The curtain concealing me was yanked away. It was all over. Two years of evading capture had ended in about two minutes. The hunter had trapped the hunted.

"Get up!" the Gestapo man shouted.

I stood and raised my hands above my head, taking quick note of the revolvers the men carried, which suffocated any urge I may have had to try to escape.

They marched me down the stairs and into the street. The crisp autumn air caressed my face as my captors shoved me into a squad car and sped towards the police station. I was frightened, and yet so grateful that I was the only one sitting in the car. Somehow, the rest of my family had evaded capture!

I suddenly sensed that I was not alone. Jesus was with me. Without thinking, I started to sing a Dutch anthem, "Whatever happens to me, I have my hand in God's hand!"

"Shut up!" shouted the SS officer.

When we arrived at the police station, they threw me into a small, empty room.

"Take off your clothes, now!" the SS officer ordered. He immediately searched my clothes and found my false identity card. Seizing it, he smiled triumphantly, and quickly left the room, locking the door behind him.

I stood there in the little room, naked, alone and scared. There was nothing for me to do but pray, "God, I need strength." I knew the Gestapo would interrogate me to find out the names of underground workers who supplied me with my false identity card. If I broke down and betrayed any information, the Nazis would also find out where my parents and George were hiding. I would also endanger the lives of about 200 other people who had helped me during the past two years. "Jesus, please help me," I pleaded.

A few moments later, an SS commandant entered the room. He had a file in his hands. He glanced at me, and did a double take when he noticed that I was not circumcised. He looked puzzled, and glanced at the file in his hand.

"You are Jewish, aren't you?" he asked.

I fought the urge to remark what a stupid question that was. Instead, I replied, "I don't know whether a Gentile or a Jewish stork laid me in the cradle, but I belong body and soul to Jesus!"

"Shut up!" replied the commandant. He opened my file and began to read it carefully.

"Your real name is Ernest Cassutto?" It was more of a statement than a question. I nodded. "Your father is Isaac Cassutto?" Again, I nodded. He turned to another page in the file. "I see we arrested your father a couple of years ago, but then he was released." Apparently, that fact displeased him.

He closed the file. "Tell me," he said, his voice slow and deliberate. "Where are your parents now?"

"I don't know," I replied, which was the truth. I had no idea where they were hiding.

"I see. And who gave you the false identity card?"

"I don't know."

He stood and his voice became louder. "Who gave you the card!" he shouted.

I too, raised my voice, "I don't know their names!" Whack! He slapped me across the face. Then he turned his back to me.

"In that case," he said coolly "You have until tomorrow morning to give us the information we want. If you do not supply us with that information, we will just have to turn you over to the Sicherheits Deinst (Security Police) in Rotterdam. They should be able to refresh your memory." He smirked at me, and motioned for the guard to take me away. The SS officer ordered me to get dressed. When I had done so, he seized me by the collar and led me down a dark, narrow corridor. He halted in front of a door, wrenched it open and sent me sprawling inside with a solid kick. "God bless you!" he laughed sarcastically.

The heavy door slammed with an echoing thud, and I was alone.

I tried to look around at the black hole into which I had been flung. Except for a bare shelf to sleep on (or at least try to), the cell was entirely empty. There wasn't even a light bulb to chase away the gloom.

During the first hours of my confinement, I knelt down and prayed. I committed my parents, Max, George, Hetty and myself to God, trusting him for everything. I was now in the hands of the Nazis whose law it was to murder the Jews. In their eyes, we were the worst foe of the German Reich. But I knew that the Jewish Messiah was mightier than Hitler. When I finished praying, I removed my collar-stud and scratched these words in Dutch on the bare cement wall: IK GELOOF IN JEZUS YESHUAUS, HALLELUJAH! (I believe in Jesus Christ, Hallelujah!)

It was hard for me to measure time in the dark, but what must have been a few hours later, there appeared through the hole in the door four slices of bread with jam on them! I was amazed, given the food shortage, and wondered who could have arranged that, certainly not the Nazis. I ate slowly, knowing it was probably the last good meal I would have in a long time. I thanked the Lord for the gift of food, and knew that even though I was in prison, Jesus was watching over me.

Early the next morning, before the sun came up, I was handcuffed and removed from my dungeon. Along with six other prisoners, I was marched at gunpoint to the train station where we boarded the train to Rotterdam. Upon arrival, I was taken to the headquarters of the S.D. (Security Police), where I had to stand for thirty minutes with my nose pressed against a wall. A German prison guard passing by paused to speak to me.

"Are you a Jew?" he asked.

"Yes," I replied. "And my soul belongs to Jesus, my Messiah and Lord."

"Poor fellow!" was his response. He escorted me to the Gestapo office. He shoved me inside and left, locking the door behind him. After a few minutes, the door opened again and three Gestapo officers entered and sat at the table with my file in front of them. My "trial" had begun.

"We know you are a Jew! Where are your parents hiding? Who gave you the black market ration cards and false identity card?" They fired questions at me, but I stood silently.

One of them grabbed me. He reached into my pocket and pulled out my engagement picture of Hetty.

"She's so beautiful," he remarked. "It really is a shame we had to kill her."

Anger burned in my throat, but I willed my face to remain expressionless.

"I see we are going to have to take more drastic measures to get the answers we want." One of the officers opened the door. "Guard!" he called. A heavyset man in Nazi uniform appeared in the doorway.

"Take this Jewish swine to the torture room," the Gestapo officer commanded.

"Let's go, Jew!" the man said. He spoke poor German in a thick Dutch brogue. Obviously he was a Dutchman turned traitor.

The torture room lived up to its name. It was decorated in "early sadistic." There were two chairs in the room, and a coal fire burned in the corner. My eyes immediately went to a long iron rod resting in the blaze. It had been heating up for awhile; its color matched the hue of the burning embers around it. I had heard people say that in interrogation sessions, the Gestapo drove a hot iron pole into the cheek of the person being interrogated. If that did not get the prisoner to talk, they pulled out his fingernails one by one, and if that did not work . . .

"Lord help me!" I prayed as my heart began to pound rapidly. I knew I would not be able to stand the pain!

The guard ordered me to squat on the floor. I did so. Then he told me to stretch my arms out in front of me. Into my arms he placed one of the heavy wooden chairs. Then he released it. "Don't drop the chair," he warned. I gritted my teeth and tried to keep from falling as beads of perspiration appeared on my forehead and the back of my neck.

The Dutch man paced around the room and sat down in the other chair. "So," he began in a conversational tone. "Tell me, why do you believe in Jesus?"

His question stunned me. I almost dropped the chair. It was difficult to breathe, let alone speak, but I replied, "The Bible says that God loves us so much he sent his Son to die as a final sacrifice for all of our sins."

"Yes, yes, I've heard that before," he said impatiently. He told me that he had become disappointed with Christianity, and that this disappointment led him to become a National Socialist. This commenced a theological dialogue! At one point during our discourse, I gently put the chair down. My tormenter didn't even notice; he was so busy ranting against organized religion.

"I understand what you are saying," I said. "But don't put your trust in religion; put it in Jesus himself!"

He looked at me, a stony expression on his face. But I could see despair in his eyes.

"There is only one god," he said. "And that is Hitler!"

A buzzer rang, indicating that we were to return at once to the waiting officers.

Startled, the Dutchman looked at me as though I had just walked into the room. He became panicky. "They'll beat me if they see that you haven't been tortured!"

"Don't worry," I replied. "I promise I'll make it look convincing."

I pretended to writhe in pain as the other Gestapo agents asked me again about the false identity and ration cards.

"I got food from many different loyal Dutch citizens, but I didn't ask their names," I said, wincing.

"Maybe he needs another torture session," one of the officers said, grinning maliciously.

"No, no!" I cried, feigning terror. I paused and furrowed my brow as if trying to remember something, and then I gave them the name of a boy who I knew had already been caught by the Nazis and executed for his role in underground activities.

That answer seemed to satisfy them, so they continued to grill me about my parents' whereabouts. I really did not know where they were staying, thank God, and my ignorance must have appeared genuine. One of the officers closed my file and said, "The question is, what do we do with this worthless, forgetful Jew now?"

The Dutchman who was supposed to interrogate me suggested that I be sent to a work camp for criminals. This provoked the Germans' wrath.

"It is we Germans who will decide where this Jew will go. Get him ready for transport to Auschwitz!" one of them retorted.

My trial was over.

CHAPTER TWENTY-SEVEN

PRISON

I was taken to the main prison in downtown Rotterdam to join other Jews and "criminals" awaiting deportation to Auschwitz. They put me in solitary confinement in a small cell that was sealed off with a solid steel door. Even an animal in a zoo could look through iron bars, but I could not even see out the peephole through which the Nazis observed me. Before they shoved me into the cell, I noticed a large yellow Star of David hung on the door to my chamber, signaling that a Jew awaiting deportation occupied the cell.

Immediately before entering the cell, I was searched again. My Bible and engagement picture of Hetty were the only things I had left. The guard looked closely at the picture of Hetty.

"I remember this girl. She was reading her Bible to the last minute," he said matter-of-factly.

The guard opened the door to my cell, and followed me in, shutting the door behind him. He still had my Bible and the picture in his hand. I expected a volley of verbal or physical abuse, but instead he handed both items back to me.

"You're letting me keep these?" I asked incredulously.

"Yes," he said in a voice barely audible. "Now listen very carefully to what I have to say, and swear that you will tell no one! If anyone finds out we had this conversation, we're both dead."

"I swear," I promised, not knowing what else to say.

"The reason I remember your fiancée so well is because of her faithfulness. I am also a Christian, and I work with the underground. I wasn't placed here in time to save her, but maybe I can save you. You must do whatever I say and follow all of my orders. Do you understand?" He waited for my response. I was still bewildered, but managed to reply. "Yes, yes I understand."

"I'm not the only guard here, so I can't guarantee that I will always be assigned to you. I can't blow my cover either, so you may not see me for a while. Just keep praying like your fiancée did."

He left quickly. "Thank you Lord, for Hetty's faithfulness!" I prayed. "And thank you for sending me another underground worker even here in prison!" I wasn't sure if this one underground worker could make any difference in a prison this large, but at least I was able to keep my Bible. That was reason enough to rejoice.

This cell had a light, a cot and a lavatory. I was alone, and yet not lonely. I knelt down on the bare ground to pray. "Lord, my fate is in your hands. Help me trust my body, soul and my loved ones to you!" I opened the Bible and began reading in the book of Daniel. When the three Hebrew children were in the fiery furnace, King Nebuchadnezzar had made a startling discovery. "'Was it not three men we cast bound into the midst of the fire?' They replied to the king, 'Certainly, O king.' He said, 'Look! I see four men loosed and walking about in the midst of the fire without harm . . .'"(Daniel 3:24-25).

The "fourth man" was also with me. No one, not even the Nazis, could shut him out. Jesus met with me in my prison cell. And he had something to ask of me.

"Can you forgive the Germans, Ernie? Can you pray for them and love them?"

"Forgive them? Love them? Oh, Jesus how can I?"

The fire raged inside me. I knew the Lord wanted me to turn the other cheek, but this was really laying it on the line.

"It's too much for me, Lord."

"This is what it is all about, Ernie," he seemed to be saying.

I remembered what Hetty had written in her diary, and a verse from the gospel of Matthew kept reverberating in my head. "Love your enemies, and pray for those who persecute you . . ."(Matthew 5:44). Until now, they had only been words. Easy to read and approve. "But Lord, they have taken me prisoner! They killed Hetty!"

In that moment, on the floor of the prison cell, I remembered that Jesus was tortured. How much he suffered! And yet he forgave his tormenters. He was not asking me to endure anything he had not already experienced. "Now is the real test, Ernie," the Lord said to me. "Can you handle it?"

"I can't Lord! But if you help me, I'll try. Please help me!"

One by one, the chains began to snap—chains of hatred, chains of bitterness—and I was set free. Even though I was behind prison walls, I was not alone. One more Hebrew child was being delivered out of a fiery furnace.

"The Nazis are the real prisoners," I thought. I felt a pang of sorrow for them. I thought of the Dutch man who was assigned to torture me. How tormented he seemed! I prayed that he would see his need for God's forgiveness.

Each day, all prisoners were allowed out of our cells for half an hour to "come up for air." We assembled in the prison courtyard. My fellow captives quickly learned that I was a "religious man." Sometimes during this half hour, they asked me to conduct religious services for them. We sang hymns quietly and cautiously, so as not to invite abuse from the Nazis. We prayed together. Sometimes we read from my precious Bible. My first "congregation" consisted entirely of prisoners.

I was never quite sure why these services were permitted. I suspected it had something to do with the Dutch underground guard, whose name, I learned, was Marinus, but I had not seen him since the day I arrived in Rotterdam.

Thoughts of deportation and death began to invade my mind like uninvited guests, forcing familiarity and demanding attention. I was among forty or so persons waiting to be sent to Auschwitz. We were the last scheduled deportation from the Rotterdam jail. Every day, I expected to be yanked from my cell and put on a train. I tried to hope and believe that I would be rescued somehow, but circumstances often prevented such optimistic thoughts.

One day, at the beginning of the half-hour break, two prison guards grabbed me and hauled me to the square in the middle of the prison compound.

"Here Jew, we have something to show you!"

In front of me, lying in a bloody heap were bodies of men. So silent and still . . . so dead. A look of horror and pain was frozen on each of their twisted faces. Pinned to the body of one of them was a note: "THIS IS WHAT WE DO WITH DUTCH RESISTANCE MOVEMENT WORKERS." It was short and concise, meant for anyone who still needed an explanation. The intent was not lost on me. I did not see Marinus in the pile of bodies, but I was almost certain that the Nazis had killed my only hope of being saved from deportation.

A few evenings after the incident in the square, I awoke in the middle of the night to the harsh clanging of heavy steel doors. Repeatedly, the sound of doors slamming shut echoed throughout the jail. The noise continued for about twenty minutes, and then it was quiet again. My groggy mind tried to figure out what was happening. Was it an inspection? Why wasn't my door opened? I waited for several minutes, listening for more telltale sounds, but all was still. I let sleep take over.

When I awoke the next morning, I received my usual meager breakfast, and then a few hours later, I heard the repeated creak of doors opening. Just as I wondered whether my door would be skipped again, it opened and Marinus stood in the doorway.

"Time to come up for air," he said. I tried to ask him what was happening.

"Shh! Don't say a word," he hissed. As he escorted me and six other prisoners to the square, I noticed that there was no Jewish star on the door of my cell. I looked at the faces of the other six prisoners that were on my block, and knew that none of them came from Jewish cells. When we reached the courtyard, the guard spoke.

"Does anyone want Ernest to lead a small service?" he asked.

"Yes," they all replied, and we started singing some familiar hymns.

After our precious half-hour, the guard escorted us back to our cells. On the way, I noticed that there were absolutely no Jewish stars on any of the cells in the prison. "Are all the Jews gone?" I wanted to ask, but didn't dare. Why had I not gone with them? Then I remembered that the Star of David was no longer on my door. Had someone removed it? I looked at the guard, but his face remained blank. When we reached my cell, I stopped in the doorway, hoping that the guard would sense my silent inquiry, "Did you take the star away?" I asked with my eyes. He was silent.

There were no more deportations to Poland from Rotterdam. The Allied forces stormed across Europe, liberating France and Belgium. Although the British and American plan to invade Germany from Arnhem in eastern Holland failed, General Montgomery ordered the rail lines destroyed. The Dutch-German border was sealed, making transport to Poland impossible. Now, the Netherlands was the only European country still under the heel of the German Reich. I missed deportation by the slimmest of chances. The Nazis chalked it up to a mistake. I view it as a miracle.

I was the only remaining Jew under German control in the Rotterdam prison. Instead of killing me, the Nazis decided that it would be wiser to use me for slave labor. They mockingly called me "Der Letzte Jude von Rotterdam" or "the last Jew of Rotterdam."

Among my fellow prisoners were a number of Gentiles who had been jailed for a variety of "crimes," ranging from running errands for the underground to offering refuge to American pilots. Along with six others, I was assigned to work days in a slave labor camp located about three and a half miles from the Rotterdam prison. The camp was a large farm that had been confiscated by the Nazis. It was used to raise cattle, other animals and vegetables, all of which were for the Germans.

Each morning, we were forced to march barefoot to the

camp in the freezing cold. We spent the day doing whatever was required. At the end of the day, we were marched back to Rotterdam to face another black night fighting fear and despair and other dark things that lurk in shadows.

Hours of uncertainty turned into days and then weeks, and by Christmas 1944, deteriorating conditions in the prison added to the growing despair. The heating system failed, the electricity went out on a routine basis and the water pressure diminished. Our diet consisted mainly of tulip bulbs and sugar beets fried in candle grease. Our digestive tracts eroded. The horrible sound and smell of prisoners vomiting was frequent. We wondered desperately if Allied forces would ever get to us and end our misery.

Though we were eating next to nothing, the Nazis planned an elaborate Christmas dinner for themselves. On Christmas Eve, at the labor camp, I was ordered to kill the goose for the Nazis' Christmas dinner. I remembered in gross detail the sight of our Indonesian cook accidentally slaughtering my pet chicken. In my mind, I saw her bleeding and fluttering with her head half off. I could hear her crying. I could bear many things, but not this. No, I would not slaughter the Christmas goose!

"Are you crazy, Ernie?" the underground guard exclaimed when I refused. "You have to do it!"

"I can't do it, and I'm not going to do it!" I cried.

"You'd better do it!" the guard answered. "Insubordination will be punished by firing squad!"

I stood my ground. The underground guard took upon himself the task of killing the goose, while I hid in a nearby shed with my hands clapped over my ears. Marinus must have thought that it would be therapeutic for me to confront my fears. Thinking he would play psychiatrist, he came back with the dead creature in his hand. Holding it before me, he said firmly, "Now look! Is it that bad?"

I flew into a rage, shouting at him to get the bird away from me, totally rejecting his misguided attempt to toughen me up. "Just leave me alone!" I begged him. "I can't take this anymore!" For a minute, I forgot all that this man had done for me, and I hated him with a passion.

My anger soon wore off, and I regained my composure as well as my appreciation for Marinus. I have no idea how we would have fared were it not for him tirelessly working on our behalf. It was apparent that he was actively trying to convince the Nazis that he was a loyal National Socialist. He made a point of doing menial tasks for them and followed their orders to the letter.

Marinus was particularly concerned for my welfare. I was rapidly losing weight and strength. Once in a while, he managed to secretly smuggle a piece of bread or a potato to me. Whenever he could, he got me assigned to KP duty, knowing I could eat the potato peels and other refuse used to feed the rabbits on the farm. Little favors like these kept me alive during the cold winter months. I thanked God for this man.

January was bitterly cold, and I had to fight the snow, hail and rain without a coat or shoes. Icy winds slapped my back and face, and my feet were so frozen it was almost impossible to carry out my farm duties. One day I received a present. During the Great War, Herr Bartels, the commandant of the prison, had been wounded and captured by the British. During this war, he was given a less rigorous assignment as commandant of the Rotterdam prison and labor camp. Remembering the humane treatment that he had received while in British custody, he was moved to give me a pair of his own shoes. I could not believe it. Just when life was at its darkest, the gift of these shoes gave me hope. They reminded me that God had not forgotten me.

Winter passed and the shifting sun dispersed its warm rays to the waiting earth, bringing us the miracle of spring. The Netherlands was faced with a new menace. The German forces pierced the dikes along the Dutch seacoast, threatening the country with flooding.

By April 1945, the Germans were themselves threatened by defeat. The Allies were closing in, and rumors of a German surrender were swarming about the prison. The Americans and

Russians had entered Berlin, and the Canadians were laying pontoon bridges over the Ijssel River in the northeast part of Holland, poised to enter the country. The atmosphere in the Rotterdam prison was frantic. Dared we hope?

CHAPTER TWENTY-EIGHT

MAY 1945

The arrival of spring could not help but lift our spirits as we trudged to the farm at the labor camp. My mind reached back and grabbed memories of Hetty and I walking among tulips on similar days. That spring seemed to belong to a world far away.

When we arrived at the barn of the farm, our guard motioned us inside. We automatically went to start feeding the cows. The guard closed the door behind him, and began to speak swiftly and quietly.

"I have a message from the underground. The Nazis know they've lost the war, so they are destroying all records and killing anyone who could testify to their crimes. They plan to shoot all of you tomorrow morning."

We were silent. The news did not surprise us. It was foolish to think they would let us live. There was no reason to spare us when so many of our Dutch countrymen were dying daily at the hands of the Nazis. Still, hearing news of the planned execution out loud was devastating. We had come so close to surviving.

The underground guard continued, "The Nazis want the firing squad to take place tomorrow morning at sunrise, but Commandant Bartels hasn't received the order yet. I have to come up with a way to get all of you out of here before then. For now, do your chores as if nothing is wrong."

Easier said than done. My mind feebly tried to think of an escape plan, but I was too weak with hunger and exhaustion to pursue anything mentally exerting. So instead I prayed for our underground resistance worker, that he would figure out a way for us to escape.

While doing the chores, one of the prisoners complained that there was no way to water the cows because the water pressure was so low. At his comment, I saw the guard's face light up.

"Continue with your chores, everyone," he said, and rushed out of the barn.

We shrugged and returned to our work. More than an hour later, he returned. "Listen everyone," he whispered. "I just saw Herr Bartels, and I got him to give us permission to go to the municipal bath house today at two o'clock." He seemed extraordinarily pleased.

"I don't get it," one of the prisoners said. "What difference does it make whether we die clean or dirty?" One or two of the other prisoners chuckled a bit at that.

"Once we are out of the camp, we are going to go straight to the underground headquarters. Any German who tries to stop us will meet with a bullet," he said. I wondered if he was as confident of his plan as he sounded.

"How did you get the passes?" one of the other prisoners asked with a hint of skepticism in his voice.

"I told Commandant Bartels that the low water pressure had prohibited you from showering or bathing for two weeks," he grinned, looking at the man who had made the comment about the low water pressure.

"And that's all it took?" the man asked.

"Well, not at first. He was a bit reluctant, but I reminded him that many of you are scheduled for KP duty." The Germans were terrified of disease. One way the underground kept the Nazis from discovering hidden Jews was by posting fake quarantine signs on the houses where Jews were hiding. The Nazis would never dare to enter a house where someone might have TB or some other disease. We congratulated the guard on his cleverness.

"So he gave passes for all six of us?" I asked warily, fearing that maybe he had refused to give me one because I was Jewish.

"Yes, for all six of you. The passes say that we are only supposed to be gone for two hours, so by the time anyone misses us, we will be in hiding. I'm told the Canadians are getting ready to liberate Holland, so hopefully, we won't have to hide for long."

A current of fear and excitement ran through the group. "Lord, this has to work!" I thought. It seemed too fantastic to believe. After eight months of imprisonment, I was just going to walk out of jail?

We met at the barn at 2:00, and made our way to the entrance of the camp. The guard at the front gate ordered us to halt. For a minute, I thought it was all over. But the guard waved us on once he saw the passes. "Lord, help me trust you," I prayed as we exited the camp.

Once on the other side of the gate, our guard marched us quickly to the site of the underground headquarters, which turned out to be a house in the countryside about five miles away. The trek seemed like it would never end. I prayed every step of the way. At every turn, we expected to be confronted by Nazis, but we arrived at our destination without incident.

Marinus deposited us in our place of shelter, and then hurried off to collect his own family before anyone discovered we were missing. A few hours later, he returned with his family, wearing civilian clothes.

"We left just in time," he informed us. At around 2:30, the SS chief had visited the plush office of Commandant Bartels and issued the orders for the firing squad. Upon hearing that Bartels had given us passes, he was livid. He immediately got on the camp loudspeakers, "Call out the guards! Prisoners have escaped!"

"Herr Bartels will pay for his blunder, I'm sure," Marinus said. "They know I've betrayed them; I'll have to stay hidden. But the Nazis have no idea that our headquarters are here, or they'd have already shown up."

We couldn't all stay at the farmhouse. Arrangements were made for me to stay at the home of a schoolteacher who lived across town. The next day, a Dutch Resistance worker, armed with a revolver, escorted me to my new hiding place. He informed me that he would not hesitate to use his weapon on anyone who tried to stop us.

I had never been so scared as I was on that tense journey across the city. Intent as I was on getting to the schoolteacher's house as swiftly as possible, I could not help but stare at the war-shredded city of Rotterdam. The destruction was too vast to comprehend. We traversed on foot, and it was the longest walk of my life. "Lord, please help us to not meet any Nazis!" I prayed, and wondered if there would ever come a day when I would not have to utter that prayer.

Finally, we arrived at the woman's home. The rules of life in hiding came back to me. The most difficult part was waiting. I anticipated either capture or liberation at every moment. How long would it be? A day? A week? A year? Who could tell?

On May 5, 1945, two days after our escape, Canadian forces liberated the Netherlands. We were free! Dutch anthems rang out across the city as throngs of joyful people danced in the streets, filling the spring air with their shouts of victory. "HOLLAND IS FREE! LONG LIVE THE QUEEN!"

The Nazi flag came down, and the red, white and blue flag of the Netherlands was raised high. Swedish and Swiss planes flew over Holland, dropping bread to her hungry citizens. American troops, equipped with a new contraption called the jeep, built roads through the partly flooded Dutch countryside. The underground came "above ground," and Nazi soldiers, their arms raised above their heads, were marched through the streets to waiting trains that would take them back to Germany.

It had been years since I had a good reason to compose music. That day, I sat down at my hostess' piano, and wrote a fervent march called, "Oranje Zal Overvinnen!" (Orange Shall Overcome). I remembered how my family often helped me with lyrics to the tunes I composed. I could not wait to proudly sing this song for my family. If they were still alive.

I decided to leave to search for them at once. My hostess

objected. "It's still dangerous out there," she warned. But I could not wait any longer to find my family.

I thanked my hostess for her generosity, and set out for the Rescue Mission in Leiden, about 30 kilometers from Rotterdam. I could not think of anywhere else to go but the Rescue Mission, even though I was scared that I would arrive only to find out that Ma and Pa Henri were no longer there.

Exuberance washed over me as I walked freely through the streets for the first time in over two years. It felt so good to stride around the city with my head held high. The sight of the Dutch flag waving in the breeze was exhilarating, and I was positively buoyant as I made my way along the narrow roads through tiny Dutch villages to the larger hamlet of Leiden. My eyes were continually delighted at the sight of tulips in full bloom under a warm spring sky.

I arrived at the Rescue Mission deliciously exhausted from my journey. Nervously, I knocked on the door, remembering the night I first came there, desperately searching for safety. Fear washed over me. What if there was no one here to greet me? What if they had been arrested months ago?

Then I heard laughter inside, the same sounds of celebration that engulfed the country. I found Ma and Pa Henri and their children. They were still alive, and they were overjoyed at my arrival. "That day I was arrested, how did you get away?" I asked Ma Henri as she hugged me.

It turned out that the day the Nazis came for me, Ma Henri gathered her children and left the area through a sewer as the Nazis were searching upstairs. They rushed to a neighbor's house, where they had a secret telephone. She phoned Pa Henri at the underground headquarters and told him that I had been captured. Pa Henri did not go home to the mission that night. Instead, the family met and went into hiding until the incident was forgotten, and they were able to resume their normal lives.

"Praise God!" I said after hearing their account. Pa Henri urged me to sit down, but I would not be seated until I asked them about my parents and George. I could not muster the courage to ask if they were still alive. Instead I asked, "What happened to my family after I was arrested?"

Ma and Pa Henri described the events that transpired the day of my arrest, eight months earlier. My mother, hearing the commotion downstairs, grabbed George and drew him into the nearest closet she could find, which was hidden by a curtain. When I ran for the attic, Father was left alone in the living room. Where could he hide? He looked around wildly, but could not find a place in time.

His eyes spotted the radio on the mantle and the stamps plastered on the wall next to it. Dutch citizens were only allowed to listen to the radio if they paid a monthly tax to the Nazi government. When the Nazis stormed into the living room, my father was ready with his exit line.

"I see you have paid your radio tax for this month," he said casually to Ma Henri. "You may continue to listen to the radio." He then tipped his hat, turned around and walked out on the unsuspecting Nazis, before they could even question him.

That sounded so much like my father, calm and quick to think. The Nazis searched the second floor of the Rescue Mission, but somehow missed the closet where my mother and George hid. After the Gestapo left, Mother and George stole away from the Rescue Mission, and joined Father at their hiding place in The Hague. From there, they had to move hastily. Staying where they were would have been foolish. For all they knew, I had already been interrogated and revealed my underground contacts. The three of them were taken to a small village named Nieuw Vennep, near Amsterdam where Mother and Father stayed hidden for the duration of the war. George had to be shuffled around a bit, but all three of them were alive and safe! I could scarcely believe it. I almost ached with the joy that was mine upon hearing the words, "They're alive." And they were only about twenty kilometers from Leiden! I could make it there in a matter of hours!

"How can I thank you?" I asked, tears appearing in my eyes as I gazed at these wonderful people who had endured so much to help strangers. In a time and place of such unspeakable cruelty, I know of no adjective that can accurately describe their actions. I hugged them both, and then I drew back. "Maybe I can visit you sometime!" I said, and we all laughed at the excitement in my voice. How incredible to be able to utter that phrase! I could visit them any time I wished! Amazing. I would have to get used to being free.

I made my way to Nieuw Vennep on a borrowed bicycle with no tires. Giving no thought to my weary state, I pedaled steadily, and arrived at Nieuw Vennep exhausted and ecstatic.

I have never had a moment quite like the one when I leaned my bike next to the door of the house. The knowledge that those walls held my family safe inside made me quiver with anticipation.

I was just going to knock on the door, but then I had an idea. Way back in the days before the occupation, I had composed a song for Hetty called "You're Like a Rose." My whole family used to sing it, or hum it; it was kind of like a family song.

I stood at the door and began to whistle the song with all my might. I heard chairs scraping the floor inside, and then the door swung open and there stood my mother and father. Their eyes widened. "Ernie!" they cried. My mother pulled me toward her, and the three of us embraced.

When we parted, I looked around and did not see George. "Where's George?" I asked, concerned.

"He's at a neighbor's house," my father said. "Don't worry, he'll be back soon. Come inside."

Just then George came running up the walk. "I heard . . . Ernie!" he shouted. "Oh, thank God!"

What a glorious reunion it was. Germany surrendered to the Allies two days later, and the war in Europe was brought to a close at last.

CHAPTER TWENTY-NINE

FREE

Elly was dreaming. In her dream she saw her parents and Henri and her friends from her school back in Amsterdam. They were all dancing in a field, and there were tulips and birds, big birds. The birds darted to and fro over their heads, and one came to rest on her shoulder. Now it was shaking her shoulder . . . no wait, that wasn't a bird. It was Tante Grietje, nudging her, dragging her from her sound sleep and the field of flowers back into her room in the house in Hazersvoude. "Wake up, Elly! Wake up, dear!"

Elly's eyes fluttered open. "What? What is it?" she asked, scared.

"We've been liberated! We're free!" Grietje exclaimed.

"Are you serious?" Elly asked, jumping out from under the covers. As her feet hit the floor, she heard the drone of airplanes flying over the tiny village. She rushed to the window, and to her amazement she saw they were Swiss and Swedish planes, and they were dropping bread and other supplies over the town. Canadian troops were riding through the streets in their jeeps, letting the villagers know that they had been liberated. Grietje's neighbors were all running out of their houses, shouting

"Holland is free! Long Live the Queen! Long Live the Queen!"

Elly got dressed in a flash, and soon was out in the village square with Tante Grietje. The homes along the square were once again flying the Dutch flag, and town people were embracing each other. Elly saw the minister and some people from the Dutch Reformed Church in the square. She went up to them and embraced them.

"I can't believe we're really free!"

The minister laid a hand on Elly's shoulder. "We are so glad this is over, especially for your sake, dear." Relief shone in his face.

"What do you mean?" she asked, but she had a feeling she knew what he was going to say.

"We've known for some time that you are Jewish," he told her.

"And you didn't tell on me? Why?" Elly was taken aback by this revelation.

A middle-aged woman standing nearby answered for him. "We never said anything to anyone. It was the least we could do for a sister of our Lord."

What could Elly say but the words she uttered, "Thank you. Thank you so much."

Later that evening, Elly told Tante Grietje what she had learned in the square. "Can you believe they kept my secret?" she asked.

"Now that's love, Elly," Grietje said, adding, "Praise God!"

"Tante Grietje, how do I find Henri and . . ." she did not finish her sentence. She did not want to think about what may have happened to her parents. Grietje let the sentence remain unfinished.

"We'll start looking as soon as possible," she said, gazing at the child tenderly.

A few days passed. Germany surrendered, and after the villagers finished celebrating, they began the enormous task of recovering from the war. There was still very little food to be had, except what was flown in by the Allies. The Red Cross came to visit Elly and Grietje, to see if they needed any medical care. Elly bravely listened as they told her that they suspected that her parents were no longer alive. They also informed Elly that her brother Henri was safe, had returned to Amsterdam and was staying at a Red Cross shelter. Elly

didn't even have to ask Tante Grietje. "Let's pack," Grietje said
as soon as she heard.

The night we found each other, my family stayed up late into the night talking, rejoicing over the fact that we were alive. It felt so strange and good to not have to keep listening for footsteps on the stairs. We could not stop looking at each other, marveling that we were all in the same room, drinking coffee together. At one point, there was a pause in the conversation. I looked at my father, who appeared to want to say something, but was struggling to do so.

"Father, what is it?" I inquired.

"Ernie, I have something to tell you," he said, and his manner was somber.

I waited patiently while he found the words to express what he wished to say.

He looked down at his coffee cup and then at me. "Do you remember when I came to visit you before we went into hiding?"

"Yes," I replied.

"Well, I was struck by your decision to become a minister. It occurred to me that your faith really had changed your life. You actually seemed hopeful despite everything. I had to approach Reverend Kwint about a place to hide anyway, and I asked him about some of the prophecies in the Tenach regarding the Messiah. We talked for a while that day, and spoke at length a few times after that. I realized that Jesus really is the Messiah."

I was astounded. Joy erupted in my heart, and I was speechless for about two minutes. Then my eyes focused on my mother, who was sitting next to my father. She was smiling. "Mother, do you believe in Jesus, too?" I asked.

She nodded. "I was very against it at first, Ernie. I thought I would have to give up my Jewish identity. Then Martin Kwint told me all of the questions you had, and I was amazed that they were the exact same questions I had. Believing in Jesus is a very Jewish thing to do, I realized. And I couldn't get over the incredible love that so many Christians were offering us. We could certainly learn a lesson from them. So yes, Ernie, I believe in Jesus, too."

"Aren't you forgetting about my part in all of this?" George spoke up.

"That's right, Ernie. Your little brother here actually helped us in our studies. He had written down all the messianic prophecies you mentioned when you lived at home, and we all looked at them together," my father interjected.

"George, you believe in Jesus?" I gasped.

He grinned. "Yes I do." He looked around the room at his family. "Now more than ever," he added.

This was almost too much to grasp. The exultation in my heart flowed into a river of thanksgiving. All I could say was, "Praise God!" I had so many reasons to thank him. My family was together again, and we had all found the Messiah. Later that night, after I went to bed, I remembered the promise I had made to God that if I made it through the war, I would devote my life to teaching my fellow Jewish people the truth about Jesus. "Well, Lord, I guess you'll have another minister," I said, smiling in the dark.

CHAPTER THIRTY

HENRI

Elly felt strange as she packed to get ready to leave the farmhouse and meet Henri. Though she was eager to see her brother again, she could not escape the fact that she was sorry to be saying good-bye to Tante Grietje.

After staying in Freisland until the summer of 1944, Henri had returned to Alphen A/D Rijn for a short time. Then he moved to Woubrugge to live with the parents of Diet Van Roosendaal. Now, Elly and Henri were to move in with their mother's sister, Tante Jo. They would live in the Victorieplein, very close to where they lived before they went into hiding, a lifetime ago.

How different it was to board a train without any thoughts of being searched or arrested. As they pulled into the Amsterdam train station, Elly gazed at the familiar neighborhoods. This was where she grew up, but she felt disconnected to the surroundings somehow. It was anguish to know that her parents would not be there to greet her. She pushed those thoughts aside, and tried to concentrate on how happy she was to see Henri. She was especially eager to tell him about Tante Grietje and her new faith in Jesus.

Elly and Grietje soon arrived at the typical stone row house in the south of Amsterdam. They rang the bell and the door opened immediately.

"Elly, it's you!" Henri cried. He hugged his sister fiercely, and they both started crying bittersweet tears. "Hello, Tante Grietje. Thank you so much for keeping my sister safe."

"There's no need to thank me, Henri. I wish I could have done more," she replied.

They were silent for a moment as they considered their absent parents. Henri abruptly said in as cheerful a tone as he could manage, "Let's go inside and say hello to Tante Jo."

They all went into the house where Tante Jo was making lunch.

"Elly's here!" Henri called into the kitchen. Tante Jo came out of the kitchen as Henri, Elly and Grietje were coming up the stairs.

"Tante Jo, I'm pleased to introduce Grietje Bogaarts," Henri said as Elly went to hug her aunt.

"Welcome, and thank you so much for taking care of Elly," Tante Jo greeted Grietje. "I trust she was a good girl?"

"Oh yes," Grietje replied, giving Elly a big hug. "Your niece is very well-behaved, and quite smart, too. She did excellently in all of her classes."

Henri smiled. "Wasn't it difficult to memorize all that Christian stuff, Elly? I thought I would go mad at times! All those hymns!" Henri was forced to pretend he was a Christian in order to keep the neighbors from suspecting him.

Elly laughed. "Actually, Henri, it wasn't all that difficult for me."

"Oh, well you've always been the brain in the family," he teased her.

"No ... I ... that's not what I meant ..." Elly fumbled, but it was apparent she was trying to say something. She looked down at her hands.

"Elly, what's wrong?" Tante Jo asked, concerned.

"Nothing's wrong, Tante Jo, that's just it. I have something I want to tell you and Henri. I'm just trying to figure out how," she explained.

"Just tell us," Henri said quietly, glancing at Grietje.

Elly took a deep breath. "I thought that I would forget all about the Christian stuff when the war was over, and that would be that," she began. "But when Mother and Father were arrested, Tante Grietje and I had to go to Dronthe for six weeks. When we got on the train, I was scared to death. I was convinced I would be captured. But then I prayed to Jesus to help me, and he did! If it weren't for him, I know they would have found me." She could see the confusion on her brother's face. She rushed on.

"You see, while I was sitting in that train, with five SS men around me, God made me see that he is powerful enough to blind the eyes of the Nazis. And if he can do that, he can bring the Messiah to earth, allow him to die on a cross and raise him from the dead. That same Messiah kept us safe."

Henri had stood silently while his sister was talking, trying to absorb what she was saying. Now he spoke in a low, even tone that Elly had never heard him use before. "Let me get this straight. You actually believe Jesus is the Messiah? That a man can be equal to God?"

"Not just any man, Henri, but Jesus isn't just any man. If you read the prophecies in the Tenach ..."

"Enough!" Henri shouted. "I can't believe I'm hearing this from my own sister! Have these Christians brainwashed you?"

"No, Henri, I came to this on my own," Elly protested.

"Elly," Tante Jo interrupted. "Your mother and father and all those people are gone ... how can you believe in Jesus after all that's happened?"

"How can you even believe in God anymore?" Henri asked.

Elly reeled under the attack from her brother and aunt. All she could bring herself to say was, "It wasn't his fault."

They were all dreadfully silent for a few minutes. When Tante Jo spoke again, her voice was cold and harsh. "If you really believe this, Elly, then you are no longer a member of the family. As far as I'm concerned, you are dead. You may as well have died like your mother and father.

"Now we will have to sit shivah for you. Please leave so we can prepare to mourn your death."

"Wait!" Elly cried. "I thought I was going to live here now!"

"You must be joking," Tante Jo exclaimed. "It's up to you. If *you want to follow this Jesus, fine, but you'll have to let him figure out where you're going to live, because it certainly won't be here! Now please for the last time, leave!"*

Elly started to sob. "You can't do this to me!"

She could not believe what was happening. Once again, Tante Grietje comforted her. "Don't worry, you can stay with me," she said, and put her arm around the devastated girl. Elly was reminded of the voice that calmed her in the train to Dronthe: "I'll be more to you than a father and a mother."

Elly turned and left the house silently, pausing to take one more look at her brother How she had looked forward to their reunion. It would have to wait, she thought. Tante Jo couldn't stay mad forever, could she?

Elly and Tante Grietje returned to Hazersvoude. Grietje immediately called the Red Cross to find out about adoption procedures. This had to be done as soon as possible in order to keep Elly from being placed in an orphanage.

The Dutch government bureau for misplaced war victims recommended that Grietje try to find some other means of support for Elly, aside from her meager schoolteacher's salary. If Grietje could find someone to help, then they would allow the adoption. Elly had an uncle in Amsterdam who was married to a Christian woman and sympathetic to her situation. He agreed to become co-guardian with Tante Grietje.

CHAPTER THIRTY-ONE

MAX

The days following the liberation were ones of celebration, as war torn Europe struggled to lift itself from the ashes of destruction and set about the enormous task of rebuilding. It would not be too difficult to raise new buildings from the ruins of old. The unseen devastation would be much harder to repair: the missing parents and children, the broken hearts, the wounded spirits, the mangled bodies—all those empty places at the dinner tables throughout the land.

The numbers were staggering. Millions of people were dead. Before the war, 140,000 Jews lived in the Netherlands. Only forty thousand remained afterwards. As the horrible details of the extermination camps filtered back to us, we were increasingly thankful that our family was intact. We were still waiting to hear about Max. All we knew was that he and Puck and their son Robert were still somewhere in Southeast Asia.

My family found an apartment in Leiden, where we stayed for a short time until we moved to a house in Scheveningen, which Father rented with some money he had received from the government. The house had been badly damaged during the war, but we worked hard to restore it to its original condition. Father resumed his work, coaching students in law, but the only law books I was determined to study were in the Torah. I enrolled at the University of Leiden and began my studies in theology, concentrating in Old Testament and prophecy.

One day, I had the chance to scan a Red Cross list of concentration camp victims, and my eyes fell upon the name

Hetty Winkel. The report said she died in January 1944, as she was walking to the gas chambers at Auschwitz. Within a few yards from the gas chambers she collapsed. A Nazi soldier took pity on her and shot her in the neck.

So there it was. Hetty was really gone. Though I had known this for quite some time, my heart still ached at the sight of her name on the never-ending list of the dead.

I decided to visit the lady with whom she had been in hiding at the time of her arrest. I held out hope that perhaps Hetty had left something of herself with her hostess, some little endearment or sweet memory that the lady would share with me. Maybe I could "touch" my fiancée in some small way through this woman with whom she had shared her last days of freedom.

I was not disappointed. "Hetty saved my life," the woman told me. When the Gestapo came to arrest her, Hetty turned to her hostess and pretended she had tricked her.

"I am sorry I never told you I was Jewish!"

Immediately catching onto Hetty's clever ruse, her hostess shouted, "You dirty liar! Now you're getting what you deserve!" The Gestapo never saw through Hetty's act. They took her away, but never returned to arrest the woman. Brave little Hetty! Wasn't that just like you?

I recognized several other names on the Red Cross list. One of them was Reverend J. Rottenberg. Like Hetty, he perished at Auschwitz. I wept as I said kaddish for both of them.

In August 1945, a new form of destruction was unleashed upon the world when atomic bombs were dropped on Hiroshima and Nagasaki, Japan, bringing about her quick surrender to the United States. "The world truly is a dangerous place to live," I said to myself.

The Second World War was over, but the ingredients of hatred and prejudice needed for making another Adolf Hitler were still very much present. There was only one answer. Hearts needed to be changed, and only the gospel of Jesus the Messiah could bring about that change. My Jewish people had suffered so much during the war. Surely, of all people, they had felt the brutal impact of a humanity that had abandoned God.

How senseless for men to settle for human nature, when God offers his own nature in the Messiah to all who will receive him. I decided to dedicate my life to spreading his gospel of peace. I threw myself into my theological studies at the University of Leiden.

My intentions had to battle my inability to concentrate, and I decided that I needed to get away from the university, and go someplace where I would not be distracted by fraternities and taverns. My grades were suffering during my first semester at school. It occurred to me that I needed a respite; I had gone straight from being a prisoner to being a student. I took an offer to go to England for a few months and recover my health. Upon my return, I enrolled in my father's alma mater, the University of Utrecht, and continued my theology studies there. Despite the longer commute from The Hague, I flourished in my new environment.

One night as I was studying my Hebrew and Aramaic, I heard the phone ring. A few minutes later, my father shouted for me to come and pick up the receiver.

"Hello, Ernest here."

"Dag, (Hello) Ernie! Do you know who this is?"

I recognized the voice immediately and almost dropped the phone.

"Max! Where are you?"

I listened intently as my brother told me what had happened to him over the past months. After the Japanese captured the Dutch East Indies, he and Puck were sent to separate Japanese work camps. Max was sent to Thailand, where he worked on the Burma Railroad, and the bridge over the Kwai River. Puck spent time in several camps in Java with her mother and my little nephew, Robert. Her father was sent to a different camp. But they had all emerged alive.

"Max," I said. "I can't believe all that's happened to you."

"I know. We have so much to tell each other." Max was

starting to sound a bit tired. "Listen," he said. "We're here at the health resort recovering. We should be arriving at the Badhuisweg in a few weeks."

"You mean you're going to be staying here with us?"

"Yes, until we get a place of our own."

"That's amazing," I said. "We'll all be together again!"

"Exactly," he said. "Well, I hear you've got exams right now, and this is costing me a fortune so I'll let you go study."

"Sure," I said. "I can't wait to see you. Did Father mention I switched my studies to theology?" I asked hesitantly.

"Yes, he did."

"So do you think I'm crazy?" I tried to keep my tone of voice light, but I wondered how my older brother would react to the family's decision to believe in Jesus.

"No, of course not," he replied. "Like I said, we have quite a bit to talk about, but for now I'll let you get back to work, and we'll see each other in a few weeks! Don't eat too much herring! I love you, Ernie!" The line crackled a bit and then was silent.

Our prayers had been answered! Max, Puck and Robert arrived a few weeks later. We had not all shared a meal in years. What a joy it was to sit down to lunch together. Each of us took turns telling my brother and sister-in-law all that we had experienced. Then Max and Puck each told us their stories in vivid detail.

"God was really faithful to us," Max concluded his narrative. We all looked at each other. God? We had never known Max to be a religious man. I looked at him; he seemed to have a sparkle in his eyes, and he was grinning. He said, "I was sort of nervous to tell you all that we had become believers in Jesus, but from what I can gather, there's no need to worry." He winked at me.

We all laughed. "How did that happen?" I asked.

"When I was working on the Kwai River bridge, there were these Catholic and Protestant missionaries who helped me several times. If it weren't for them, I would be dead. One day I asked them what would make them want to help me at such a risk. They answered, 'It was what Jesus told us to do.'"

"Sounds familiar," my mother said.

"They were convinced that helping me was just like doing something to help God. So I wanted to know about this Jesus that these wonderful people followed, and I came to believe that he was the Messiah. Little did I know that Puck had also heard about Jesus while she was in prison and had come to believe that he is the Messiah as well."

We all sat quietly for a moment, and then I started to pray out loud. "Lord, thank you so much for bringing us together again. Thank you that the Messiah has made atonement for our sins, and that we can share this new bond of faith. Lord, the whole world stands guilty before you. Help us to always remember who we are and what our people have suffered because we are children of Abraham. Lord, we know that because of our faith, many Jewish people will see us as traitors. Show us how to share our hope and our Messiah with our Jewish brothers and sisters."

"Amen," they all said. Though outside the weather was icy cold, our home was warmer than I could ever remember it being.

CHAPTER THIRTY-TWO

LOVE

Tante Grietje and Elly were no longer Dutch woman and Jewish girl, they were mother and daughter. Eventually, Elly was invited to visit her brother and aunt on special occasions, on the condition that she not mention Jesus or the New Testament. Her visits to Amsterdam were bittersweet. She was happy to see her brother, but grieved that he had emerged from the war so bitter and angry. For Henri, the question of how God could allow six million Jews to die so plagued him that he turned his back on his faith altogether and refused even to become a bar mitzvah. Elly could see he was hurting, but any attempt she made to comfort him was met with suspicious reproach.

One night, after returning from a trip to Amsterdam, Elly's face was cloudy, and Grietje asked her what was troubling her.

"I'm just frustrated. Henri said he heard someone say the other day that the reason all the Jews died is because we have rejected the Messiah. And I know that's not true. The Messiah had to die. It was God's will. But I don't know how to communicate that to Henri. I have a difficult time coming up with the words. Maybe it's because I have questions, too. There are many things I don't understand." She sat forward and put her head in her hands. "I feel like I have my hands tied behind my back, like I'm the only one in the world who struggles with this. Maybe it is just me."

Grietje joined her on the couch. "I'm glad you told me," she said, patting Elly's back. "Unfortunately, I'm not sure how to

153

tell you to approach your family. But I think I may know of someone who can help you."

Elly looked up. "Really? Who?"

"Well, as it turns out, you are not the only Jewish person in the world who believes in Jesus. Our minister told me this weekend about a group he heard about called the Hebrew Christian Youth Organization. They also go by the name Haderech. They meet on Saturdays in Utrecht."

"Really?" Elly was growing more and more excited. "How many of them are there, do you know?"

"I heard that there are about two hundred and fifty of them. The Queen gave them a citation a few months ago, so apparently they are a strong group."

"Unbelievable!" Elly exclaimed, and jumped up from where they were sitting. "Mother, can we go there sometime?"

Grietje laughed. "How about this Saturday? I'll go with you."

On Saturday, they boarded the train to the large city of Utrecht in the center of Holland. Thankfully, the Nazis had left this cultural and academic "hub" of the Netherlands pretty much alone. There was nothing of military importance here, unlike the seaport of Rotterdam. The "Dom," the Roman Catholic Church from the twelfth century, with its towering steeple and bell, was still standing in the center of town. It had been changed to a Dutch Reformed Church during the Reformation, and was a familiar national monument for all Dutch citizens. The Haderech was holding their meeting in a hall nearby.

Elly and Grietje arrived at the hall, and walked in to see a mixture of Jewish people, ranging from age sixteen through thirty-five. They were all singing songs of praise to Jesus. Elly felt at home immediately. She introduced herself to those gathered, and they asked if she would mind taking notes for the day. She was delighted to be of help, and decided that she would return the following Saturday.

Before too long, Elly's life became increasingly busy with Haderech activities. Between her responsibilities at church, school, music lessons and Haderech, she had little time for much else. Her interests began to include boys. There was one young man in town whom she wanted to date, but Grietje was very parochial when it came to that subject. Elly was only sixteen, so Grietje only allowed her to see him in a group, at church or other social occasions. "There's plenty of time for dating later," Grietje said.

In the spring of 1948, the Haderech announced it was having a large weekend meeting in Amsterdam to commemorate the third anniversary of the Liberation. Elly wanted to go, but she knew Grietje would object. Timidly, she approached her.

"Mother, can I ask you something?"

"Sure sweetheart. What is it?"

"The Haderech is having a big four-day meeting in Amsterdam, and I really should go since I'm on the newsletter staff . . ."

"You mean you want to spend four days in Amsterdam by yourself? I don't know, Elly."

"But we'll be with adults! We'll be chaperoned and supervised at all times," she tried to convince her mother.

"I guess if that's the case, you can go, but you better be careful. I know you grew up there, but Amsterdam is a big place."

"Really? I can go? Oh thank you!" She gave her mother a big hug and a kiss.

Elly packed her suitcase, and was off to Amsterdam for the Haderech meeting. It was the weekend of May 5, 1948, and not only was it the anniversary of the Netherlands' liberation, but when Elly arrived, she was told they had another reason to celebrate; a new state had been formed: the State of Israel!

I really don't want to go, I thought when I reached into my pocket and found the crumpled invitation to the Haderech meeting in Amsterdam.

I was in Rotterdam. A year had passed since I completed my

Bachelor's degree in Old Testament theology, and I was working on my Master's degree, aiming for my ecclesiastical examination for ordination in the Dutch Reformed Church.

The spring semester was over, and I felt a need to take a break from studying. Then I heard about a large Dutch Reformed Church convention being held in Rotterdam on the anniversary of the Liberation.

I thought it would be interesting to see how the Marshall Plan to rebuild Europe had affected that city. Three years had passed since the war had ended, and slowly the ugly scars were beginning to vanish from the Dutch countryside. As I made my way from Leiden to Rotterdam by bike, I noticed the transformation. Here were new buildings rising up out of the ruins of the old, changing the city skylines, and giving Holland a new look. The refashioned city center was more open, with wide boulevards bordering large green parks and lush gardens. Once again, ships crowded the harbor beneath giraffe-like cranes, loading and unloading cargo from all over the world. The Netherlands was again a land of plenty, with a huge agricultural export market. No longer was it difficult to buy the most expensive foods and Indonesian spices so many Hollanders enjoyed. The dikes along the coast had been repaired, and whirring windmills pumped water from the once flooded land back to the sea.

I had a wonderful time at the conference. I had brought my bugle and guitar along, and the conference leaders decided to make me the official bugler, and asked me to play guitar as well. The conference ended on a Sunday at noon, after the morning worship service. I was tired and looking forward to going back to Leiden and taking the rest of Sunday off. On Monday, I planned to get up early and work on my thesis.

The day before, I had met one of the two men who had formed an organization called Haderech. He was at the conference to speak to the candidates about the need to bring the Gospel to the Jewish people in Europe and Israel. I thoroughly enjoyed the lecture, and after the meeting, he invited me to attend a Haderech gathering concurrently taking place in Amsterdam. I had not thought much about going, but as I prepared to mount my bike, I put my hand in my pocket and found the invitation the man had given me to an Old Dutch Reformed Church in the suburbs of Amsterdam. The directions were written on the back.

I did not really feel like going, but from somewhere inside me, I felt a tug, like someone was poking me. My inner protests were overruled. If I pedaled real fast and took a few shortcuts, I could make it to the afternoon session.

Elly was having the time of her life at the Haderech meeting in Amsterdam. The leaders of the conference asked if she would provide the musical program. Elly could play the piano very well, but she wished that someone there played the guitar. "It would be really helpful for some of the Middle Eastern music," she thought. "Israeli folk music isn't really Israeli folk music without it." She started asking around, but out of all of the members there, she found nobody who could accompany her. She resolved to do the best she could.

On Sunday, Elly, her friends on the musical team and the conference speakers were having lunch at the church so they could go over the afternoon's music and worship service. When they were almost done eating, one of the leaders pulled Elly aside.

"Elly, there may be a chance that we'll have a guest performer this afternoon."

"Great," she replied. "My voice could use a rest. Who is coming?"

"A young man who's been very busy studying for ordination. He hasn't been to any of our meetings yet. I saw him perform at a convention in Rotterdam yesterday, and he was great!"

"Really, what does he do?"

"He plays both the guitar and the piano. He was a jazz band leader before the war, and he has written many of his own compositions."

"Wow, that's just what this conference needs, a guitar player! We were going to do Psalm 150 and some other Israeli and Yiddish melodies this afternoon, in honor of Israel's statehood, but they don't work on just the piano. Maybe he knows how to play them on the guitar!"

"Oh, I'm sure he does. I'll let you get back to your group now."

Elly returned to her friends, who were fervently discussing the topic of the day; the second coming of the Messiah. That Sunday, the topic for the morning Bible study and worship service had been the prophecies concerning the re-gathering of the Jewish people to Israel, and its relationship to the second coming of the Messiah. The conference speakers were warning the group to remember that Y'shua had said himself that no one knows the hour of his return.

"Yes, we all realize that," Elly responded to their warnings. "We're not trying to say that Messiah is going to come back today, tomorrow or next week. All we are trying to say is that the statehood of Israel is a significant fulfillment of prophecy."

In the past few years, Elly had become well versed in messianic prophecies, poring over them whenever she could. The convention members were slowly returning from their lunchtime break and filtered into the hall to listen to the lively discussion.

"According to the book of Jeremiah, Israel must be a nation, and the Jewish people must be allowed to live safely in it before the trumpets can herald Jesus' return." Elly said emphatically.

Suddenly, the wail of a trumpet resounded through the courtyard. From their seats inside, the group heard the blast and leapt to their feet. "What in the world can that be?" someone asked.

"Maybe the Messiah has returned," someone said, laughing as they all raced to the courtyard to see what was going on.

I biked for an hour straight in order to get to the conference in Amsterdam in time for the afternoon session. Huffing and puffing, I arrived at the old Dutch Reformed Church, which had been a monastery back in the 1500s. I hastily dismounted my bike, untied my bugle and guitar, and walked across the church lawn to the inner court of the large building. I looked around and noticed a maze of doors. Which door would bring me to where the group was meeting? I was too tired to go searching around. Rather than knock on all of them, I took my bugle to my mouth and blew it loud and long, hoping someone would hear it and come to my aid.

Suddenly, the doors were thrown open and around sixty people rushed to the courtyard. They almost overran me. I was not expecting such a throng. I stopped blowing the bugle, and faced the crowd.

"Are you the Messiah?" someone asked, laughing.

Startled, I could only answer, "Pardon me?"

I figured at that point an introduction was due. "Hello. I'm Ernie Cassutto. I didn't know which door to go through, so . . ."

Everyone started laughing hysterically. I was beginning to think this group was a little odd. "What's so funny," I asked, confused.

A young woman came forward. Her face was red from laughing. "Well, you aren't going to believe this, but right when you blew your bugle, we were discussing how when the Messiah comes again, the trumpets will blast!" She broke off in a fit of uncontrollable giggles. "They thought you were the Messiah," she said over the peals of laugher.

"What do you mean 'they' thought this," one of the group members chided her.

"I knew it wasn't the Messiah. I just wanted to see who would have the chutzpah to blow a bugle in the middle of a conference," she exclaimed in her defense.

"Well, unless the Messiah is a stocky bald man with glasses, I'm afraid you are out of luck," I said. I smiled, dropped my knapsack and extended my hand to this young woman.

"Consider me his lowly servant."

"Elly Rodrigues," she said, shaking my hand. "Pleased to meet you. I hear you play the guitar."

I liked her immediately. I liked the way her dark eyes sparkled. I liked the way I felt when those eyes met mine.

"That's true," I said.

"I'm in charge of the music program, and I heard that you might be willing and able to play for us this afternoon," she said.

"That's why I'm here," I replied. "Your wish is my command. When does the afternoon session start?"

"Two o'clock," she replied, then added, "Yiddish time," and winked. That meant that the session would start a little later. "So we have some time to go over the music before then." She was witty, I could tell. I liked that. I followed the group inside to the small stage where the piano was. Elly called the vocalists together to rehearse. I was impressed at the maturity of this young woman. She seemed to be very much in control.

The service went well. Everyone seemed pleased with the music. Later, a group of us took a walk. Elly and I walked together, a little ahead of the others.

"Thank you very much for helping us with the music, Ernest," she said gratefully.

"You are welcome," I replied. "It was a pleasure."

"I heard that you used to lead a jazz band, and that you've composed your own music. Is that true? I would love to hear some of your songs sometime."

My heart warmed at this. "I don't want to play my compositions here," I said. "But maybe I can visit you some time, and play them for you then. Where do you live?" As soon as I said it, I was embarrassed. I had said too much too soon.

"I live in Hazersvoude with my foster mother, Grietje Bogaarts," Elly answered easily, allaying my fears that I had ventured into inappropriate territory.

"Where are your parents?" I asked, and then fervently wished that those words had not come out of my mouth. "What a stupid question," I thought, inwardly scolding myself. "I'm sorry ... I know they must ..." I fumbled around a bit.

"It's alright," she said, gently rescuing me from my blunder. "They're both gone. I don't mind talking about it. God has really helped me through all of this. I miss them terribly, but I can talk about it."

How brave she seemed. Since Hetty, I had not been able to feel any sort of attachment to any woman. But Elly possessed a strength in her that reminded me of Hetty. I was drawn to her. We spent the rest of the afternoon together, walking along the canals side by side; laughing, singing and falling in love.

We spent the rest of the conference at each other's side. When it came time to eat, I realized I had forgotten to bring my own eating utensils. Elly shared hers with me. At the end of the conference, I asked Elly if we could exchange addresses. She smiled at me and said yes.

We were engaged in a matter of weeks. There was still much we did not know about each other and our future, and I had to pass Tante Grietje's scrutiny, but the months following our engagement were some of the happiest of our lives.

In July 1948, on one beautiful summer day, Elly was at my house chatting with my family about wedding plans when the phone rang. My mother answered it and told me I had a call.

I went to the phone. "Hello?" A woman's voice said, "Ernest Cassutto?" I did not recognize the speaker. "That's me," I said.

The caller was Mrs. Bartels, the wife of Herr Bartels, the commandant of the prison where I had been detained. She told me that Herr Bartels had been sentenced to death for his role in Hitler's Final Solution, but that he had been exempted due to severe illness. He was dying.

"He asked to see you," Mrs. Bartels said. "It's his final wish to see you." I could tell the request was awkward for her to make. I did not know what to say. I was preparing to be a minister. I had given sermons on the need to forgive. But I did not want to go and visit a Nazi, even one on his deathbed.

"Will you come?" his wife was asking.

I mumbled to her that I would think about it. Then I hung

up the phone and called for Elly. She came into the room. "What is it?" she asked, seeing my disturbed expression. When I told her my dilemma, she pondered for a moment, then said, "How can you refuse a dying man?"

"But Elly, what will my parents think?"

"What will your parents think about what?" my father asked, entering the room.

I told him about my phone call. "Father, the prison was horrible. There was a dentist, who was in prison just for treating Jews. One night he was forced to watch his son die in a firing squad. We heard him crying and screaming all night. I really am not interested in easing the commandant's conscience."

"I know, Ernie," he said. "But Jesus tells us we must forgive our enemies. Go see him."

I could not argue with what my father said. So I caught the next train. I could not remember what the man was dying of, only that it was some sort of lung disease. When I saw the former commandant lying in bed, he was white as wax. He was weak and struggling to breathe, and I wondered just how contagious he was.

"Go kiss him," a voice from inside me urged.

I could not believe what I had heard. Kiss him? I wasn't sure what bothered me the most: the thought of kissing someone with a fatal and possibly contagious disease, or the thought of kissing a Nazi.

"I will protect you. Kiss him." The voice would not keep quiet. My heart's pace quickened, and I found myself moving toward Herr Bartel's bedside. Timidly, I leaned forward and kissed his forehead. He burst into tears. "Cassutto," he wheezed. He placed his pale hand in mine. "The Last Jew of Rotterdam," he mumbled. As he wept, he apologized over and over for the wrong he had done, and I knew that he didn't just need my forgiveness; he needed God's mercy. I told him about Jesus; that the Jewish Messiah had to die to atone for the sins of the world. "The only way we can stand before a holy God is to accept that Jesus made atonement for our sins," I said. "Would you like to pray with me and ask for forgiveness on that basis?" He nodded silently, and right then and there, I had the privilege of praying with him. Afterwards, Herr Bartels whispered, "Thank God you came. Thank God you said my last prayer with me. Thank God." Those were his last words. Before I left, the dying man lapsed into a coma from which he never recovered consciousness. The Lord had taught me one more lesson on how to love my enemy, and this time, he had also taught my enemy to love me.

I recounted the story to Elly as we walked in the cool summer evening. "It's incredible what God gives us the strength to do," she remarked, looking at the sun setting over the coastal town of Scheveningen.

"Indeed," I said. "Hetty was the one who first told me we had to pray for the Nazis. She wrote it in her diary. She knew that they were the prime example of what men would do if left to their own devices."

Elly listened thoughtfully. "Hetty was your fiancée before the war, right? When I met you, you were still wearing an engagement ring."

"Yes," I said. "When you told me today that I had to go see Herr Bartels, your compassion reminded me of her. So I thought you might like to see this." I reached into my pocket and took out Hetty's diary. I handed it to Elly. She held it for a minute, then delicately turned some of its pages. Her eyes watered when she read some of the words Hetty had penned. She closed the book, held it to her chest, and then she placed it back in my hands. Her gaze was pensive as she watched the sun's rays stroke the clouds above. Her dark curly hair waved in the breeze. After a few minutes, she turned and faced me.

"When we have our first daughter," she said, "We will name her Hetty."

LAST (JEW) BUT NOT LEAST

A Son's Tribute

Reverend Kwint was speaking, but my father's eyes were focused upon his lovely young bride. Her soft white veil followed her dark hair to her shoulders and ran down her back in long graceful folds. She held a bouquet of white flowers.

"I Ernest, take thee Elisabeth . . ."

My parents, Ernest and Elly, exchanged wedding vows on April 22, 1949, one day before my mother's eighteenth birthday.

The radiant couple were surrounded by friends and family. On Ernest's right stood his brother and best man, George. Watching and beaming with joy were Isaac and Caroline, Max and Puck, and, of course, Tante Grietje.

Elly wished her parents were there to claim the portion of joy that should have been theirs. But as she took her eyes away from Ernest's glowing face for a brief moment, her gaze drifted over the pews to the place where her brother Henri was sitting, and inwardly, she thanked God for all of her blessings.

My father remembered the promise he had made to God, and he and my mother set out to tell anyone who would listen about the hope that preserved them both during one of the world's darkest decades. Their yearning to tell other Jewish people about Jesus the Messiah took them first to Paris, then to New York and New Jersey. Ernest served as a missionary with the American

Board of Missions to the Jews (ABMJ) and as a pastor in the Dutch Reformed Church in the Netherlands as well as in America.

Their first child was born in February 1951, while they were in Holland awaiting long-term visas for the United States. She was a beautiful baby girl, and Elly kept her word. Without a moment's hesitation, they named her Hetty.

The Cassuttos had four more children; two sets of twins named Carolyn and Marilyn (1952) and my brother George and me (1960). All are married and currently living in the United States.

In September 1955, Isaac and Caroline Cassutto came to the United States to visit their three grandchildren, Hetty, Carolyn and Marilyn. Two weeks after Isaac and Caroline returned to Holland, our telephone rang. My father answered it. Caroline Cassutto was on the other end of the phone. Isaac had suffered a heart attack while on the return voyage. When he arrived in Holland, he was taken to the hospital, where he passed away in his sleep. Shortly after his father's death, my father received a package in the mail. Opening it, he found a gold ring inside and read the inscription engraved in jade: "I.C."

Tante Grietje died in 1964. Years later, Elly submitted the name of her foster mother to the United States Holocaust Memorial Museum as one of the righteous Gentiles who protected Europe's Jews during World War II. Grietje Bogaarts' name can be found on the Wall of Rescuers in the museum.

One day in early 1968, while we were living in New Jersey, my father saw an advertisement in the back of the magazine he was reading:

Full-time minister needed. Must have strong background in Old Testament theology and witnessing to the Jewish people. Applicant must be able to read Hebrew and be well versed in Hebrew liturgy and the Jewish feasts. For further information, send resume to Emmanuel Hebrew Christian Presbyterian Congregation in Baltimore, Maryland.

"Elly!" he called from his study. "I think I've found our new home!"

On July 4, 1968, we moved from Passaic, New Jersey to Baltimore, where my father assumed the leadership of

Emmanuel Hebrew Christian Presbyterian Congregation (known as Emmanuel Messianic Jewish Congregation today). Ernest and Elly served there until 1979, when Ernest had to leave his position due to his failing health. Also in 1979, my grandmother Caroline passed away.

Max L.H. Cassuto[1] currently resides in The Hague, the Netherlands. He and Puck had three children, Robert, Albert and Irene, who all currently live in the Netherlands. Puck died in 1997. George H. Cassuto studied theology just like his older brother Ernie, and became a minister for the Dutch Reformed Church in the Netherlands. For the next 40 years, he shared his brother's zeal for preaching the good news of Jesus, with an emphasis on trying to understand the Jewishness of Jesus. At age 65, he developed colon cancer, and two years later, during Yom Kippur 1996, he passed away in the Netherlands. He is survived by his wife, Hanneke, and three children, Michele, Davide and Carine Cassuto, all of whom reside in the Netherlands.

Henri Rodrigues moved to the United States in 1949, where he met Renee Dubinsky. They were married July 12, 1951. Henri and Renee Rodrigues have resided in Queens, New York for the past 45 years. They have two children, Albert and Leah. Over the years, the Rodrigues and Cassutto families were able to visit each other often, due to their close proximity. Elly's prayers that she and her brother would be close despite their different beliefs, were answered.

In addition to serving with her husband at the Messianic congregation, Elly became a high school foreign language teacher, certified to instruct in both French and German. It was with mixed emotions that she accepted a Fulbright foreign language scholarship to teach in Germany for a year in 1983.

After only three months in Germany, Elly received a telephone call. My father, whose health was deteriorating, had fallen in the bathroom, and was in Sinai Hospital. He had bruised his kidney and suffered a mild heart attack. My mother took the next plane home.

Hetty, Carolyn, George, and I all went to meet her at the airport. Immediately, we all noticed there was something wrong with her face. The left side of her cheek was drooping. When we asked her if she had noticed the condition, she said she felt fine, just a little tired, and that it was nothing to worry about. The following morning, while getting ready to visit Ernest, Elly passed out in Hetty's bathroom. She was rushed to a local Baltimore hospital. The doctors informed us that she had a suspicious lesion in her brain, but that it was small, nothing to worry about. However, a few days later, the small lesion had become a fast growing brain tumor, which required immediate surgery. About two weeks later, neurosurgeons performed major laser surgery on Elly, but they were only able to remove 20 percent of my mother's tumor. During this period of time, my father remained in the hospital diagnosed with a condition similar to Alzheimer's disease.

My mother underwent eight weeks of radiation therapy, but it did not reduce the tumor. While she was in the hospital, she was contacted by the television show "This is Your Life." They planned to have a man named Barry Spaanjaard[2] as a guest on the show. They wanted Elly to appear on the show as the "childhood sweetheart" whom Barry was so fond of during the war. The family declined on Elly's behalf.

When the radiation failed to eradicate Elly's brain tumor, the doctors suggested experimental chemotherapy, but she refused. She just wanted to go home. She came to live in the apartment my brother George and I shared, and stayed for six months with home hospice care. On May 5, 1984, 39 years after the liberation of the Netherlands from Nazi occupation, Elisabeth Rodrigues Cassutto died at our home.

Meanwhile, the doctors tried to treat my father's symptoms with anti-depressants and anti-Parkinson's disease medications, which helped for a short period of time. However, by January 1985, Dad was transferred to a nursing home in Columbia, Maryland. We visited him every week until he died on March 18, 1985.

The initial publication of *The Last Jew of Rotterdam* in 1974 generated much attention in the Baltimore area. My parents became more well known. Over the years, they spoke to many groups about their miraculous story. From the Jewish bubbes who oohed and aahed in Yiddish over the Cassutto babies when Ernest took them for a walk in the oversized baby buggy affectionately called "the Cadillac," to the scores of Jewish people who crossed their paths at the messianic congregation, Ernest and Elly shared the love of Jesus with our Jewish people.

I am most thankful that they chose to share the hope of Jesus the Jewish Messiah with me and my siblings. I truly could not have asked for better parents. I stand in awe of them and the God who rescued them and brought them together, all the while writing an incredible testimony of his faithfulness on their hearts.

Although I miss my parents every day, I treasure the legacy they left in my life and the lives of my brothers and sisters. They gave us breath and love and showed us all a faith for which I am eternally grateful.

Have hope,
Benjamin Cassutto
Spring, 2001

1. In Holland, Cassutto is spelled with one "t."
2. Barry, who was sent from Westerbork to Bergen-Belsen, lives in Canyon County, California with his wife, Bunny. Barry's story is chronicled in the book, *Don't Fence Me In: An American Teenager in the Holocaust.* At present, he still travels across America, speaking to students and others about his wartime experiences.

ACKNOWLEDGMENTS

I am grateful to my brother George H. Cassutto, whose work as the volunteer Cassutto historian made this book a reality. Thanks are due to my dear sister, Hetty Cassutto Haden, whose computer I used, pictures I borrowed and food I ate during many long hours of conversation concerning family history. Your good memory and even better heart keeps all our history together. To Hetty's son, my nephew Calvin Haden, thank you for your computer help and photo expertise. To my sisters Carolyn and Marilyn, your good humor, prayers, love and constant encouragement made me press on.

To my wife Elizabeth Ann Cassutto, whose love for me reminds me that love is always of God, thanks for your writing and editing help, but most of all for believing in me.

To my family in Holland, Uncle Max L.H. Cassuto, cousins Robert H. Cassuto and Albert H. Cassuto, Tante Hanneke Cassuto, and Uncle Henri Rodrigues, thank you for your time, love and help. My cousins Michele and Davide Cassuto, playing my parents' music gave real soul to this work. Carine Cassuto and Albert Cassutto, thanks for allowing us to bunk at your places while we researched.

—Benjamin Cassutto

171

4

SIGNALEMENT — DESCRIPTION

	Echtgenote - femme - w
Plaats en datum van geboorte Lieu et date de naissance Place and date of birth	*Amsterdam* *23 April 1931*
Woonplaats Domicile Domicile	*zie blad.* *voir page* *see page*
Gelaatsvorm Visage Face	*ovaal*
Kleur der ogen Couleur des yeux Colour of eyes	*groen* *blauw*
Kleur der haren Couleur des cheveux Colour of hair	*bruin*
Bijzondere kentekenen Signes particuliers Special marks	